To Peter —
For the "boy"
who will always
bubble within —
Love,
Carol

GULLIVER'S
TRAVELS

Other Gramercy Books Classics:

The Works of Edgar Allan Poe

The Works of Mark Twain

The Works of Charles Dickens

The Works of Lewis Carroll

The Works of Jules Verne

The Works of Jack London

The Complete Works of Shakespeare

The Works of Nathaniel Hawthorne

The Works of O. Henry

GULLIVER'S TRAVELS

A Novel by
JONATHAN SWIFT

ILLUSTRATED BY
ARTHUR RACKHAM

Gramercy Books
New York • Avenel

Biographical Note and Introduction
copyright ©1995 by Gramercy Books
All Rights Reserved.

This 1995 edition published by Gramercy Books,
Distributed by Random HouseValue Publishing, Inc.
40 Engelhard Avenue,
Avenel, New Jersey 07001.

This book was published previously in a slightly different form
under the title, *Gulliver's Travels into Several Remote Nations
of the World.*

Random House
New York • Toronto • London • Sydney • Auckland

Printed and bound in the United States

Library of Congress Cataloging-in-Publication Data
Swift, Jonathan, 1667-1745
    Gulliver's travels.
     I. Title.
PR3724.G7 1985 823'.5 84-24293
ISBN 0-517-46611-2

8 7 6 5 4 3 2 1

CONTENTS

PART I

A VOYAGE TO LILLIPUT

CHAPTER I

CHAPTER II

CHAPTER III

CHAPTER IV

CHAPTER V

CHAPTER VI

CONTENTS

PART III

A VOYAGE TO LAPUTA, BALNIBARBI, LUGGNAGG, GLUBBDUBDRIB AND JAPAN

CONTENTS

PART IV

A VOYAGE TO THE COUNTRY OF THE HOUYHNHNMS

CHAPTER I

CHAPTER II

CHAPTER III

CHAPTER IV

CHAPTER V

CHAPTER VI

BIOGRAPHICAL NOTE

In any listing of British writers whose work has endured long past the span of their lives, Jonathan Swift's name will always appear. Born in Dublin, Ireland, on November 30, 1667, Swift's life was, for his seventy-eight years, filled with change and unorthodoxy rare for a man of his background and times.

Holding formalized education in great disdain, Swift was nonetheless required, thanks to an uncle's provision, to adhere to the routines and regulations for which he had so little regard, and eventually obtained his degree from Trinity College in Dublin. The Revolution of 1688 drove him out of Ireland to England, where he became secretary to Sir William Temple, a statesman of considerable culture, and it was here that Swift honed his writing talents. Soon, though, he tired even of his work with Sir Temple, and returned to Ireland where he entered the Church.

A restless, basically dissatisfied man, Swift's career as prelate and politician never garnered the praise nor the popularity of his pen, for as a master of "humor, irony, and invective he has no superior," it was said. He was no more successful in affairs of the heart than in those of the church or state, having several love affairs that ended poorly, although his passions for Esther Johnson, or "Stella," and for Vanessa—Miss Vanhomrigh—are considered critical inspirations for the works that immortalized them.

First published in 1726, **Gulliver's Travels** has long been the embodiment of satire at its best, with its open ridicule of pomp and pretense. Only Swift's diabolically clever wit and intelligence prevented its suppression at the time, but what has lasted through the centuries is his superbly keen and ironic observations on the frailities of human nature, the humor of which, as well as the sad truths, are as remarkably pertinent today as when first written.

FOREWARD

Much as Lewis Carroll's beloved *Alice in Wonderland* and *Alice Through the Looking Glass* have long been considered classics for children, while having levels of meaning apparent and comprehensible only to adults, so, too, is Jonathan Swift's classic of satiric observation, **Gulliver's Travels**, a novel for both young and old alike.

A delightful work of adventure to exotic lands, created and peopled by a master of the imagination, **Gulliver's Travels** was originally intended by its author to be an indictment of the British society in which he found himself, a story meant to "vex the world rather than divert it." Instead, it proved a vastly popular entertainment for those who could not, or would not, grasp its more barbed meanings. And in the decades that have followed since its original publication in 1726, **Gulliver's Travels** has enjoyed the same bilevel reception—a classic of the imagination for children, a classic of satire and wit for adults.

To read **Gulliver's Travels** with a true understanding of the author's intent, it is helpful to understand the author himself, and the misanthropic view he had of society, the church, state, humanity in general. In his travels to Lilliput, the land of the pygmies, and to Brobdingnag, the land of the giants, Gulliver is being manipulated by Swift to reveal his attitudes toward the English court during the reign of George I, and how Swift himself envisioned the ideal ruler and government. The journey to Laputa is an indictment of the British Royal Society, while the visit to Houyhnhnms is a bold and brazen stroke of biting wit against humanity at large.

The watercolor paintings of the talented British illustrator, Arthur Rackham, which enhance this edition, are as timeless as the tale itself. With a brilliant sense of imaginative fantasy, a keenly critical eye, and a pen pointed enough for the task, Swift created a masterpiece for all ages, for all the ages.

Eve Nancy

1995

PART I

CHAPTER I

MY father had a small estate in Nottinghamshire; I was the third of five sons. He sent me to Emanuel College in Cambridge, at fourteen years old, where I resided three years, and applied myself close to my studies; but the charge of maintaining me (although I had a very scanty allowance) being too great for a narrow fortune, I was bound apprentice to Mr. James Bates, an eminent surgeon in London, with whom I continued four years; and my father now and then sending me small sums of money, I laid them out in learning navigation, and other parts of the mathematics, useful to those who intend to travel, as I always believed it would be some time or other my fortune to do. When I left Mr. Bates, I went down to my father; where, by the assistance of him and my uncle John, and some other relations, I got forty pounds, and a promise of thirty pounds a year to maintain me at Leyden: there I studied physic two years and seven months, knowing it would be useful in long voyages.

Soon after my return from Leyden, I was recommended by my good master Mr. Bates, to be surgeon to the *Swallow*, Captain Abraham Pannell, commander; with whom I continued three years and a half, making a voyage or two into the Levant, and some other parts. When I came back, I resolved to settle in London, to which Mr. Bates, my master, encouraged me, and by him I was recommended to several patients. I took part of a small house in the Old Jewry; and being advised to alter my condition, I married Mrs. Mary Burton, second daughter to Mr. Edmund Burton, hosier, in Newgate Street, with whom I received four hundred pounds for a portion.

But, my good master Bates dying in two years after, and I having few friends, my business began to fail; for my conscience would not suffer me to imitate the bad practice of too many among my brethren. Having therefore consulted with my wife, and some of my acquaintance, I determined to go again to sea. I was surgeon successively in two ships, and made several voyages for six years to the East and West Indies, by which I got some addition to my fortune. My hours of leisure I spent in reading the best authors, ancient and modern, being always provided with a good number of books; and when I was ashore, in observing the manners and dispositions of the people, as well as learning their language, wherein I had a great facility by the strength of my memory.

The last of these voyages not proving very fortunate, I grew weary of the sea, and intended to stay at home with my wife and family. I removed from the Old Jewry to Fetter Lane, and from thence to Wapping, hoping to get business among the sailors; but it would not turn to account. After three years' expectation that things would mend, I accepted an advantageous offer from Captain William Pritchard, master of the *Antelope*, who was making a voyage to the South Sea. We set sail from Bristol, May 4th, 1699, and our voyage at first was very prosperous.

It would not be proper, for some reasons, to trouble the reader with the particulars of our adventures in those seas: Let it suffice to inform him, that, in our passage from thence to the East Indies, we were driven by a violent storm to the north-west of Van Diemen's Land. By an observation we found ourselves in the latitude of 30 degrees 2 minutes south. Twelve of our crew were dead by immoderate labour, and ill food, the rest were in a very weak condition. On the fifth of November, which was the beginning of summer in those parts, the weather being very hazy, the seamen spied a rock, within half a cable's length of the ship; but the wind was so strong, that we were driven directly upon it, and immediately split. Six of the crew, of whom I was one, having let down the boat into the sea, made a shift to get clear of the ship and the rock. We rowed, by my computation, about three leagues, till we were able to work no longer, being already spent with labour while we were in the ship. We therefore trusted ourselves to the mercy of the waves, and in about half an hour the boat was overset by a sudden flurry from the north. What became of my companions in the boat, as well as of those who escaped on the rock, or were left in the vessel, I cannot tell; but conclude they were all lost. For my own part, I swam as fortune directed me, and was pushed forward by wind and tide. I often let my legs drop, and could feel no bottom: but when I was almost gone, and able to struggle no longer, I found myself within my depth; and by this time the storm was much abated. The declivity was so small, that I walked near a mile before I got to the shore, which I conjectured was about eight o'clock in the evening. I then advanced forward near half a mile, but could not discover any sign of houses or inhabitants; at least I was in so weak a condition that I did not observe them. I was extremely tired, and with that, and the heat of the weather, and about half a pint of brandy that I drank as I left the ship, I found myself much inclined to sleep. I lay down on the grass, which was very short and soft, where I slept sounder than ever I remembered to have done in my life, and, as I reckoned, about nine hours; for when I awaked it was just daylight. I attempted to rise, but was not able to stir: for as I happened to lie on my back, I found my arms and legs were strongly fastened on each side to the ground; and my hair, which was long and thick, tied down in the same manner. I likewise felt several slender ligatures across my body, from my arm-pits to my thighs. I could only look upwards, the sun began to grow hot, and the light offended my eyes. I heard a confused noise about me, but, in the posture I lay, could see nothing except the sky. In a little time I felt something alive moving on my left leg, which advancing gently forward, over my breast, came almost up to my chin; when bending my eyes downward as much as I could, I perceived it to be a human creature not six inches high, with a bow and arrow in his hands, and a quiver at his back. In the meantime, I felt at least forty more of the same kind (as I conjectured) following the first. I was in the utmost astonishment, and roared so loud, that they all ran back in a fright; and some of them, as I was afterwards told, were hurt with the falls they got by leaping from my sides upon the ground. However, they soon returned, and one of them, who ventured so far as to get a full sight of my face, lifting up his hands and eyes by way of admiration, cried out in a shrill but distinct voice, *Hekinah degul* : the others repeated the same words several times, but I then knew not what they meant. I lay all this while, as the reader may believe, in great uneasiness; at length, struggling to get loose, I had the fortune to break the strings, and wrench out the pegs that fastened my left arm to the ground; for, by lifting it up to my face, I discovered the methods they had taken to bind me, and, at the same time, with a violent

pull, which gave me excessive pain, I a little loosened the
strings that tied down my hair on the left side, so that I
was just able to turn my head about two inches. But the
creatures ran off a second time, before I could seize them;
whereupon there was a great shout in a very shrill accent,
and after it ceased, I heard one of them cry aloud, *Tolgo
phonac;* when in an instant I felt above an hundred arrows
discharged on my left hand, which pricked me like so many
needles; and besides, they shot another flight into the air,
as we do bombs in Europe, whereof many I suppose fell on
my body (though I felt them not), and some on my face,
which I immediately covered with my left hand. When
this shower of arrows was over, I fell a groaning with grief
and pain, and then striving again to get loose, they discharged another volley larger than the first, and some of
them attempted with spears to stick me in the sides; but,
by good luck, I had on me a buff jerkin, which they could
not pierce. I thought it the most prudent method to lie
still, and my design was to continue so till night, when my
left hand being already loose, I could easily free myself:
and as for the inhabitants, I had reason to believe I might
be a match for the greatest army they could bring against
me, if they were all of the same size with him that I saw.
But fortune disposed otherways of me. When the people
observed I was quiet, they discharged no more arrows:
but, by the noise I heard, I knew their numbers increased;
and about four yards from me, over against my right ear,
I heard a knocking for above an hour, like that of people at
work; when turning my head that way, as well as the pegs
and strings would permit me, I saw a stage erected, about
a foot and half from the ground, capable of holding four of
the inhabitants, with two or three ladders to mount it:
from whence one of them, who seemed to be a person of
quality, made me a long speech, whereof I understood not
one syllable. But I should have mentioned, that before
the principal person began his oration, he cried out three

times, *Langro dehul san* (these words and the former were afterwards repeated and explained to me). Whereupon immediately about fifty of the inhabitants came and cut the strings that fastened the left side of my head, which gave me the liberty of turning it to the right, and of observing the person and gesture of him that was to speak. He appeared to be of a middle age, and taller than any of the other three who attended him, whereof one was a page that held up his train, and seemed to be somewhat longer than my middle finger; the other two stood one on each side to support him. He acted every part of an orator, and I could observe many periods of threatenings, and others of promises, pity, and kindness. I answered in a few words, but in the most submissive manner, lifting up my left hand and both my eyes to the sun, as calling him for a witness; and, being almost famished with hunger, having not eaten a morsel for some hours before I left the ship, I found the demands of nature so strong upon me, that I could not forbear shewing my impatience (perhaps against the strict rules of decency) by putting my finger frequently to my mouth, to signify that I wanted food. The Hurgo (for so they call a great lord, as I afterwards learnt) understood me very well. He descended from the stage, and commanded that several ladders should be applied to my sides, on which above an hundred of the inhabitants mounted, and walked towards my mouth, laden with baskets full of meat, which had been provided and sent thither by the king's orders, upon the first intelligence he received of me. I observed there was the flesh of several animals, but could not distinguish them by the taste. There were shoulders, legs, and loins, shaped like those of mutton, and very well dressed, but smaller than the wings of a lark. I eat them by two or three at a mouthful, and took three loaves at a time, about the bigness of musket bullets. They supplied me as they could, shewing a thousand marks of wonder and astonishment at my bulk and appetite. I then made another sign that I wanted drink. They found by my eating, that a small quantity would not suffice me, and being a most ingenious people, they flung up with great dexterity one of their largest hogsheads, then rolled it towards my hand, and beat out the top; I drank it off at a draught, which I might well do, for it did not hold half a pint, and tasted like a small wine of Burgundy, but much more delicious. They brought me a second hogshead, which I drank in the same manner, and made signs for more; but they had none to give me. When I had performed these wonders, they shouted for joy, and danced upon my breast, repeating several times as they did at first, *Hekinah degul*. They made me a sign that I should throw down the two hogsheads, but first warning the people below to stand out of the way, crying aloud, *Borach mivola*, and when they saw the vessels in the air, there was an universal shout of *Hekinah degul*. I confess, I was often tempted, while they were passing backwards and forwards on my body, to seize forty or fifty of the first that came in my reach, and dash them against the ground. But the remembrance of what I had felt, which probably might not be the worst they could do, and the promise of honour I made them, for so I interpreted my submissive behaviour, soon drove out these imaginations. Besides, I now considered myself as bound by the laws of hospitality to a people who had treated me with so much expense and magnificence. However, in my thoughts, I could not sufficiently wonder at the intrepidity of these diminutive mortals, who durst venture to mount and walk upon my body, while one of my hands was at liberty, without trembling at the very sight of so prodigious a creature, as I must appear to them. After some time, when they observed that I made no more demands for meat, there appeared before me a person of high rank from his Imperial Majesty. His Excellency, having mounted on the small of my right leg, advanced forwards up to my face, with about a dozen of his retinue. And producing his credentials under the Signet Royal, which he applied close to my eyes, spoke about ten minutes, without any signs of anger, but with a kind of determinate resolution; often pointing forwards, which, as I afterwards found, was towards the capital city, about half a mile distant, whither, it was agreed by his Majesty in council, that I must be conveyed. I answered in few words, but to no purpose, and made a sign with my hand that was loose, putting it to the other (but over his Excellency's head, for fear of hurting him or his train) and then to my own head and body, to signify that I desired my liberty. It appeared that he understood me well enough, for he shook his head by way of disapprobation, and held his hand in a posture, to shew that I must be carried as a prisoner. However, he made other signs to let me understand that I should have meat and drink enough, and very good treatment. Whereupon I once more thought of attempting to break my bonds; but again, when I felt the smart of their arrows, upon my face and hands, which were all in blisters, and many of the darts still sticking in them; and observing likewise that the number of my enemies increased, I gave tokens, to let them know that they might do with me what they pleased. Upon this, the Hurgo and his train withdrew, with much civility and cheerful countenances. Soon after, I heard a general shout, with frequent repetitions of the words, *Peplom selan*, and I felt great numbers of people on my left side, relaxing the cords to such a degree, that I was able to turn upon my right. But before this, they had daubed my face, and both my hands, with a sort of ointment very pleasant to the smell, which in a few minutes removed all the smart of their arrows. These circumstances, added to the refreshment I had received by their victuals and drink, which were very nourishing, disposed me to sleep. I slept about eight hours, as I was afterwards assured; and it was no wonder, for the physicians, by the

Emperor's order, had mingled a sleepy potion in the hogsheads of wine.

It seems that, upon the first moment I was discovered
sleeping on the ground after my landing, the Emperor had
early notice of it by an express; and determined in council
that I should be tied in the manner I have related (which
was done in the night while I slept), that plenty of meat
and drink should be sent to me, and a machine prepared
to carry me to the capital city.

This resolution, perhaps, may appear very bold and
dangerous, and I am confident, would not be imitated by
any prince in Europe, on the like occasion; however, in my
opinion, it was extremely prudent, as well as generous:
for, supposing these people had endeavoured to kill me
with their spears and arrows, while I was asleep, I should
certainly have awaked with the first sense of smart, which
might so far have roused my rage and strength, as to have
enabled me to break the strings wherewith I was tied; after
which, as they were not able to make resistance, so they
could expect no mercy.

These people are most excellent mathematicians, and
arrived to a great perfection in mechanics, by the countenance and encouragement of the Emperor, who is a renowned
patron of learning. This prince hath several machines
fixed on wheels, for the carriage of trees, and other great
weights. He often builds his largest men-of-war, whereof
some are nine feet long, in the woods where the timber
grows, and has them carried on these engines three or four
hundred yards to the sea. Five hundred carpenters and
engineers were immediately set at work to prepare the
greatest engine they had. It was a frame of wood raised
three inches from the ground, about seven feet long, and
four wide, moving upon twenty-two wheels. The shout I
heard was upon the arrival of this engine, which, it seems,
set out in four hours after my landing. It was brought
parallel to me as I lay. But the principal difficulty was, to

raise and place me in this vehicle. Eighty poles, each of one foot high, were erected for this purpose, and very strong cords, of the bigness of pack-thread, were fastened by hooks to many bandages, which the workmen had girt round my neck, my hands, my body, and my legs. Nine hundred of the strongest men were employed to draw up these cords by many pulleys fastened on the poles, and thus, in less than three hours, I was raised, and flung into the engine, and there tied fast. All this I was told, for, while the whole operation was performing, I lay in a profound sleep, by the force of that soporiferous medicine infused into my liquor. Fifteen hundred of the Emperor's largest horses, each about four inches and an half high, were employed to draw me towards the Metropolis, which, as I said, was half a mile distant.

About four hours after we began our journey, I awaked by a very ridiculous accident; for the carriage being stopped a while to adjust something that was out of order, two or three of the young natives had the curiosity to see how I looked when I was asleep; they climbed up into the engine, and advancing very softly to my face, one of them, an officer in the Guards, put the sharp end of his half-pike a good way up into my left nostril, which tickled my nose like a straw, and made me sneeze violently: whereupon they stole off unperceived, and it was three weeks before I knew the cause of my awaking so suddenly. We made a long march the remaining part of that day, and rested at night with five hundred guards on each side of me, half with torches, and half with bows and arrows, ready to shoot me, if I should offer to stir. The next morning at sun-rise we continued our march, and arrived within two hundred yards of the city gates about noon. The Emperor, and all his court, came out to meet us, but his great officers would by no means suffer his Majesty to endanger his person by mounting on my body.

At the place where the carriage stopped, there stood

an ancient temple, esteemed to be the largest in the whole
kingdom, which, having been polluted some years before
by an unnatural murder, was, according to the zeal of
those people, looked on as profane, and therefore had been
applied to common use, and all the ornaments and furniture
carried away. In this edifice it was determined I should
lodge. The great gate fronting to the north, was about four
feet high, and almost two feet wide, through which I could
easily creep. On each side of the gate was a small window,
not above six inches from the ground: into that on the
left side, the King's smith conveyed fourscore and eleven
chains, like those that hang to a lady's watch in Europe,
and almost as large, which were locked to my left leg, with
six and thirty padlocks. Over against this temple, on
t'other side of the great highway, at twenty feet distance,
there was a turret at least five feet high. Here the Emperor
ascended, with many principal lords of his court, to have
an opportunity of viewing me, as I was told, for I could
not see them. It was reckoned, that above an hundred
thousand inhabitants came out of the town upon the same
errand; and, in spite of my guards, I believe there could
not be fewer than ten thousand, at several times, who
mounted my body by the help of ladders. But a proclamation was soon issued to forbid it, upon pain of death.
When the workmen found it was impossible for me to break
loose, they cut all the strings that bound me; whereupon I
rose up with as melancholy a disposition as ever I had in my
life. But the noise and astonishment of the people, at seeing
me rise and walk, are not to be expressed. The chains
that held my left leg, were about two yards long,
and gave me not only the liberty of walking
backwards and forwards in a semi-circle,
but, being fixed within four inches
of the gate, allowed me to
creep in, and lie at my full
length in the temple.

CHAPTER II

WHEN I found myself on my feet I looked about me, and must confess I never beheld a more entertaining prospect. The country round appeared like a continual garden, and the enclosed fields, which were generally forty feet square, resembled so many beds of flowers. These fields were intermingled with woods of half a stang, and the tallest trees, as I could judge, appeared to be seven feet high. I viewed the town on my left hand, which looked like the painted scene of a city in a theatre.

The Emperor was already descended from the tower, and advancing on horseback towards me, which had like to have cost him dear; for the beast, though very well trained, yet wholly unused to such a sight, which appeared as if a mountain moved before him, reared up on his hinder feet: but that Prince, who is an excellent horseman, kept his seat, till his attendants ran in, and held the bridle, while his Majesty had time to dismount. When he alighted, he surveyed me round with great admiration, but kept without the length of my chain. He ordered his cooks and butlers, who were already prepared, to give me victuals and drink, which they pushed forward in a sort of vehicles on wheels, till I could reach them. I took these vehicles, and soon emptied them all; twenty of them were filled with meat, and ten with liquor. Each of the former afforded me two or three good mouthfuls, and I emptied the liquor of ten vessels, which was contained in earthen vials, into one vehicle, drinking it off at a draught, and so I did with the rest. The Empress and young Princes of the blood, of both sexes, attended by many ladies, sat at some distance in their chairs; but, upon the accident that happened to the Emperor's horse, they alighted, and came near his

person, which I am now going to describe. He is taller by
almost the breadth of my nail, than any of his court, which,
alone, is enough to strike an awe into the beholders. His
features are strong and masculine, with an Austrian lip
and arched nose, his complexion olive, his countenance
erect, his body and limbs well proportioned, all his motions
graceful, and his deportment majestic. He was then past
his prime, being twenty-eight years and three quarters old,
of which he had reigned about seven, in great felicity, and
generally victorious. For the better convenience of beholding him, I lay on my side, so that my face was parallel to
his, and he stood but three yards off: however, I had him
since many times in my hand, and, therefore, cannot be
deceived in the description. His dress was very plain and
simple, and the fashion of it, between the Asiatic and the
European: but he had on his head a light helmet of gold,
adorned with jewels, and a plume on the crest. He held
his sword drawn in his hand, to defend himself, if I should
happen to break loose; it was almost three inches long,
the hilt and scabbard were gold enriched with diamonds.
His voice was shrill, but very clear and articulate, and I
could distinctly hear it when I stood up. The ladies and
courtiers were all most magnificently clad, so that the spot
they stood upon, seemed to resemble a petticoat spread on
the ground, embroidered with figures of gold and silver.
His Imperial Majesty spoke often to me, and I returned
answers, but neither of us could understand a syllable.
There were several of his priests and lawyers present (as I
conjectured by their habits) who were commanded to
address themselves to me, and I spoke to them in as many
languages as I had the least smattering of, which were
High and Low Dutch, Latin, French, Spanish, Italian, and
Lingua Franca; but all to no purpose. After about two
hours the court retired, and I was left with a strong guard,
to prevent the impertinence, and probably, the malice of
the rabble, who were very impatient to crowd about me as

near as they durst, and some of them had the impudence to shoot their arrows at me as I sat on the ground by the door of my house, whereof one very narrowly missed my left eye. But the colonel ordered six of the ringleaders to be seized, and thought no punishment so proper, as to deliver them bound into my hands, which some of his soldiers accordingly did, pushing them forwards with the butt ends of their pikes into my reach; I took them all in my right hand, put five of them into my coat pocket, and as to the sixth, I made a countenance as if I would eat him alive. The poor man squalled terribly, and the colonel and his officers were in much pain, especially when they saw me take out my penknife: but I soon put them out of fear; for, looking mildly, and immediately cutting the strings he was bound with, I set him gently on the ground, and away he ran. I treated the rest in the same manner, taking them, one by one, out of my pocket, and I observed both the soldiers and people were obliged at this mark of my clemency, which was represented very much to my advantage at court.

Towards night I got with some difficulty into my house, where I lay on the ground, and continued to do so about a fortnight; during which time, the Emperor gave orders to have a bed prepared for me. Six hundred beds of the common measure were brought in carriages, and worked up in my house. An hundred and fifty of their beds, sewn together, made up the breadth and length; and these were four double, which, however, kept me but very indifferently from the hardness of the floor, that was of smooth stone. By the same computation, they provided me with sheets, blankets, and coverlets, tolerable enough for one who had been so long inured to hardships.

As the news of my arrival spread through the kingdom, it brought prodigious numbers of rich, idle, and curious people to see me, so that the villages were almost emptied, and great neglect of tillage and household affairs must have ensued, if his Imperial Majesty had not provided, by several proclamations and orders of State, against this inconveniency. He directed that those who had already beheld me should return home, and not presume to come within fifty yards of my house, without licence from court; whereby the Secretaries of State got considerable fees.

In the meantime, the Emperor had frequent councils, to debate what course should be taken with me; and, I was afterwards assured by a particular friend, a person of great quality, who was looked upon to be as much in the secret as any, that the court was under many difficulties concerning me. They apprehended my breaking loose, that my diet would be very expensive, and might cause a famine. Sometimes they determined to starve me, or at least to shoot me in the face and hands with poisoned arrows, which would soon despatch me; but again they considered, that the stench of so large a carcase might produce a plague in the metropolis, and probably spread through the whole kingdom. In the midst of these consultations, several officers of the army went to the door of the great council chamber, and two of them, being admitted, gave an account of my behaviour to the six criminals above mentioned, which made so favourable an impression in the breast of his Majesty, and the whole board, in my behalf, that an Imperial Commission was issued out, obliging all the villages, nine hundred yards round the city, to deliver in every morning six beeves, forty sheep, and other victuals, for my sustenance; together with a proportionable quantity of bread, and wine, and other liquors; for the due payment of which, his Majesty gave assignments upon his treasury. For this prince lives chiefly upon his own demesnes, seldom, except upon great occasions, raising any subsidies upon his subjects, who are bound to attend him in his wars, at their own expense. An establishment was also made of six hundred persons to be my domestics, who had board wages allowed for their maintenance, and tents built for them very conveniently on each side of my door. It was likewise ordered, that three hundred tailors should make me a suit of clothes, after the fashion of the country: that six of his Majesty's greatest scholars should be employed to instruct me in their language, and, lastly, that the Emperor's horses, and those of the nobility, and troops of guards, should be frequently exercised in my sight, to accustom themselves to me. All these orders were duly put in execution, and, in about three weeks, I made a great progress in learning their language, during which time, the Emperor frequently honoured me with his visits, and was pleased to assist my masters in teaching me. We began already to converse together in some sort; and the first words I learnt were to express my desire that he would please to give me my liberty, which I every day repeated on my knees. His answer, as I could apprehend it, was, that this must be a work of time, not to be thought on without the advice of his council, and that first I must *Lumos kelmin peffo defmar lon Emposo;* that is, swear a peace with him and his kingdom. However, that I should be used with all kindness; and he advised me to acquire, by my patience and discreet behaviour, the good opinion of himself and his subjects. He desired I would not take it ill, if he gave orders to certain proper officers to search me; for probably I might carry about me several weapons, which must needs be dangerous things, if they answered the bulk of so prodigious a person. I said, his Majesty should be satisfied, for I was ready to strip myself, and turn up my pockets before him. This I delivered, part in words, and part in signs. He replied, that by the laws of the kingdom I must be searched by two of his officers; that he knew this could not be done without my consent and assistance; that he had so good an opinion of my generosity and justice, as to trust their persons in my hands; that whatever they took from me, should be returned when I left the country, or paid for at the rate which I would set upon them. I took up the two officers in my hands, put them first into my coat pockets, and then into every other pocket about me, except my two fobs, and another secret pocket I had no mind should be searched, wherein I had some little necessaries that were of no consequence to any but myself. In one of my fobs there was a silver watch, and in the other a small quantity of gold in a purse. These gentlemen, having pen, ink, and paper, about them, made an exact inventory of everything they saw, and, when they had done, desired I would set them down, that they might deliver it to the Emperor. This inventory I afterwards translated into English, and is word for word as follows:—

" *Imprimis*, In the right coat pocket of the ' Great Man Mountain ' (for so I interpret the *Quinbus Flestrin*), after the strictest search, we found only one great piece of coarse cloth, large enough to be a foot-cloth for your Majesty's chief room of state. In the left pocket we saw a huge silver chest, with a cover of the same metal, which we, the searchers, were not able to lift. We desired it should be opened, and one of us stepping into it, found himself up to the mid leg in a sort of dust, some part whereof, flying up to our faces, set us both a sneezing for several times together. In his right waistcoat pocket, we found a pro-digious bundle of white, thin substances, folded one over another, about the bigness of three men, tied with a strong ᴄable, and marked with black figures; which we humbly conceive to be writings, every letter almost half as large as the palm of our hands. In the left there was a sort of engine, from the back of which were extended twenty long poles, resembling the palisadoes before your Majesty's court; wherewith we conjecture the Man-Mountain combs his head, for we did not always trouble him with questions, because we found it a great difficulty to make him under-stand us. In the large pocket on the right side of his

middle cover (so I translate the word *Ranfu-Lo*, by which
they meant my breeches), we saw a hollow pillar of iron,
about the length of a man, fastened to a strong piece of
timber, larger than the pillar; and upon one side of the
pillar were huge pieces of iron sticking out, cut into strange
figures, which we know not what to make of. In the left
pocket, another engine of the same kind. In the smaller
pocket, on the right side, were several round flat pieces of
white and red metal, of different bulk; some of the white,
which seemed to be silver, were so large and heavy, that
my comrade and I could hardly lift them. In the left
pocket were two black pillars, irregularly shaped; we
could not, without difficulty, reach the top of them, as we
stood at the bottom of his pocket. One of them was
covered, and seemed all of a piece; but, at the upper end
of the other, there appeared a white round substance, about
twice the bigness of our heads. Within each of these was
enclosed a prodigious plate of steel; which, by our orders,
we obliged him to shew us, because we apprehended they
might be dangerous engines. He took them out of their
cases, and told us, that in his own country, his practice was
to shave his beard with one of these, and to cut his meat
with the other. There were two pockets which we could
not enter: these he called his fobs; they were two large
slits cut into the top of his middle cover, but squeezed
close by the pressure of his belly. Out of the right fob
hung a great silver chain, with a wonderful kind of engine
at the bottom. We directed him to draw out whatever
was fastened to that chain; which appeared to be a globe,
half silver, and half of some transparent metal: for on the
transparent side, we saw certain strange figures, circularly
drawn, and thought we could touch them, till we found
our fingers stopped by that lucid substance. He put this
engine to our ears, which made an incessant noise, like that
of a water-mill. And we conjecture, it is either some unknown animal, or the god that he worships: but we are

more inclined to the latter opinion, because he assured us
(if we understood him right, for he expressed himself very
imperfectly) that he seldom did anything without consulting it. He called it his oracle, and said it pointed out the
time for every action of his life. From the left fob he
took out a net almost large enough for a fisherman, but
contrived to open and shut like a purse, and served him
for the same use: we found therein several massy pieces
of yellow metal, which, if they be real gold, must be of
immense value.

"Having thus, in obedience to your Majesty's commands, diligently searched all his pockets, we observed a
girdle about his waist, made of the hide of some prodigious
animal, from which, on the left side, hung a sword of the
length of five men; and on the right, a bag or pouch,
divided into two cells, each cell capable of holding three of
your Majesty's subjects. In one of these cells were several
globes, or balls, of a most ponderous metal, about the bigness of our heads, and required a strong hand to lift them.
The other cell contained a heap of certain black grains, but
of no great bulk or weight, for we could hold above fifty of
them in the palms of our hands.

"This is an exact inventory of what we found about
the body of the Man-Mountain, who used us with great
civility, and due respect to your Majesty's commission.
Signed and sealed, on the fourth day of the eighty-ninth
moon of your Majesty's auspicious reign.

"CLEFRIN FRELOCK, MARSI FRELOCK."

When this inventory was read over to the Emperor, he
directed me, although in very gentle terms, to deliver up
the several particulars. He first called for my scimitar,
which I took out, scabbard and all. In the meantime, he
ordered three thousand of his choicest troops (who then
attended him) to surround me at a distance, with their
bows and arrows just ready to discharge: but I did not

observe it, for mine eyes were wholly fixed upon his Majesty. He then desired me to draw my scimitar, which, although it had got some rust by the sea-water, was in most parts exceeding bright. I did so, and immediately all the troops gave a shout, between terror and surprise; for the sun shone clear, and the reflection dazzled their eyes, as I waved the scimitar to and fro in my hand. His Majesty, who is a most magnanimous prince, was less daunted than I could expect; he ordered me to return it into the scabbard, and cast it on the ground as gently as I could, about six feet from the end of my chain. The next thing he demanded, was one of the hollow iron pillars, by which he meant my pocket pistols. I drew it out, and at his desire, as well as I could, expressed to him the use of it; and charging it only with powder, which, by the closeness of my pouch, happened to escape wetting in the sea (an inconvenience against which all prudent mariners take special care to provide), I first cautioned the Emperor not to be afraid, and then I let it off into the air. The astonishment here was much greater than at the sight of my scimitar. Hundreds fell down, as if they had been struck dead; and even the Emperor, although he stood his ground, could not recover himself in some time. I delivered up both my pistols in the same manner as I had done my scimitar, and then my pouch of powder and bullets; begging him, that the former might be kept from the fire, for it would kindle with the smallest spark, and blow up his imperial palace into the air. I likewise delivered up my watch, which the Emperor was very curious to see, and commanded two of his tallest yeomen of the guards to bear it on a pole upon their shoulders, as dray-men in England do a barrel of ale. He was amazed at the continual noise it made, and the motion of the minute-hand, which he could easily discern (for their sight is much more acute than ours), and asked the opinions of his learned men about him, which were various and remote, as the reader may well imagine without my repeating; although, indeed, I could not very perfectly understand them. I then gave up my silver and copper money, my purse with nine large pieces of gold, and some smaller ones; my knife and razor, my comb and silver snuff-box, my handkerchief, and journal-book. My scimitar, pistols, and pouch were conveyed in carriages to his Majesty's stores; but the rest of my goods were returned me.

I had, as I before observed, one private pocket which escaped their search, wherein there was a pair of spectacles (which I sometimes use for the weakness of my eyes), a pocket perspective, and several other little conveniences, which being of no consequence to the Emperor, I did not think myself bound in honour to discover, and I apprehended they might be lost or spoiled, if I ventured them out of my possession.

CHAPTER III

My gentleness and good behaviour had gained so far on the Emperor and his court, and indeed upon the army and people in general, that I began to conceive hopes of getting my liberty in a short time. I took all possible methods to cultivate this favourable disposition. The natives came, by degrees, to be less apprehensive of any danger from me. I would sometimes lie down and let five or six of them dance on my hand; and, at last, the boys and girls would venture to come and play at hide and seek in my hair. I had now made a good progress in understanding and speaking their language. The Emperor had a mind, one day, to entertain me with several of the country shows, wherein they exceed all nations I have known, both for dexterity and magnificence. I was diverted with none so much as that of the rope-dancers performed upon a slender white thread, extended about two feet, and twelve inches from the ground. Upon which I shall desire liberty, with the reader's patience, to enlarge a little.

This diversion is only practised by those persons who are candidates for great employments, and high favour at court. They are trained in this art from their youth, and are not always of noble birth, or liberal education. When a great office is vacant, either by death or disgrace (which often happens), five or six of those candidates petition the Emperor to entertain his Majesty and the court with a dance on the rope, and whoever jumps the highest, without falling, succeeds in the office. Very often the chief ministers themselves are commanded to shew their skill, and to convince the Emperor that they have not lost their faculty. Flimnap, the treasurer, is allowed to cut a caper on the strait rope at least an inch higher than any other lord in the whole empire. I have seen him do the somerset several times together, upon a trencher fixed on the rope, which is no thicker than a common pack-thread in England. My friend Reldresal, principal secretary for private affairs, is, in my opinion, if I am not partial, the second after the treasurer; the rest of the great officers are much upon a par.

These diversions are often attended with fatal accidents, whereof great numbers are on record. I myself have seen two or three candidates break a limb. But the danger is much greater when the ministers themselves are com- manded to show their dexterity; for, by contending to excel themselves and their fellows, they strain so far, that there is hardly one of them who hath not received a fall, and some of them two or three. I was assured, that, a year or two before my arrival, Flimnap would have infallibly broke his neck, if one of the king's cushions, that acci- dentally lay on the ground, had not weakened the force of his fall.

There is likewise another diversion, which is only shewn before the Emperor and Empress, and first minister, upon particular occasions. The Emperor lays on the table three fine silken threads of six inches long; one is blue, the other red, and the third green. These threads are pro- posed as prizes for those persons whom the Emperor hath a mind to distinguish by a peculiar mark of his favour. The ceremony is performed in his Majesty's great chamber of state, where the candidates are to undergo a trial of dexterity very different from the former, and such as I have not observed the least resemblance of in any other country of the old or new world. The Emperor holds a stick in his hands, both ends parallel to the horizon, while the candidates advancing, one by one, sometimes leap over the stick, sometimes creep under it backwards and forwards several times, according as the stick is advanced or de- pressed. Sometimes the Emperor holds one end of the stick, and his first minister the other; sometimes the minister has it entirely to himself. Whoever performs his part with most agility, and holds out the longest in leaping and creeping, is rewarded with the blue-coloured silk, the red is given to the next, and the green to the third, which they all wear girt twice round about the middle, and you see few great persons about this court who are not adorned with one of these girdles.

The horses of the army, and those of the royal stables, having been daily led before me, were no longer shy, but would come up to my very feet without starting. The riders would leap them over my hand as I held it on the ground, and one of the Emperor's huntsmen, upon a large courser, took my foot, shoe and all: which was, indeed, a prodigious leap. I had the good fortune to divert the Emperor, one day, after a very extraordinary manner: I desired he would order several sticks of two feet high, and the thickness of an ordinary cane, to be brought me; whereupon his Majesty commanded the master of his woods to give directions accordingly, and the next morning six woodmen arrived with as many carriages, drawn by eight horses to each. I took nine of these sticks, and fixing them firmly in the ground, in a quadrangular figure, two feet and a half square, I took four other sticks, and tied them parallel at each corner, about two feet from the ground; then I fastened my handkerchief to the nine sticks that stood erect, and extended it on all sides till it was as tight as the top of a drum; and the four parallel sticks, rising about five inches higher than the handkerchief, served as ledges on each side. When I had finished my work, I desired the Emperor to let a troop of his best horse, twenty-four in number, come and exercise upon this plain. His Majesty approved of the proposal, and I took them up one by one in my hands, ready mounted and armed, with the proper officers to exercise them. As soon as they got in order, they divided into two parties, performed mock skirmishes, discharged blunt arrows, drew their swords, fled and pursued, attacked and retired, and in short discovered the best military discipline I ever beheld. The parallel sticks secured them and their horses from falling over the stage; and the Emperor was so much delighted that he ordered this entertainment to be repeated several days, and once was pleased to be lifted up, and give the word of command; and, with great difficulty, persuaded even the Empress herself to let me hold her in her close chair within two yards of the stage, from whence she was able to take a full view of the whole performance. It was by good fortune that no ill accident happened in these entertainments, only once a fiery horse, that belonged to one of the captains, pawing with his hoof, struck a hole in my handkerchief, and his foot slipping, he overthrew his rider and himself; but I immediately relieved them both, and covering the hole with one hand, I set down the troop with the other, in the same manner as I took them up. The horse that fell was strained in the left shoulder, but the rider got no hurt, and I repaired my handkerchief as well as I could; however, I would not trust to the strength of it any more in such dangerous enterprises.

About two or three days before I was set at liberty, as I was entertaining the court with these kind of feats, there arrived an express to inform his Majesty, that some of his subjects, riding near the place where I was first taken up, had seen a great black substance lying on the ground, very oddly shaped, extended its edges round as wide as his Majesty's bed-chamber, and rising up in the middle as high as a man; that it was no living creature, as they at first apprehended, for it lay on the grass without motion; and some of them had walked round it several times: that, by mounting upon each other's shoulders, they had got to the top, which was flat and even, and, stamping upon it, they found it was hollow within; that they humbly conceived it might be something belonging to the Man-Mountain;

and if his Majesty pleased, they would undertake to bring
it with only five horses. I presently knew what they
meant, and was glad at heart to receive this intelligence.
It seems upon my first reaching the shore, after our ship-
wreck, I was in such confusion, that, before I came to the
place where I went to sleep, my hat, which I had fastened
with a string to my head while I was rowing, and had stuck
on all the time I was swimming, fell off after I came to land;
the string, as I conjecture, breaking by some accident which
I never observed, but thought my hat had been lost at sea.
I intreated his Imperial Majesty to give orders it might be
brought to me as soon as possible, describing to him the use
and the nature of it; and the next day the waggoners
arrived with it, but not in a very good condition; they had
bored two holes in the brim, within an inch and a half of
the edge, and fastened two hooks in the holes; these hooks
were tied by a long cord to the harness, and thus my hat
was dragged along for above half an English mile; but,
the ground in that country being extremely smooth and
level, it received less damage than I expected.

Two days after this adventure, the Emperor having
ordered that part of his army, which quarters in and about
his metropolis, to be in readiness, took a fancy of diverting
himself in a very singular manner: he desired I would
stand like a colossus, with my legs as far asunder as I conveniently could; he then commanded his general (who
was an old experienced leader, and a great patron of mine)
to draw up the troops in close order, and march them under
me; the foot by twenty-four in a breast, and the horse by
sixteen, with drums beating, colours flying, and pikes
advanced. This body consisted of three thousand foot, and
a thousand horse.

I had sent so many memorials and petitions for my
liberty, that his Majesty at length mentioned the matter
first in the cabinet, and then in a full council; where it
was opposed by none, except Skyresh Bolgolam, who was

pleased, without any provocation, to be my mortal enemy. But it was carried against him by the whole board, and confirmed by the Emperor. That minister was Galbet, or Admiral of the realm, very much in his master's confidence, and a person well versed in affairs, but of a morose and sour complexion. However, he was at length persuaded to comply; but prevailed that the articles and conditions upon which I should be set free, and to which I must swear, should be drawn up by himself. These articles were brought to me by Skyresh Bolgolam in person, attended by two under-secretaries, and several persons of distinction. After they were read, I was demanded to swear to the performance of them; first in the manner of my own country, and afterwards in the method prescribed by their laws, which was to hold my right foot in my left hand, and to place the middle finger of my right hand on the crown of my head, and my thumb on the tip of my right ear. But, because the reader may be curious to have some idea of the style and manner of expression peculiar to that people, as well as to know the articles upon which I recovered my liberty, I have made a translation of the whole instrument, word for word, as near as I was able, which I here offer to the public.

" GOLBASTO MOMAREN EVLAME GURDILO SHEFIN MULLY ULLY GUE, most mighty Emperor of Lilliput, delight and terror of the universe, whose dominions extend five thousand blustrugs (about twelve miles in circumference), to the extremities of the globe; monarch of all monarchs, taller than the sons of men; whose feet press down to the center, and whose head strikes against the sun; at whose nod the princes of the earth shake their knees; pleasant as the spring, comfortable as the summer, fruitful as autumn, dreadful as winter. His most sublime Majesty proposeth to the Man-Mountain, lately arrived to our celestial dominions, the following articles, which, by a solemn oath, he shall be obliged to perform:

" 1st. The Man-Mountain shall not depart from our dominions without our licence under our great seal.

" 2d. He shall not presume to come into our metropolis without our express order; at which time the inhabitants shall have two hours warning to keep within their doors.

" 3d. The said Man-Mountain shall confine his walks to our principal high roads, and not offer to walk or lie down in a meadow or field of corn.

" 4th. As he walks the said roads he shall take the utmost care not to trample upon the bodies of any of our loving subjects, their horses, or carriages, nor take any of our subjects into his hands, without their own consent.

" 5th. If an express requires extraordinary despatch, the Man-Mountain shall be obliged to carry in his pocket the messenger and horse a six days' journey once in every moon, and return the said messenger back (if so required) safe to our imperial presence.

" 6th. He shall be our ally against our enemies in the Island of Blefuscu, and do his utmost to destroy their fleet, which is now preparing to invade us.

" 7th. That the said Man-Mountain shall, at his times of leisure, be aiding and assisting to our workmen, in helping to raise certain great stones, towards covering the wall of the principal park, and other our royal buildings.

" 8th. That the said Man-Mountain shall, in two moons time, deliver in an exact survey of the circumference of our dominions, by a computation of his own paces round the coast.

" Lastly, That, upon his solemn oath to observe all the above articles, the said Man-Mountain shall have a daily allowance of meat and drink sufficient for the support of 1724 of our subjects, with free access to our royal person, and other marks of our favour. Given at our palace at Belfaborac, the twelfth day of the ninety-first moon of our reign."

I swore and subscribed to these articles with great cheerfulness and content, although some of them were not so honourable as I could have wished; which proceeded wholly from the malice of Skyresh Bolgolam, the high admiral; whereupon my chains were immediately unlocked, and I was at full liberty; the Emperor himself in person did me the honour to be by at the whole ceremony. I made my acknowledgments, by prostrating myself at his Majesty's feet, but he commanded me to rise; and after many gracious expressions, which, to avoid the censure of vanity, I shall not repeat, he added that he hoped I should prove a useful servant, and well deserve all the favours he had already conferred upon me, or might do for the future.

The reader may please to observe, that, in the last article for the recovery of my liberty, the Emperor stipulates to allow me a quantity of meat and drink sufficient for the support of 1724 Lilliputians. Some time after, asking a friend at court, how they came to fix on that determinate number, he told me that his Majesty's mathematicians, having taken the height of my body by the help of a quadrant, and finding it to exceed theirs in the proportion of twelve to one, they concluded, from the similarity of their bodies, that mine must contain, at least, 1724 of theirs, and, consequently, would require as much food as was necessary to support that number of Lilliputians. By which, the reader may conceive an idea of the ingenuity of that people, as well as the prudent and exact economy of so great a prince.

CHAPTER IV

THE first request I made, after I had obtained my liberty, was that I might have licence to see Mildendo, the metropolis; which the Emperor easily granted me, but with a special charge to do no hurt either to the inhabitants or their houses. The people had notice by proclamation of my design to visit the town. The wall which encompassed it is two feet and a half high, and at least eleven inches broad, so that a coach and horses may be driven very safely round it; and it is flanked with strong towers, at ten feet distance. I stepped over the great Western Gate, and passed very gently and sideling through the two principal streets, only in my short waistcoat, for fear of damaging the roofs and eaves of the houses with the skirts of my coat. I walked with the utmost circumspection, to avoid treading on any stragglers that might remain in the streets, although the orders were strict that all people should keep in their houses at their own peril. The garret-windows and tops of houses were so crowded with spectators that I thought, in all my travels, I had not seen a more populous place. The city is an exact square, each side of the wall being five hundred feet long. The two great streets, which run cross, and divide it into four quarters, are five feet wide. The lanes and alleys, which I could not enter, but only viewed them as I passed, are from twelve to eighteen inches. The town is capable of holding five hundred thousand souls. The houses are from three to five stories. The shops and markets well provided.

The Emperor's palace is in the centre of the city, where the two great streets met. It is inclosed by a wall of two feet high, and twenty feet distance from the buildings. I had his Majesty's permission to step over this wall; and, the space being so wide between that and the palace, I could easily view it on every side. The outward court is a square of forty feet, and includes two other courts: in the inmost are the royal apartments, which I was very desirous to see, but found it extremely difficult; for the great gates, from one square into another, were but eighteen inches high, and seven inches wide. Now, the buildings of the outer court were at least five feet high, and it was impossible for me to stride over them without infinite damage to the pile, though the walls were strongly built of hewn stone, and four inches thick. At the same time, the Emperor had a great desire that I should see the magnificence of his palace; but this I was not able to do till three days after, which I spent in cutting down with my knife some of the largest trees in the royal park, about an hundred yards distance from the city. Of these trees I made two stools, each about three feet high, and strong enough to bear my weight. The people having received notice a second time, I went again through the city to the palace, with my two stools in my hands. When I came to the side of the outer court, I stood upon one stool, and took the other in my hand; this I lifted over the roof, and gently set it down on the space between the first and second court, which was eight feet wide. I then stepped over the building very conveniently, from one stool to the other, and drew up the first after me with a hooked stick. By this contrivance I got into the inmost court; and, lying down upon my side, I applied my face to the windows of the middle stories, which were left open on purpose, and discovered the most splendid apartments that can be imagined. There I saw the Empress, and the young Princes, in their several lodgings, with their chief attendants about them. Her

Imperial Majesty was pleased to smile very graciously upon me, and gave me out of the window her hand to kiss.

But I shall not anticipate the reader with farther descriptions of this kind, because I reserve them for a greater work, which is now almost ready for the press, containing a general description of this empire, from its first erection, through a long series of princes, with a particular account of their wars and politics, laws, learning, and religion: their plants and animals, their peculiar manners and customs, with other matters very curious and useful; my chief design at present being only to relate such events and transactions as happened to the public or to myself during a residence of about nine months in that empire.

One morning, about a fortnight after I had obtained my liberty, Reldresal, principal secretary (as they style him) of private affairs, came to my house, attended only by one servant. He ordered his coach to wait at a distance, and desired I would give him an hour's audience; which I readily consented to, on account of his quality, and personal merits, as well as the many good offices he had done me during my solicitations at court. I offered to lie down, that he might the more conveniently reach my ear; but he chose rather to let me hold him in my hand during our conversation. He began with compliments on my liberty; said, he might pretend to some merit in it; but, however, added, that, if it had not been for the present situation of things at court, perhaps I might not have obtained it so soon. "For," said he, "as flourishing a condition as we may appear to be in to foreigners, we labour under two mighty evils; a violent faction at home, and the danger of an invasion by a most potent enemy from abroad. As to the first, you are to understand that, for above seventy moons past, there have been two struggling parties in this empire, under the names of Tramecksan and Slamecksan, from the high and low heels of their shoes, by which they distinguish themselves. It is alleged indeed, that the high heels are most agreeable to our ancient constitution; but, however this be, his Majesty hath determined to make use of only low heels in the administration of the government, and all offices in the gift of the crown, as you cannot but observe; and particularly, that his Majesty's imperial heels are lower at least by a drurr than any of his court (drurr is a measure about the fourteenth part of an inch). The animosities between these two parties run so high that they will neither eat nor drink nor talk with each other. We compute the Tramecksan, or high heels, to exceed us in number; but the power is wholly on our side. We apprehend his Imperial Highness, the heir to the crown, to have some tendency towards the high heels; at least, we can plainly discover that one of his heels is higher than the other, which gives him a hobble in his gait. Now, in the midst of these intestine disquiets, we are threatened with an invasion from the island of Blefuscu, which is the other great empire of the universe, almost as large and powerful as this of his Majesty. For as to what we heard you affirm, that there are other kingdoms and states in the world, inhabited by human creatures, as large as yourself, our philosophers are in much doubt, and would rather conjecture that you dropped from the moon, or one of the stars; because it is certain that an hundred mortals of your bulk would, in a short time, destroy all the fruits and cattle of his Majesty's dominions. Besides, our histories of six thousand moons make no mention of any other regions than the two great empires of Lilliput and Blefuscu, which two mighty powers have, as I was going to tell you, been engaged in a most obstinate war for six and thirty moons past. It began upon the following occasion: It is allowed on all hands that the primitive way of breaking eggs before we eat them was upon the larger end; but his present Majesty's grandfather, while he was a boy, going to eat an egg, and breaking it according to the ancient practice, happened to cut one of his fingers. Whereupon the

Emperor, his father, published an edict, commanding all
his subjects, upon great penalties, to break the smaller end
of their eggs.   The people so highly resented this law, that
our histories tell us, there have been six rebellions raised on
that account; wherein one emperor lost his life, and another
his crown.   These civil commotions were constantly
fomented by the monarchs of Blefuscu; and when they
were quelled, the exiles always fled for refuge to that
empire.   It is computed that eleven thousand persons have
at several times suffered death rather than submit to break
their eggs at the smaller end.   Many hundred large volumes
have been published upon this controversy; but the books
of the Big-endians have been long forbidden, and the whole
party rendered incapable by law of holding employments.
During the course of these troubles the emperors of
Blefuscu did frequently expostulate by their ambassadors,
accusing us of making a schism in religion, by offending
against a fundamental doctrine of our great Prophet
Lustrog, in the fifty-fourth chapter of the Blundecral
(which is their Alcoran).   This, however, is thought to be
a mere strain upon the text; for the words are these: That
all true believers break their eggs at the convenient end.
And which is the convenient end seems, in my humble
opinion, to be left to every man's conscience, or at least in
the power of the chief magistrate to determine.   Now,
the Big-endian exiles have found so much credit in the
Emperor of Blefuscu's court and so much private assistance and encouragement from their party here at home,
that a bloody war hath been carried on between the two
empires for thirty-six moons, with various success; during
which time we have lost forty capital ships, and a much
greater number of smaller vessels, together with thirty
thousand of our best seamen and soldiers; and the damage
received by the enemy is reckoned to be somewhat greater
than ours.   However, they have now equipped a numerous
fleet, and are just preparing to make a descent upon us;

and his Imperial Majesty, placing great confidence in your valour and strength, hath commanded me to lay this account of his affairs before you."

I desired the secretary to present my humble duty to the Emperor, and to let him know that I thought it would not become me, who was a foreigner, to interfere with parties; but I was ready, with the hazard of my life, to defend his person and state against all invaders.

CHAPTER V

THE empire of Blefuscu is an island, situated to the north-east side of Lilliput, from whence it is parted only by a channel of eight hundred yards wide. I had not yet seen it, and upon this notice of an intended invasion, I avoided appearing on that side of the coast, for fear of being discovered by some of the enemy's ships, who had received no intelligence of me, all intercourse between the two empires having been strictly forbidden during the war, upon pain of death, and an embargo laid by our Emperor upon all vessels whatsoever. I communicated to his Majesty a project I had formed of seizing the enemy's whole fleet: which, as our scouts assured us, lay at anchor in the harbour ready to sail with the first fair wind. I consulted the most experienced seamen upon the depth of the channel, which they had often plumbed, who told me, that in the middle, at high water, it was seventy glumgluffs deep, which is about six feet of European measure; and the rest of it fifty glumgluffs at most. I walked towards the north-east coast, over against Blefuscu; where, lying down behind a hillock, I took out my small perspective glass, and viewed the enemy's fleet at anchor, consisting of about fifty men-of-war, and a great number of transports: I then came back to my house, and gave order (for which I had a warrant) for a great quantity of the strongest cable and bars of iron. The cable was about as thick as pack-thread, and the bars of the length and size of a knitting needle. I trebled the cable to make it stronger, and, for the same reason, I twisted three of the iron bars together, binding the extremities into a hook. Having thus fixed fifty hooks to as many cables, I went back to the north-east coast, and putting off my coat, shoes, and stockings, walked into the sea, in my leathern jerkin, about an hour before high water. I waded with what haste I could, and swam in the middle about thirty yards, till I felt ground; I arrived to the fleet in less than half an hour. The enemy was so frighted when they saw me, that they leaped out of their ships, and swam to the shore, where there could not be fewer than thirty thousand souls. I then took my tackling, and, fastening a hook to the hole at the prow of each, I tied all the cords together at the end. While I was thus employed, the enemy discharged several thousand arrows, many of which stuck in my hands and face: and, besides the excessive smart, gave me much disturbance in my work. My greatest apprehension was for mine eyes, which I should have infallibly lost, if I had not suddenly thought of an expedient. I kept among other little necessaries a pair of spectacles in a private pocket, which, as I observed before, had escaped the Emperor's searchers. These I took out and fastened as strongly as I could upon my nose, and, thus armed, went on boldly with my work in spite of the enemy's arrows, many of which struck against the glasses of my spectacles, but without any other effect, farther than a little to discompose them. I had now fastened all the hooks, and, taking the knot in my hand, began to pull, but not a ship would stir, for they were all too fast held by their anchors, so that the boldest part of my enterprise remained. I therefore let go the cord, and leaving the hooks fixed to the ships, I resolutely cut with my knife the cables that fastened the anchors, receiving above two hundred shots in my face and hands; then I took up the knotted end of the cables to which my hooks were tied, and with great ease drew fifty of the enemy's largest men-of-war after me.

The Blefuscudians, who had not the least imagination of what I intended, were at first confounded with astonishment. They had seen me cut the cables, and thought my design was only to let the ships run adrift, or fall foul on each other: but when they perceived the whole fleet moving in order, and saw me pulling at the end, they set up such a scream of grief and despair, that it is almost impossible to describe or conceive. When I had got out of danger, I stopt a while to pick out the arrows that stuck in my hands and face; and rubbed on some of the same ointment that was given me at my first arrival, as I have formerly mentioned. I then took off my spectacles, and, waiting about an hour till the tide was a little fallen, I waded through the middle with my cargo, and arrived safe at the royal port of Lilliput.

The Emperor and his whole court stood on the shore expecting the issue of this great adventure. They saw the ships move forward in a large half-moon, but could not discern me, who was up to my breast in water. When I advanced to the middle of the channel, they were yet in more pain, because I was under water to my neck. The Emperor concluded me to be drowned, and that the enemy's fleet was approaching in a hostile manner: but he was soon eased of his fears, for the channel growing shallower every step I made, I came in a short time within hearing, and, holding up the end of the cable by which the fleet was fastened, I cried in a loud voice, Long live the most puissant Emperor of Lilliput! This great prince received me at my landing with all possible encomiums, and created me a nardac upon the spot, which is the highest title of honour among them.

His Majesty desired I would take some other opportunity of bringing all the rest of his enemy's ships into his ports. And so unmeasurable is the ambition of princes, that he seemed to think of nothing less than reducing the whole empire of Blefuscu into a province, and governing it by a viceroy; of destroying the Big-endian exiles, and compelling that people to break the smaller end of their eggs, by which he would remain the sole monarch of the whole world. But I endeavoured to divert him from his design, by many arguments drawn from the topics of policy as well as justice: and I plainly protested, that I would never be an instrument of bringing a free and brave people into slavery. And, when the matter was debated in council, the wisest part of the ministry were of my opinion.

This open bold declaration of mine was so opposite to the schemes and politics of his Imperial Majesty, that he could never forgive me; he mentioned it in a very artful manner at council, where I was told that some of the wisest appeared, at least, by their silence, to be of my opinion; but others, who were my secret enemies, could not forbear some expressions, which by a side-wind reflected on me. And from this time began an intrigue between his Majesty and a junto of ministers maliciously bent against me, which broke out in less than two months, and had like to have ended in my utter destruction. Of so little weight are the greatest services to princes, when put into the balance with a refusal to gratify their passions.

About three weeks after this exploit, there arrived a solemn embassy from Blefuscu, with humble offers of a peace; which was soon concluded upon conditions very advantageous to our Emperor, wherewith I shall not trouble the reader. There were six ambassadors, with a train of about five hundred persons, and their entry was very magnificent, suitable to the grandeur of their master, and the importance of their business. When their treaty was finished, wherein I did them several good offices by the credit I now had, or at least appeared to have at court, their Excellencies, who were privately told how much I had been their friend, made me a visit in form. They began with many compliments upon my valour and generosity, invited me to that kingdom in the Emperor their master's name, and desired me to shew them some proofs of my prodigious strength, of which they had heard so many

wonders; wherein I readily obliged them, but shall not
trouble the reader with the particulars.

When I had for some time entertained their Excellencies to their infinite satisfaction and surprise, I desired
they would do me the honour to present my most humble
respects to the Emperor their master, the renown of whose
virtues had so justly filled the whole world with admiration, and whose royal person I resolved to attend before I
returned to my own country: accordingly, the next time
I had the honour to see our Emperor, I desired his general
licence to wait on the Blefuscudian monarch, which he was
pleased to grant me, as I could plainly perceive, in a very
cold manner; but could not guess the reason, till I had a
whisper from a certain person, that Flimnap and Bolgolam
had represented my intercourse with those ambassadors as
a mark of disaffection, from which I am sure my heart was
wholly free. And this was the first time I began to conceive some imperfect idea of courts and ministers.

It is to be observed, that these ambassadors spoke to
me by an interpreter, the languages of both empires differ-
ing as much from each other as any two in Europe, and
each nation priding itself upon the antiquity, beauty, and
energy of their own tongues, with an avowed contempt for
that of their neighbour; yet our Emperor, standing upon
the advantage he had got by the seizure of their fleet,
obliged them to deliver their credentials and make their
speech in the Lilliputian tongue. And it must be confessed that, from the great intercourse of trade and commerce between both realms, from the continual reception
of exiles, which is mutual among them, and from the custom
in each empire to send their young nobility and richer
gentry to the other, in order to polish themselves by seeing
the world, and understanding men and manners, there are
few persons of distinction, or merchants, or seamen, who
dwell in the maritime parts, but what can hold conversation in both tongues; as I found some weeks after, when I

went to pay my respects to the Emperor of Blefuscu,
which, in the midst of great misfortunes through the malice
of my enemies, proved a very happy adventure to me, as I
shall relate in its proper place.

The reader may remember, that, when I signed those
articles upon which I recovered my liberty, there were
some which I disliked upon account of their being too
servile, neither could anything but an extreme necessity
have forced me to submit. But, being now a nardac of
the highest rank in that Empire, such offices were looked
upon as below my dignity, and the Emperor (to do him
justice) never once mentioned them to me.

CHAPTER VI

ALTHOUGH I intend to leave the description of this empire to a particular treatise, yet, in the meantime, I am content to gratify the curious reader with some general ideas. As the common size of the natives is somewhat under six inches high, so there is an exact proportion in all other animals, as well as plants and trees: for instance, the tallest horses and oxen are between four and five inches in height, the sheep an inch and half, more or less; their geese about the bigness of a sparrow, and so the several gradations downwards, till you come to the smallest, which, to my sight, were almost invisible; but nature hath adapted the eyes of the Lilliputians to all objects proper for their view: they see with great exactness, but at no great distance. And, to shew the sharpness of their sight towards objects that are near, I have been much pleased with observing a cook pulling a lark, which was not so large as a common fly, and a young girl threading an invisible needle with invisible silk. Their tallest trees are about seven feet high; I mean some of those in the great Royal Park, the tops whereof I could but just reach with my fist clinched. The other vegetables are in the same proportion; but this I leave to the reader's imagination.

I shall say but little at present of their learning, which for many ages hath flourished in all its branches among them: but their manner of writing is very peculiar, being neither from the left to the right, like the Europeans; nor from the right to the left, like the Arabians; nor from up to down, like the Chinese; but aslant from one corner of the paper to the other, like ladies in England.

They bury their dead with their heads directly downwards, because they hold an opinion that in eleven thousand moons they are all to rise again, in which period the earth (which they conceive to be flat) will turn upside down, and by this means they shall, at their resurrection, be found ready standing on their feet. The learned among them confess the absurdity of this doctrine, but the practice still continues, in compliance to the vulgar.

There are some laws and customs in this empire very peculiar; and, if they were not so directly contrary to those of my own dear country, I should be tempted to say a little in their justification. It is only to be wished they were as well executed. The first I shall mention relates to informers. All crimes against the State are punished here with the utmost severity; but, if the person accused maketh his innocence plainly to appear upon his trial, the accuser is immediately put to an ignominious death; and, out of his goods or lands, the innocent person is quadruply recompensed for the loss of his time, for the danger he underwent, for the hardship of his imprisonment, and for all the charges he hath been at in making his defence. Or, if that fund be deficient, it is largely supplied by the crown. The Emperor does also confer on him some public mark of his favour, and proclamation is made of his innocence through the whole city.

They look upon fraud as a greater crime than theft, and therefore seldom fail to punish it with death; for they allege, that care and vigilance, with a very common under-standing, may preserve a man's goods from thieves, but honesty has no fence against superior cunning; and since it is necessary that there should be a perpetual intercourse of buying and selling, and dealing upon credit, where fraud is permitted and connived at, or hath no law to punish it, the honest dealer is always undone, and the knave gets the advantage. I remember when I was once interceding with the king for a criminal, who had wronged his master of a great sum of money, which he had received by order and

ran away with; and happening to tell his Majesty, by way
of extenuation, that it was only a breach of trust; the
Emperor thought it monstrous in me to offer, as a defence,
the greatest aggravation of the crime: and truly I had little
to say in return, farther than the common answer, that
different nations had different customs; for, I confess, I
was heartily ashamed.

Although we usually call reward and punishment the
two hinges upon which all Government turns, yet I could
never observe this maxim to be put in practice by any
nation except that of Lilliput. Whoever can there bring
sufficient proof that he hath strictly observed the laws of
his country for seventy-three moons, hath a claim to certain
privileges, according to his quality and condition of life,
with a proportionable sum of money out of a fund appropriated for that use: he likewise acquires the title of Snil-
pall, or legal, which is added to his name, but does not
descend to posterity. And these people thought it a prodigious defect of policy among us when I told them that
our laws were enforced only by penalties, without any
mention of reward. It is upon this account that the
image of Justice, in their courts of judicature, is formed
with six eyes, two before, as many behind, and on each side
one, to signify circumspection; with a bag of gold open in
her right hand, and a sword sheathed in her left, to shew
she is more disposed to reward than to punish.

In choosing persons for all employments, they have
more regard to good morals than to great abilities; for,
since Government is necessary to mankind, they believe
that the common size of human understandings is fitted to
some station or other, and that Providence never intended
to make the management of public affairs a mystery, to be
comprehended only by a few persons of sublime genius, of
which there seldom are three born in an age; but they
suppose truth, justice, temperance, and the like, to be in
every man's power, the practice of which virtues, assisted by

experience and a good intention, would qualify any man for the service of his country, except where a course of study is required. But they thought the want of moral virtues was so far from being supplied by superior endowments of the mind, that employments could never be put into such dangerous hands as those of persons so qualified; and at least, that the mistakes, committed by ignorance in a virtuous disposition, would never be of such fatal consequence to the public weal as the practices of a man whose inclinations led him to be corrupt, and had great abilities to manage and multiply and defend his corruptions.

In like manner the disbelief of a Divine Providence renders a man incapable of holding any public station; for, since kings avow themselves to be the deputies of Providence, the Lilliputians think nothing can be more absurd than for a Prince to employ such men as disown the authority under which they act.

In relating these and the following laws, I would only be understood to mean the original institutions, and not the most scandalous corruptions into which these people are fallen by the degenerate nature of man. For as to that infamous practice of acquiring great employments by dancing on the ropes, or badges of favour and distinction by leaping over sticks and creeping under them, the reader is to observe that they were first introduced by the grandfather of the Emperor now reigning, and grew to the present height by the gradual increase of party and faction.

Ingratitude is among them a capital crime, as we read it to have been in some other countries; for they reason thus, that whoever makes ill returns to his benefactor, must needs be a common enemy to the rest of mankind, from whom he hath received no obligation, and therefore such a man is not fit to live.

Their notions relating to the duties of parents and children differ extremely from ours. Their opinion is, that parents are the last of all others to be trusted with the education of their own children; and therefore they have in every town public nurseries, where all parents, except cottagers and labourers, are obliged to send their infants of both sexes to be reared and educated when they come to the age of twenty moons, at which time they are supposed to have some rudiments of docility. These schools are of several kinds, suited to different qualities, and to both sexes. They have certain professors well skilled in preparing children for such a condition of life as befits the rank of their parents, and their own capacities as well as inclinations. I shall first say something of the male nurseries, and then of the female.

The nurseries for males of noble or eminent birth are provided with grave and learned professors, and their several deputies. The clothes and food of the children are plain and simple. They are bred up in the principles of honour, justice, courage, modesty, clemency, religion, and love of their country; they are always employed in some business, except in the times of eating and sleeping, which are very short, and two hours for diversions, consisting of bodily exercises. They are dressed by men till four years of age, and then are obliged to dress themselves, although their quality be ever so great; and the women attendants, who are aged proportionably to ours at fifty, perform only the most menial offices. They are never suffered to converse with servants, but go together in smaller and greater numbers to take their diversions, and always in the presence of a professor, or one of his deputies; whereby they avoid those early bad impressions of folly and vice to which our children are subject. Their parents are suffered to see them only twice a year; the visit is to last but an hour. They are allowed to kiss the child at meeting and parting; but a professor, who always stands by on those occasions, will not suffer them to whisper, or use any fondling expressions, or bring any presents of toys, sweet-meats, and the like.

The pension from each family for the education and entertainment of a child, upon failure of due payment, is levied by the Emperor's officers.

The nurseries for children of ordinary gentlemen, merchants, traders, and handicrafts, are managed proportionably after the same manner; only those designed for trades are put out apprentices at eleven years old, whereas those of persons of quality continue in their exercises till fifteen, which answers to twenty-one with us: but the confinement is gradually lessened for the last three years.

In the female nurseries, the young girls of quality are educated much like the males, only they are dressed by orderly servants of their own sex; but always in the presence of a professor or deputy, till they come to dress themselves, which is at five years old. And if it be found that these nurses ever presume to entertain the girls with frightful or foolish stories, they are publicly whipped thrice about the city, imprisoned for a year, and banished for life to the most desolate part of the country. Thus the young ladies there are as much ashamed of being cowards and fools as the men, and despise all personal ornaments beyond decency and cleanliness: neither did I perceive any difference in their education made by their difference of sex, only that the exercises of the females were not altogether so robust; and that some rules were given them relating to domestic life, and a smaller compass of learning was enjoined them: For their maxim is, that, among people of quality, a wife should be always a reasonable and agreeable companion, because she cannot always be young. When the girls are twelve years old, which among them is the marriageable age, their parents or guardians take them home, with great expressions of gratitude to the professors, and seldom without tears of the young lady and her companion.

In the nurseries of the females of the meaner sort, the

children are instructed in all kinds of works proper for their sex, and their several degrees: those intended for apprentices, are dismissed at seven years old, the rest are kept to eleven.

The meaner families, who have children at these nurseries, are obliged, besides their annual pension, which is as low as possible, to return to the steward of the nursery a small monthly share of their gettings, to be a portion for the child: and therefore all parents are limited in their expenses by the law. For the Lilliputians think nothing can be more unjust, than for people to bring children into the world, and leave the burthen of supporting them on the public. As to persons of quality, they give security to appropriate a certain sum for each child, suitable to their condition; and these funds are always managed with good husbandry, and the most exact justice.

The cottagers and labourers keep their children at home, their business being only to till and cultivate the earth, and therefore their education is of little consequence to the public: but the old and diseased among them are supported by hospitals, for begging is a trade unknown in this empire.

And here it may, perhaps, divert the curious reader, to give some account of my domestic life, and my manner of living in this country, during a residence of nine months and thirteen days. Having a head mechanically turned, and being likewise forced by necessity, I had made for myself a table and chair convenient enough, out of the largest trees in the royal park. Two hundred sempstresses were employed to make me shirts, and linen for bed and table, all of the strongest and coarsest kind they could get; which, however, they were forced to quilt together in several folds, for the thickest was some degrees finer than lawn. Their linen is usually three inches wide, and three feet make a piece. The sempstresses took my measure as I lay on the ground, one standing at my neck, and another at

my mid-leg, with a strong cord extended, that each held
by the end, while the third measured the length of the cord
with a rule of an inch long.   Then they measured my right
thumb and desired no more; for, by a mathematical computation, that twice round the thumb is once round the
wrist, and so on to the neck and the waist; and by the help
of my old shirt, which I displayed on the ground before
them for a pattern, they fitted me exactly.   Three hundred
tailors were employed in the same manner to make me
clothes; but they had another contrivance for taking my
measure.   I kneeled down, and they raised a ladder from
the ground to my neck; upon this ladder one of them
mounted, and let fall a plumb-line from my collar to the
floor, which just answered the length of my coat; but my
waist and arms I measured myself.   When my clothes were
finished, which was done in my house (for the largest of
theirs would not have been able to hold them) they looked
like the patch-work made by the ladies in England, only
that mine were all of a colour.

I had three hundred cooks to dress my victuals, in little
convenient huts built about my house, where they and
their families lived, and prepared me two dishes a-piece.   I
took up twenty waiters in my hand, and placed them on
the table; an hundred more attended below on the ground,
some with dishes of meat, and some with barrels of wine
and other liquors, slung on their shoulders, all of which the
waiters above drew up as I wanted, in a very ingenious
manner, by certain cords, as we draw the bucket up a well
in Europe.   A dish of their meat was a good mouthful, and
a barrel of their liquor a reasonable draught.   Their mutton
yields to ours, but their beef is excellent.   I have had a
surloin so large, that I have been forced to make three
bites of it; but this is rare.   My servants were astonished
to see me eat it, bones and all, as in our country we do the
leg of a lark.   Their geese and turkeys I usually eat at a
mouthful; and, I must confess, they far exceed ours.   Of

their smaller fowl, I could take up twenty or thirty at the end of my knife.

One day his Imperial Majesty, being informed of my way of living, desired that himself and his royal consort, with the young princes of the blood of both sexes, might have the happiness (as he was pleased to call it) of dining with me. They came accordingly, and I placed them upon chairs of state on my table, just over against me, with their guards about them. Flimnap, the lord high treasurer, attended there likewise, with his white staff; and I observed he often looked on me with a sour countenance, which I would not seem to regard, but eat more than usual, in honour to my dear country, as well as to fill the court with admiration. I have some private reasons to believe that this visit from his Majesty gave Flimnap an opportunity of doing me ill offices to his master. That minister had always been my secret enemy, though he outwardly caressed me more than was usual to the moroseness of his nature. He represented to the Emperor the low condition of his treasury; that he was forced to take up money at great discount; that exchequer bills would not circulate under nine per cent. below par; that, in short, I had cost his Majesty above a million and a half of sprugs (their greatest gold coin, about the bigness of a spangle) and, upon the whole, that it would be advisable in the Emperor to take the first fair occasion of dismissing me.

On occasions when a servant gave me notice of the arrival of a coach, my custom was to go immediately to the door; and, after paying my respects, to take up the coach and two horses very carefully in my hands (for, if there were six horses, the postillion always unharnessed four) and place them on a table, where I had fixed a moveable rim quite round, of five inches high, to prevent accidents. And I have often had four coaches and horses at once on my table full of company, while I sat in my chair, leaning my face towards them; and, when I was engaged with one set, the coachman would gently drive the others round my table. I have passed many an afternoon very agreeably in these conversations. But I defy the treasurer to prove that any person ever came to me incognito, except the secretary Reldresal, who was sent by express command of his Imperial Majesty, as I have before related. I then had the honour to be a nardac, which the treasurer himself is not; for all the world knows that he is only a glumglum, a title inferior by one degree, as that of a marquis is to a duke in England, although I allow he preceded me in right of his post. These false informations made Flimnap, the treasurer, shew me an ill countenance; and although he were at last undeceived, yet I lost all credit with him, and found my interest decline very fast with the Emperor himself, who was, indeed, too much governed by that favourite.

CHAPTER VII

BEFORE I proceed to give an account of my leaving this kingdom, it may be proper to inform the reader of a private intrigue which had been for two months forming against me.

I had been hitherto all my life a stranger to courts, for which I was unqualified by the meanness of my condition. I had, indeed, heard and read enough of the dispositions of great princes and ministers; but never expected to have found such terrible effects of them in so remote a country, governed, as I thought, by very different maxims from those in Europe.

When I was just preparing to pay my attendance on the Emperor of Blefuscu, a considerable person at court (to whom I had been very serviceable, at a time when he lay under the highest displeasure of his Imperial Majesty) came to my house very privately at night in a close chair, and, without sending his name, desired admittance. The chairmen were dismissed; I put the chair, with his lordship in it, into my coat pocket; and, giving orders to a trusty servant to say I was indisposed and gone to sleep, I fastened the door of my house, placed the chair on the table, according to my usual custom, and sat down by it. After the common salutations were over, observing his lordship's countenance full of concern, and enquiring into the reason, he desired I would hear him with patience, in a matter that highly concerned my honour and my life. His speech was to the following effect, for I took notes of it as soon as he left me.

" You are to know," said he, " that several committees of council have been lately called in the most private manner on your account; and it is but two days since his Majesty came to a full resolution.

" You are very sensible that Skyresh Bolgolam (galbet, or high admiral) hath been your mortal enemy almost ever since your arrival: his original reasons I know not; but his hatred is increased since your great success against Blefuscu, by which his glory, as admiral, is much obscured. This lord, in conjunction with Flimnap, the high treasurer, whose enmity against you is notorious on account of his lady, Limtoc the general, Lalcon the chamberlain, and Balmuff the grand justiciary, have prepared articles of impeachment against you, for treason, and other capital crimes."

This preface made me so impatient, being conscious of my own merits and innocence, that I was going to interrupt; when he intreated me to be silent, and thus proceeded:

" Out of gratitude for the favours you have done me, I procured information of the whole proceedings, and a copy of the articles, wherein I venture my head for your service.

Articles of Impeachment against QUINBUS FLESTRIN *(the* MAN-MOUNTAIN*).*

ARTICLE I

" ' That the said Quinbus Flestrin having brought the imperial fleet of Blefuscu into the royal port, and being afterwards commanded by his Imperial Majesty to seize all the other ships of the said empire of Blefuscu, and reduce that empire to a province, to be governed by a viceroy from hence, and to destroy and put to death not only all the Big-endian exiles, but likewise all the people of that empire, who would not immediately forsake the Big-endian heresy: he, the said Flestrin, like a false traitor against his most auspicious, serene, Imperial Majesty, did petition to be excused from the said service, upon pretence of unwillingness to force the consciences, or destroy the liberties and lives of innocent people.

ARTICLE II

" ' That, whereas certain ambassadors arrived from the court of Blefuscu, to sue for peace in his Majesty's court: he the said Flestrin did, like a false traitor, aid, abet, comfort, and divert the said ambassadors, although he knew them to be servants to a prince who was lately an open enemy to his Imperial Majesty, and in open war against his said Majesty.

ARTICLE III

" ' That the said Quinbus Flestrin, contrary to the duty of a faithful subject, is now preparing to make a voyage to the court and empire of Blefuscu, for which he hath received only verbal licence from his Imperial Majesty; and under colour of the said licence doth falsely and traitorously intend to take the said voyage, and thereby to aid, comfort, and abet the Emperor of Blefuscu, so late an enemy, and in open war with his Imperial Majesty aforesaid.'

" There are some other articles, but these are the most important, of which I have read you an abstract.

" In the several debates upon this impeachment, it must be confessed that his Majesty gave many marks of his great lenity, often urging the services you had done him, and endeavouring to extenuate your crimes. The treasurer and admiral insisted that you should be put to the most painful and ignominious death, by setting fire on your house at night, and the general was to attend with twenty thousand men armed with poisoned arrows, to shoot you on the face and hands. Some of your servants were to have private orders to strew a poisonous juice on your shirts and sheets, which would soon make you tear your own flesh, and die in the utmost torture. The general came into the same opinion; so that for a long time there was a majority against you: but his Majesty resolving, if possible, to spare your life, at last brought off the chamberlain.

" Upon this incident, Reldresal, principal secretary for private affairs, who always approved himself your true friend, was commanded by the Emperor to deliver his opinion, which he accordingly did: and therein justified the good thoughts you have of him. He allowed your crimes to be great, but that still there was room for mercy, the most commendable virtue in a prince, and for which his Majesty was so justly celebrated. He said the friendship between you and him was so well known to the world, that perhaps the most honourable board might think him partial. However, in obedience to the command he had received, he would freely offer his sentiments. That if his Majesty, in consideration of your services, and pursuant to his own merciful disposition, would please to spare your life, and only give order to put out both your eyes, he humbly conceived, that, by this expedient, justice might in some measure be satisfied, and all the world would applaud the lenity of the Emperor, as well as the fair and generous proceedings of those who have the honour to be his counsellors. That the loss of your eyes would be no impediment to your bodily strength, by which you might still be useful to his Majesty. That blindness is an addition to courage, by concealing dangers from us; that the fear you had for your eyes was the greatest difficulty in bringing over the enemy's fleet, and it would be sufficient for you to see by the eyes of the ministers, since the greatest princes do no more.

" This proposal was received with the utmost disapprobation by the whole board. Bolgolam, the admiral, could not preserve his temper; but, rising up in fury, said, he wondered how the secretary durst presume to give his opinion for preserving the life of a traitor: that the services you had performed were, by all true reasons of state, the

great aggravation of your crimes; that the same strength,
which enabled you to bring over the enemy's fleet, might
serve, upon the first discontent, to carry it back; that he
had good reasons to think you were a Big-endian in your
heart; and as treason begins in the heart, before it appears
in overt acts, so he accused you as a traitor on that account,
and therefore insisted you should be put to death.

" The treasurer was of the same opinion. He showed
to what straits his Majesty's revenue was reduced by the
charge of maintaining you, which would soon grow insupportable: that the secretary's expedient of putting out
your eyes was so far from being a remedy against this evil,
it would probably increase it, as it is manifest from the
common practice of blinding some kind of fowl, after which
they fed the faster, and grew sooner fat; that his sacred
Majesty and the council, who are your judges, were in
their own consciences fully convinced of your guilt, which
was a sufficient argument to condemn you to death, without
the formal proofs required by the strict letter of the law.

" But his Imperial Majesty, fully determined against
capital punishment, was graciously pleased to say, that,
since the council thought the loss of your eyes too easy a
censure, some other may be inflicted hereafter. And your
friend, the secretary, humbly desiring to be heard again,
in answer to what the treasurer had objected concerning
the great charge his Majesty was at in maintaining you,
said that his Excellency, who had the sole disposal of the
Emperor's revenue, might easily provide against that evil
by gradually lessening your establishment, by which, for
want of sufficient food, you would grow weak and faint, and
lose your appetite, and consume in a few months; neither
would the stench of your carcase be then so dangerous,
when it should become more than half diminished; and
immediately, upon your death, five or six thousand of his
Majesty's subjects might, in two or three days, cut your
flesh from your bones, take it away by cartloads, and bury

it in distant parts to prevent infection, leaving the skeleton as a monument of admiration to posterity.

" Thus, by the great friendship of the secretary, the whole affair was compromised. It was strictly enjoined that the project of starving you, by degrees, should be kept a secret, but the sentence of putting out your eyes was entered on the books; none dissenting except Bolgolam, the admiral, who, being a creature of the Empress, was perpetually instigated by her Majesty to insist upon your death.

" In three days, your friend, the secretary, will be directed to come to your house, and read before you the articles of impeachment; and then to signify the great lenity and favour of his Majesty and council, whereby you are only condemned to the loss of your eyes, which his Majesty doth not question you will gratefully and humbly submit to; and twenty of his Majesty's surgeons will attend, in order to see the operation well performed, by discharging very sharp-pointed arrows into the balls of your eyes as you lie on the ground.

" I leave to your prudence what measures you will take; and, to avoid suspicion, I must immediately return in as private manner as I came."

His lordship did so, and I remained alone, under many doubts and perplexities of mind.

It was a custom introduced by this prince and his ministry (very different, as I have been assured, from the practices of former times) that after the court had decreed any cruel execution, either to gratify the monarch's resentment or the malice of a favourite, the Emperor always made a speech to his whole council, expressing his great lenity and tenderness, as qualities known and confessed by all the world. This speech was immediately published through the kingdom; nor did anything terrify the people so much as those encomiums on his Majesty's mercy, because it was observed, that, the more these praises were enlarged and insisted on, the more inhuman was the punishment, and the sufferer more innocent. And as to myself, I must confess, having never been designed for a courtier, either by my birth or education, I was so ill a judge of things, that I could not discover the lenity and favour of this sentence, but conceived it (perhaps erroneously) rather to be rigorous than gentle. I sometimes thought of standing my trial; for, although I could not deny the facts alleged in the several articles, yet I hoped they would admit of some extenuation. But having in my life perused many state-trials, which I ever observed to terminate as the judges thought fit to direct, I durst not rely on so dangerous a decision in so critical a juncture, and against such powerful enemies. Once I was strongly bent upon resistance, for, while I had liberty, the whole strength of that empire could hardly subdue me, and I might easily with stones pelt the metropolis to pieces; but I soon rejected that project with horror, by remembering the oath I had made to the Emperor, the favours I received from him, and the high title of nardac he conferred upon me. Neither had I so soon learned the gratitude of courtiers, to persuade myself that his Majesty's present severities acquitted me of all past obligations.

At last I fixed upon a resolution, for which it is probable I may incur some censure, and not unjustly; for I confess I owe the preserving my eyes, and consequently my liberty, to my own great rashness, and want of experience; because, if I had then known the nature of princes and ministers, which I have since observed in many other courts, and their methods of treating criminals less obnoxious than myself, I should with great alacrity and readiness have submitted to so easy a punishment. But hurried on by the precipitancy of youth, and having his Imperial Majesty's licence to pay my attendance upon the Emperor of Blefuscu, I took this opportunity, before the three days were elapsed, to send a letter to my friend the secretary, signifying my resolution of setting out that morning for Blefuscu, pursuant to the leave I had got; and, without waiting for an answer, I went to that side of the island where our fleet lay. I seized a large man-of-war, tied a cable to the prow, and, lifting up the anchors, I stript myself, put my clothes (together with my coverlet, which I brought under my arm) into the vessel, and drawing it after me, between wading and swimming, arrived at the royal port of Blefuscu, where the people had long expected me; they lent me two guides to direct me to the capital city, which is of the same name. I held them in my hands till I came within two hundred yards of the gate, and desired them to signify my arrival to one of the secretaries, and let him know, I there waited his Majesty's command. I had an answer in about an hour, that his Majesty, attended by the royal family and great officers of the court, was coming out to receive me. I advanced a hundred yards. The Emperor and his train alighted from their horses, the Empress and ladies from their coaches, and I did not perceive they were in any fright or concern. I lay on the ground to kiss his Majesty's and the Empress's hand. I told his Majesty that I was come according to my promise, and with the licence of the Emperor my master, to have the honour of seeing so mighty a monarch, and to offer him any service in my power consistent with my duty to my own prince; not mentioning a word of my disgrace, because I had hitherto no regular information of it, and might suppose myself wholly ignorant of any such design; neither could I reasonably conceive that the Emperor would discover the secret while I was out of his power; wherein, however, it soon appeared I was deceived.

I shall not trouble the reader with the particular account of my reception at this court, which was suitable to the generosity of so great a prince; nor of the difficulties I was in for want of a house and bed, being forced to lie on the ground, wrapped up in my coverlet.

CHAPTER VIII

THREE days after my arrival, walking out of curiosity to
the north-east coast of the island, I observed, about half
a league off, in the sea, somewhat that looked like a boat
overturned. I pulled off my shoes and stockings, and,
wading two or three hundred yards, I found the object to
approach nearer by force of the tide; and then plainly
saw it to be a real boat, which I supposed might, by some
tempest, have been driven from a ship. Whereupon I
returned immediately towards the city, and desired his
Imperial Majesty to lend me twenty of the tallest vessels
he had left after the loss of his fleet, and three thousand
seamen, under the command of the vice-admiral. This
fleet sailed round, while I went back the shortest way to
the coast, where I first discovered the boat; I found the
tide had driven it still nearer. The seamen were all provided with cordage, which I had beforehand twisted to a
sufficient strength. When the ships came up, I stripped
myself, and waded till I came within an hundred yards of
the boat, after which I was forced to swim till I got up to it.
The seamen threw me the end of the cord, which I fastened
to a hole in the fore-part of the boat, and the other end to a
man-of-war. But I found all my labour to little purpose;
for, being out of my depth, I was not able to work. In
this necessity, I was forced to swim behind, and push the
boat forwards as often as I could, with one of my hands;
and, the tide favouring me, I advanced so far, that I could
just hold up my chin and feel the ground. I rested two or
three minutes, and then gave the boat another shove, and
so on, till the sea was no higher than my arm-pits; and
now, the most laborious part being over, I took out my

other cables, which were stowed in one of the ships, and fastened them first to the boat, and then to nine of the vessels which attended me; the wind being favourable, the seamen towed, and I shoved till we arrived within forty yards of the shore, and, waiting till the tide was out, I got dry to the boat, and by the assistance of two thousand men, with ropes, and engines, I made a shift to turn it on its bottom, and found it was but little damaged.

I shall not trouble the reader with the difficulties I was under, by the help of certain paddles, which cost me ten days making, to get my boat to the royal port of Blefuscu, where a mighty concourse of people appeared upon my arrival, full of wonder at the sight of so prodigious a vessel. I told the Emperor that my good fortune had thrown this boat in my way, to carry me to some place from whence I might return into my native country, and begged his Majesty's orders for getting materials to fit it up, together with his licence to depart, which, after some kind expostulations, he was pleased to grant.

I did very much wonder, in all this time, not to have heard of any express relating to me from our Emperor to the court of Blefuscu. But I was afterwards given privately to understand that his Imperial Majesty, never imagining I had the least notice of his designs, believed I was only gone to Blefuscu, in performance of my promise, according to the licence he had given me, which was well known at our court, and would return in a few days, when the ceremony was ended. But he was at last in pain at my long absence; and, after consulting with the treasurer and the rest of that cabal, a person of quality was dispatched with the copy of the articles against me. This envoy had instructions to represent to the monarch of Blefuscu the great lenity of his master, who was content to punish me no farther than with the loss of my eyes; that I had fled from justice, and, if I did not return in two hours, I should be deprived of my title of nardac, and declared a traitor.

The envoy further added, that in order to maintain the peace and amity between both empires, his master expected that his brother of Blefuscu would give orders to have me sent back to Lilliput, bound hand and foot, to be punished as a traitor.

The Emperor of Blefuscu, having taken three days to consult, returned an answer, consisting of many civilities and excuses. He said that as for sending me bound, his brother knew it was impossible; that although I had deprived him of his fleet, yet he owed great obligations to me for many good offices I had done him in making the peace: that, however, both their Majesties would soon be made easy; for I had found a prodigious vessel on the shore, able to carry me on the sea, which he had given order to fit up with my own assistance and direction; and he hoped, in a few weeks, both empires would be freed from so insupportable an incumbrance.

With this answer the envoy returned to Lilliput, and the monarch of Blefuscu related to me all that had passed; offering me at the same time (but under the strictest confidence) his gracious protection, if I would continue in his service; wherein, although I believed him sincere, yet I resolved never more to put any confidence in princes or ministers, where I could possibly avoid it, and, therefore, with all due acknowledgments for his favourable intentions, I humbly begged to be excused. I told him, that since fortune, whether good or evil, had thrown a vessel in my way, I was resolved to venture myself in the ocean rather than be an occasion of difference between two such mighty monarchs. Neither did I find the Emperor at all displeased, and I discovered, by a certain accident, that he was very glad of my resolution, and so were most of his ministers.

These considerations moved me to hasten my departure somewhat sooner than I intended; to which the court, impatient to have me gone, very readily contributed.

Five hundred workmen were employed to make two sails to my boat, according to my directions, by quilting thirteen fold of their strongest linen together. I was at the pains of making ropes and cables, by twisting ten, twenty, or thirty of the thickest and strongest of theirs. A great stone that I happened to find, after a long search by the sea-shore, served me for an anchor. I had the tallow of three hundred cows for greasing my boat and other uses. I was at incredible pains in cutting down some of the largest timber-trees for oars and masts, wherein I was, however, much assisted by his Majesty's ship-carpenters, who helped me in smoothing them after I had done the rough work.

In about a month, when all was prepared, I sent to receive his Majesty's commands, and to take my leave. The Emperor and royal family came out of the palace; I lay down on my face to kiss his hand, which he very graciously gave me; so did the Empress, and young princes of the blood. His Majesty presented me with fifty purses of two hundred sprugs a-piece, together with his picture at full length, which I put immediately into one of my gloves, to keep it from being hurt. The ceremonies at my departure were too many to trouble the reader with at this time.

I stored the boat with the carcases of an hundred oxen, and three hundred sheep, with bread and drink proportionable, and as much meat ready dressed as four hundred cooks could provide. I took with me six cows and two bulls alive, with as many ewes and rams, intending to carry them into my own country and propagate the breed. And, to feed them on board, I had a good bundle of hay, and a bag of corn. I would gladly have taken a dozen of the natives, but this was a thing the Emperor would by no means permit; and, besides a diligent search into my pockets, his Majesty engaged my honour not to carry away any of his subjects, although with their own consent and desire.

Having thus prepared all things as well as I was able, I set sail on the twenty-fourth day of September 1701, at six in the morning; and when I had gone about four leagues to the northward, the wind being at south-east, at six in the evening I descried a small island about half a league to the north-west. I advanced forward, and cast anchor on the lee-side of the island, which seemed to be uninhabited. I then took some refreshment and went to my rest. I slept well, and I conjecture at least six hours, for I found the day broke in two hours after I awaked. It was a clear night. I eat my breakfast before the sun was up; and heaving anchor, the wind being favourable, I steered the same course that I had done the day before, wherein I was directed by my pocket-compass. My intention was to reach, if possible, one of those islands which I had reason to believe lay on the north-east of Van Diemen's Land. I discovered nothing all that day; but upon the next, about three in the afternoon, when I had by my computation made twenty-four leagues from Blefuscu, I descried a sail steering to the south-east; my course was due east. I hailed her, but could get no answer; yet I found I gained upon her, for the wind slackened. I made all the sail I could, and in half an hour she spied me, then hung out her ancient, and discharged a gun. It is not easy to express the joy I was in upon the unexpected hope of once more seeing my beloved country, and the dear pledges I had left in it. The ship slackened her sails, and I came up with her between five and six in the evening, September 26; but my heart leapt within me to see her English colours. I put my cows and sheep into my coat-pockets, and got on board with all my little cargo of provisions. The vessel was an English merchantman, returning from Japan by the north and south seas, the captain, Mr. John Biddel of Deptford, a very civil man, and an excellent sailor. We were now in the latitude of 30 degrees south; there were about fifty men in the ship; and here I met an old comrade of mine, one Peter Williams, who gave me a good character to the captain. This gentleman treated me with kindness, and desired I

would let him know what place I came from last and whither
I was bound; which I did in few words, but he thought I
was raving, and that the dangers I underwent had disturbed
my head; whereupon I took my black cattle and sheep out
of my pocket, which, after great astonishment, clearly convinced him of my veracity. I then shewed him the gold
given me by the Emperor of Blefuscu, together with his
Majesty's picture at full length, and some other rarities
of that country. I gave him two purses of two hundred
sprugs each, and promised, when we arrived in England, to
make him a present of a cow and a sheep big with young.

I shall not trouble the reader with a particular account
of this voyage, which was very prosperous for the most
part. We arrived in the Downs on the 13th of April 1702.
I had only one misfortune, that the rats on board carried
away one of my sheep; I found her bones in a hole, picked
clean from the flesh. The rest of my cattle I got safe
a-shore, and set them a-grazing in a bowling-green at
Greenwich, where the fineness of the grass made them feed
very heartily, though I had always feared the contrary:
neither could I possibly have preserved them in so long a
voyage if the captain had not allowed me some of his best
biscuit, which rubbed to powder, and mingled with water,
was their constant food. The short time I continued in
England, I made a considerable profit by shewing my
cattle to many persons of quality and others: and, before
I began my second voyage, I sold them for six hundred
pounds. Since my last return, I find the breed is con-
siderably increased, especially the sheep, which I hope will
prove much to the advantage of the woollen manufacture,
by the fineness of the fleeces.

I stayed but two months with my wife and family; for
my insatiable desire of seeing foreign countries would suffer
me to continue no longer. I left fifteen hundred pounds
with my wife, and fixed her in a good house at Redriff. My
remaining stock I carried with me, part in money and part

in goods, in hopes to improve my fortunes. My eldest
uncle John had left me an estate in land, near Epping, of
about thirty pounds a year; and I had a long lease of the
Black Bull in Fetter Lane, which yielded me as much more:
so that I was not in any danger of leaving my family upon
the parish. My son Johnny, named so after his uncle, was
at the Grammar School, and a towardly child. My daughter
Betty (who is now well married, and has children) was then
at her needlework. I took leave of my wife, and boy and
girl, with tears on both sides, and went on board the *Adventure*, a merchant ship, of three hundred tons, bound for
Surat, Captain John Nicholas of Liverpool, commander.
But my account of this voyage must be referred to the second
part of my travels.

THE END OF THE FIRST PART

PART 2

CHAPTER I

HAVING been condemned by nature and fortune to an active and restless life, in two months after my return I again left my native country, and took shipping in the Downs on the 20th day of June 1702, in the *Adventure*, Captain John Nicholas, a Cornish man, commander, bound for Surat. We had a very prosperous gale till we arrived at the Cape of Good Hope, where we landed for fresh water, but, discovering a leak, we unshipped our goods, and wintered there; for the captain falling sick of an ague, we could not leave the Cape till the end of March. We then set sail, and had a good voyage till we passed the Straits of Madagascar; but having got northward of that island, and to about five degrees south latitude, the winds, which in those seas were observed to blow a constant equal gale between the north and west, from the beginning of December to the beginning of May, on the 9th of April began to blow with much greater violence, and more westerly than usual, continuing so for twenty days together, during which time we were driven a little to the east of the Molucca islands, and about three degrees northward of the line, as our captain found by an observation he took the 2nd of May, at which time the wind ceased, and it was a perfect calm, whereat I was not a little rejoiced. But he, being a man experienced in the navigation of those seas, bid us all prepare against a storm, which accordingly happened the day following: for a southern wind, called the southern monsoon, began to set in.

Finding it was like to overblow, we took in our sprit-sail, and stood by to hand the foresail; but, making foul weather, we looked the guns were all fast, and handed the mizzen. The ship lay very broad off, so we thought it better spooning before the sea, than trying or hulling. We reefed the foresail and set him, and hawled aft the fore-sheet; the helm was hard a weather. The ship wore bravely. We belayed the fore down-hall; but the sail was split, and we hawled down the yard, and got the sail into the ship, and unbound all the things clear of it. It was a very fierce storm; the sea broke strange and dangerous. We hawled off upon the lanyard of the whipstaff, and helped the man at the helm. We would not get down our top-mast, but let all stand, because she scudded before the sea very well, and we knew that, the top-mast being aloft, the ship was the wholesomer, and made better way through the sea, seeing we had sea-room. When the storm was over, we set foresail and main-sail, and brought the ship to. Then we set the mizzen, main top-sail, and the fore top-sail. Our course was east north-east, the wind was at south-west. We got the starboard tacks aboard, we cast off our weather braces and lifts; we set in the lee-braces, and hawled forward by the weather-bowlings, and hawled them right, and belayed them, and hawled over the mizzen tack to windward, and kept her full and by as near as she would lie.

During this storm, which was followed by a strong wind west south-west, we were carried by my computation about

five hundred leagues to the east, so that the oldest sailor
aboard could not tell in what part of the world we were.
Our provisions held out well, our ship was staunch, and our
crew all in good health; but we lay in the utmost distress
for water. We thought it best to hold on the same course,
rather than turn more northerly, which might have brought
us to the north-west parts of Great Tartary, and into the
frozen sea.

On the 16th day of June 1703, a boy on the top-mast
discovered land. On the 17th, we came in full view of
a great island or continent (for we knew not whether) on
the south side whereof was a small neck of land jutting
out into the sea, and a creek too shallow to hold a ship
of above one hundred tons. We cast anchor within a league
of this creek, and our captain sent a dozen of his men well
armed in the long boat, with vessels for water, if any could
be found. I desired his leave to go with them, that I might
see the country, and make what discoveries I could. When
we came to land, we saw no river or spring, nor any sign
of inhabitants. Our men therefore wandered on the shore,
to find out some fresh water near the sea, and I walked alone
about a mile on the other side, where I observed the country
all barren and rocky. I now began to be weary, and, seeing
nothing to entertain my curiosity, I returned gently down
towards the creek; and the sea being full in my view, I saw
our men already got into the boat, and rowing for life to
the ship. I was going to holloa after them, although it had
been to little purpose, when I observed a huge creature
walking after them in the sea, as fast as he could: he waded
not much deeper than his knees, and took prodigious strides;
but our men had the start of him half a league, and, the sea
thereabouts being full of sharp-pointed rocks, the monster
was not able to overtake the boat. This, I was afterwards
told, for I durst not stay to see the issue of the adventure;
but ran as fast as I could the way I first went, and then
climbed up a steep hill, which gave me some prospect of

the country. I found it fully cultivated; but that which first surprised me was the length of the grass, which, in those grounds that seemed to be kept for hay, was about twenty feet high.

I fell into a high road, for so I took it to be, though it served to the inhabitants only as a footpath through a field of barley. Here I walked on for some time, but could see little on either side, it being now at least harvest, and the corn rising near forty feet. I was an hour walking to the end of this field, which was fenced in with a hedge of at least one hundred and twenty feet high, and the trees so lofty that I could make no computation of their altitude. There was a stile to pass from this field into the next. It had four steps, and a stone to cross over when you came to the uppermost. It was impossible for me to climb this stile, because every step was six feet high, and the upper stone above twenty. I was endeavouring to find some gap in the hedge, when I discovered one of the inhabitants in the next field, advancing towards the stile, of the same size with him I saw in the sea, pursuing our boat. He appeared as tall as an ordinary spire-steeple, and took about ten yards at every stride, as near as I could guess. I was struck with the utmost fear and astonishment, and ran to hide myself in the corn, from whence I saw him at the top of the stile, looking back into the next field on the right hand, and heard him call in a voice many degrees louder than a speaking-trumpet; but the noise was so high in the air, that at first I certainly thought it was thunder. Whereupon, seven monsters like himself came towards him with reaping-hooks in their hands, each hook about the largeness of six scythes.

These people were not so well clad as the first, whose servants or labourers they seemed to be; for, upon some words he spoke, they went to reap the corn in the field where I lay. I kept from them at as great a distance as I could, but was forced to move with extreme difficulty, for the stalks of the corn were sometimes not above a foot distant, so that I could hardly squeeze my body betwixt them. However, I made shift to go forward, till I came to a part of the field where the corn had been laid by the rain and wind. Here it was impossible for me to advance a step; for the stalks were so interwoven that I could not creep through, and the beards of the fallen ears so strong and pointed that they pierced through my cloaths into my flesh. At the same time I heard the reapers not above an hundred yards behind me.

Being quite dispirited with toil, and wholly overcome by grief and despair, I lay down between two ridges, and heartily wished I might there end my days. I bemoaned my desolate widow, and fatherless children. I lamented my own folly and wilfulness in attempting a second voyage, against the advice of all my friends and relations. In this terrible agitation of mind I could not forbear thinking of Lilliput, whose inhabitants looked upon me as the greatest prodigy that ever appeared in the world: where I was able to draw an imperial fleet in my hand, and perform those other actions which will be recorded for ever in the chronicles of that empire, while posterity shall hardly believe them, although attested by millions. I reflected what a mortification it must prove to me to appear as inconsiderable in this nation as one single Lilliputian would be among us. But this, I conceived, was to be the least of my misfortunes, for, as human creatures are observed to be more savage and cruel in proportion to their bulk, what could I expect but to be a morsel in the mouth of the first among these enormous barbarians that should happen to seize me? Undoubtedly philosophers are in the right when they tell us that nothing is great or little otherwise than by comparison. It might have pleased fortune to let the Lilliputians find some nation where the people were as diminutive with respect to them as they were to me. And who knows but that even this prodigious race of mortals might be equally overmatched in some distant part of the world, whereof we have yet no discovery?

Scared and confounded as I was, I could not forbear going on with these reflections, when one of the reapers, approaching within ten yards of the ridge where I lay, made me apprehend that with the next step I should be squashed to death under his foot, or cut in two with his reaping-hook. And, therefore, when he was again about to move, I screamed as loud as fear could make me. Whereupon the huge creature trod short, and, looking round about under him for some time, at last espied me as I lay on the ground. He considered a while, with the caution of one who endeavours to lay hold on a small, dangerous animal, in such a manner that it may not be able either to scratch or to bite him, as I myself have sometimes done with a weasel in England. At length he ventured to take me up behind by the middle, between his forefinger and thumb, and brought me within three yards of his eyes, that he might behold my shape more perfectly. I guessed his meaning, and my good fortune gave me so much presence of mind, that I resolved not to struggle in the least as he held me in the air, about sixty feet from the ground, although he grievously pinched my sides, for fear I should slip through his fingers. All I ventured was to raise my eyes towards the sun, and place my hands together in a supplicating posture, and to speak some words in an humble, melancholy tone, suitable to the condition I then was in. For I apprehended every moment that he would dash me against the ground, as we usually do any little hateful animal which we have a mind to destroy. But my good star would have it that he appeared pleased with my voice and gestures, and began to look upon me as a curiosity, much wondering to hear me pronounce articulate words, although he could not understand them. In the meantime I was not able to forbear groaning and shedding tears, and turning my head towards my sides, letting him know, as well as I could, how cruelly I was hurt by the pressure of his thumb and finger. He seemed to apprehend my meaning; for, lifting up the lappet of his coat, he put me gently into it, and immediately ran along with me to his master, who was a substantial farmer, and the same person I had first seen in the field.

The farmer having (as I suppose by their talk) received such an account of me as his servant could give him, took a piece of a small straw, about the size of a walking-staff, and therewith lifted up the lappets of my coat, which, it seems, he thought to be some kind of covering that Nature had given me. He blew my hair aside to take a better view of my face. He called his hinds about him, and asked them (as I afterwards learned) whether they had ever seen in the fields any little creature that resembled me: he then placed me softly on the ground, upon all-four, but I got immediately up, and walked slowly backwards and forwards, to let those people see I had no intent to run away. They all sat down in a circle about me, the better to observe my motions. I pulled off my hat, and made a low bow towards the farmer. I fell on my knees, and lifted up my hands and eyes, and spoke several words as loud as I could: I took a purse of gold out of my pocket, and humbly presented it to him. He received it on the palm of his hand, then applied it close to his eye, to see what it was, and afterwards turned it several times with the point of a pin (which he took out of his sleeve) but could make nothing of it. Whereupon I made a sign that he should place his hand on the ground. I then took the purse, and opening it, poured all the gold into his palm. There were six Spanish pieces, of four pistoles each, besides twenty or thirty smaller coins. I saw him wet the tip of his little finger upon his tongue, and take up one of my largest pieces, and then another, but he seemed to be wholly ignorant what they were. He made me a sign to put them again into my purse, and the purse again into my pocket, which, after offering it to him several times, I thought it best to do.

The farmer by this time was convinced I must be a rational creature. He spoke often to me, but the sound of his voice pierced my ears like that of a water-mill, yet his words were articulate enough. I answered as loud as I could in several languages, and he often laid his ear within two yards of me; but all in vain, for we were wholly unintelligible to each other. He then sent his servants to their work, and, taking his handkerchief out of his pocket, he doubled and spread it on his left hand, which he placed flat on the ground, with the palm upwards, making me a sign to step into it, as I could easily do, for it was not above a foot in thickness. I thought it my part to obey, and, for fear of falling, laid myself at length upon the handkerchief, with the remainder of which he lapped me up to the head for farther security, and in this manner carried me home to his house. There he called his wife and showed me to her; but she screamed and ran back, as women in England do at the sight of a toad or a spider. However, when she had a while seen my behaviour, and how well I observed the signs her husband made, she was soon reconciled, and, by degrees, grew extremely tender of me.

It was about twelve at noon, and a servant brought in dinner. It was only one substantial dish of meat (fit for the plain condition of an husbandman), in a dish of about four and twenty feet diameter. The company were the farmer and his wife, three children, and an old grandmother. When they were set down, the farmer placed me at some distance from him on the table, which was thirty feet high from the floor. I was in a terrible fright, and kept as far as I could from the edge, for fear of falling. The wife minced a bit of meat, then crumbled some bread on a trencher, and placed it before me. I made her a low bow, took out my knife and fork, and fell to eat, which gave them exceeding delight. The mistress sent her maid for a small dram cup, which held about two gallons, and filled it with drink; I took up the vessel with much difficulty in both hands, and in a most respectful manner, drank to her lady-ship's health, expressing the words as loud as I could in English, which made the company laugh so heartily that I was almost deafened with the noise. This liquor tasted like a small cyder, and was not unpleasant. Then the master made me a sign to come to his trencher-side; but as I walked on the table, being in great surprise all the time, as the indulgent reader will easily conceive and excuse, I happened to stumble against a crust, and fell flat on my face, but received no hurt. I got up immediately, and observing the good people to be in much concern, I took my hat (which I held under my arm out of good manners) and, waving it over my head, made three huzzas, to show I had got no mischief by my fall. But advancing forward towards my master (as I shall henceforth call him) his youngest son, who sat next him, an arch boy of about ten years old, took me up by the legs, and held me so high in the air that I trembled every limb; but his father snatched me from him, and at the same time gave him such a box on the left ear as would have felled an European troop of horse to the earth, ordering him to be taken from the table. But being afraid the boy might owe me a spite, and well remembering how mischievous all children among us naturally are to sparrows, rabbits, young kittens, and puppy dogs, I fell on my knees, and, pointing to the boy, made my master to understand, as well as I could, that I desired his son might be pardoned. The father complied, and the lad took his seat again; whereupon I went to him and kissed his hand, which my master took and made him stroke me gently with it.

In the midst of dinner my mistress's favourite cat leapt into her lap. I heard a noise behind me like that of a dozen stocking-weavers at work; and, turning my head, I found it proceeded from the purring of that animal, who seemed to be three times larger than an ox, as I computed by the view of her head and one of her paws while her mistress was feeding

and stroking her. The fierceness of this creature's countenance altogether discomposed me, though I stood at the
further end of the table above fifty feet off, and although
my mistress held her fast for fear she might give a spring
and seize me in her talons. But it happened there was no
danger, for the cat took not the least notice of me when my
master placed me within three yards of her. And as I have
been always told, and found true by experience in my travels,
that flying or discovering fear, before a fierce animal, is a
certain way to make it pursue or attack you, so I resolved,
in this dangerous juncture, to show no manner of concern.
I walked with intrepidity five or six times before the very
head of the cat, and came within half a yard of her; whereupon she drew herself back, as if she were more afraid of me.
I had less apprehension concerning the dogs, whereof three
or four came into the room, as it is usual in farmers' houses,
one of which was a mastiff, equal in bulk to four elephants,
and a greyhound somewhat taller than the mastiff, but not
so large.

When dinner was almost done, the nurse came in with
a child of a year old in her arms, who immediately spied
me, and began a squall that you might have heard from
London Bridge to Chelsea, after the usual oratory of infants,
to get me for a plaything. The mother out of pure indulgence took me up, and put me towards the child, who
presently seized me by the middle, and got my head into
his mouth, where I roared so loud that the urchin was
frighted and let me drop, and I should infallibly have
broken my neck if the mother had not held her apron under
me. The nurse to quiet her babe made use of a rattle, which
was a kind of hollow vessel filled with great stones, and
fastened by a cable to the child's waist; but all in vain, so
that she was forced to apply the last remedy by giving it
suck. I had a near sight of her, she sitting down the more
conveniently to give suck, and I standing on the table.
This made me reflect upon the fair skins of our English

ladies, who appear so beautiful to us, only because they are of our own size, and their defects not to be seen but through a magnifying-glass, where we find by experiment that the smoothest and whitest skins look rough and coarse, and ill-coloured.

I remember, when I was at Lilliput, the complexions of those diminutive people appeared to me the fairest in the world; and talking upon this subject with a person of learning there, who was an intimate friend of mine, he said that my face appeared much fairer and smoother when he looked on me from the ground, than it did upon a nearer view when I took him up in my hand and brought him close, which he confessed was at first a very shocking sight. He said he could discover great holes in my skin; that the stumps of my beard were ten times stronger than the bristles of a boar, and my complexion made up of several colours altogether disagreeable: although I must beg leave to say for myself, that I am as fair as most of my sex and country, and very little sunburnt by travels. On the other side, discoursing of the ladies in that Emperors' court, he used to tell me, one had freckles, another too wide a mouth, a third too large a nose, nothing of which I was able to distinguish. I confess, this reflection was obvious enough; which, however, I could not forbear, lest the reader might think those vast creatures were actually deformed: for I must do them justice to say they are a comely race of people; and particularly the features of my master's countenance, although he were but a farmer, when I beheld him from the height of sixty feet, appeared very well proportioned.

When dinner was done, my master went out to his labourers, and, as I could discover by his voice and gesture, gave his wife a strict charge to take care of me. I was very much tired, and disposed to sleep, which my mistress perceiving, she put me on her own bed, and covered me with a clean white handkerchief, but larger and coarser than the main-sail of a man-of-war.

I slept about two hours, and dreamed I was at home with my wife and children, which aggravated my sorrows when I awaked, and found myself alone in a vast room, between two and three hundred feet wide, and above two hundred high, lying in a bed twenty yards wide. My mistress was gone about her household affairs, and had locked me in. The bed was eight yards from the floor. I durst not presume to call, and, if I had, it would have been in vain, with such a voice as mine, at so great a distance as from the room where I lay to the kitchen where the family kept. While I was under these circumstances, two rats crept up the curtains, and ran smelling backwards and forwards on the bed. One of them came up almost to my face, whereupon I rose in a fright, and drew out my hanger to defend myself. These horrible animals had the boldness to attack me on both sides, and one of them held his fore-feet at my collar; but I had the good fortune to rip up his belly before he could do me any mischief. He fell down at my feet, and the other, seeing the fate of his comrade, made his escape, but not without one good wound on the back, which I gave him as he fled, and made the blood run trickling from him. After this exploit, I walked gently to and fro on the bed, to recover my breath and loss of spirits. These creatures were of the size of a large mastiff, but infinitely more nimble and fierce, so that, if I had taken off my belt before I went to sleep I must have infallibly been torn to pieces and devoured. I measured the tail of the dead rat, and found it to be two yards long, wanting an inch; but it went against my stomach to drag the carcass off the bed, where it lay still bleeding; I observed it had yet some life, but, with a strong slash across the neck, I thoroughly despatched it.

Soon after, my mistress came into the room, who, seeing me all bloody, ran and took me up in her hand. I pointed to the dead rat, smiling, and making other signs, to shew I was not hurt, whereat she was extremely rejoiced, calling the maid to take up the dead rat with a pair of tongs and throw it out of the window. Then she set me on a table, where I shewed her my hanger all bloody, and, wiping it on the lappet of my coat, returned it to the scabbard.

I hope the gentle reader will excuse me for dwelling on particulars, which, however insignificant they may appear to grovelling vulgar minds, yet will certainly help a philosopher to enlarge his thoughts and imagination, and to apply them to a benefit of public as well as private life, which was my sole design in presenting this and other accounts of my travels to the world; wherein I have been chiefly studious of truth, without affecting any ornaments of learning or of style. But the whole scene of this voyage made so strong an impression on my mind, and is so deeply fixed in my memory, that, in committing it to paper, I did not omit one material circumstance: however, upon a strict review, I blotted out several passages of less moment which were in my first copy, for fear of being censured as tedious and trifling, whereof travellers are often, perhaps not without justice, accused.

CHAPTER II

MY mistress had a daughter of nine years old, a child of
towardly parts for her age, very dexterous at her needle,
and skilful at dressing her baby. Her mother and she
contrived to fit up the baby's cradle for me against night:
The cradle was put into a small drawer placed upon a hanging
shelf for fear of the rats. This was my bed all the time I
stayed with those people, though made more convenient
by degrees, as I began to learn their language, and make
my wants known. This young girl was so handy, that, after
I had once or twice pulled off my clothes before her, she was
able to dress and undress me, though I never gave her that
trouble when she would let me do either myself. She made
me seven shirts, and some other linen, of as fine cloth as
could be got, which, indeed, was coarser than sack-cloth;
and these she constantly washed for me with her own
hands. She was likewise my school-mistress, to teach me
the language. When I pointed to any thing, she told me the
name of it in her own tongue, so that, in few days, I was
able to call for whatever I had a mind to. She was very
good-natured, and not above forty feet high, being little
for her age. She gave me the name of Grildrig, which the
family took up, and afterwards the whole kingdom. The
word imports what the Latins call Nanunculus, the Italians
Homunceletino, and the English Mannikin. To her I
chiefly owe my preservation in that country: we never
parted while I was there; I called her my Glumdalclitch,
or little nurse; and should be guilty of great ingratitude, if
I omitted this honourable mention of her care and affection
towards me, which I heartily wish it lay in my power to
requite as she deserves, instead of being the innocent but

unhappy instrument of her disgrace, as I have too much reason to fear.

It now began to be known and talked of in the neighbourhood that my master had found a strange animal in the field, about the bigness of a *splacknuck*, but exactly shaped in every part like a human creature, which it likewise imitated in all its actions; seemed to speak in a little language of its own, had already learned several words of theirs, went erect upon two legs, was tame and gentle, would come when it was called, do whatever he was bid, had the finest limbs in the world, and a complexion fairer than a nobleman's daughter of three years old. Another farmer, who lived hard by, and was a particular friend of my master, came on a visit on purpose to enquire into the truth of this story. I was immediately produced, and placed upon a table, where I walked as I was commanded, drew my hanger, put it up again, made my reverence to my master's guest, asked him in his own language how he did, and told him he was welcome, just as my little nurse had instructed me. This man, who was old and dim-sighted, put on his spectacles to behold me better, at which I could not forbear laughing very heartily, for his eyes appeared like the full moon shining into a chamber at two windows. Our people, who discovered the cause of my mirth, bore me company in laughing, at which the old fellow was fool enough to be angry and out of countenance. He had the character of a great miser, and, to my misfortune, he well deserved it, by the cursed advice he gave my master to show me as a sight upon a market-day in the next town, which was half an hour's riding, about two and twenty miles from our house. I guessed there was some mischief contriving, when I observed my master and his friend whispering long together, sometimes pointing at me; and my fears made me fancy that I overheard and understood some of their words. But the next morning Glumdalclitch, my little nurse, told me the whole matter, which she had cunningly picked out from

her mother. The poor girl laid me on her bosom, and fell
a weeping with shame and grief. She apprehended some
mischief would happen to me from rude vulgar folks, who
might squeeze me to death, or break one of my limbs, by
taking me in their hands. She had also observed how
modest I was in my nature, how nicely I regarded my honour,
and what an indignity I should conceive it to be exposed for
money as a public spectacle to the meanest of the people.
She said, her papa and mamma had promised that Grildrig
should be hers, but now she found they meant to serve her
as they did last year, when they pretended to give her a
lamb, and yet, as soon as it was fat, sold it to a butcher.
For my own part, I may truly affirm that I was less concerned
than my nurse. I had a strong hope, which never left me,
that I should one day recover my liberty; and as to the
ignominy of being carried about for a monster, I considered
myself to be a perfect stranger in the country, and that such
a misfortune could never be charged upon me as a reproach,
if ever I should return to England; since the king of Great
Britain himself, in my condition, must have undergone the
same distress.

My master, pursuant to the advice of his friend, carried
me in a box the next market-day to the neighbouring
town, and took along with him his little daughter, my
nurse, upon a pillion behind him. The box was close on
every side, with a little door for me to go in and out, and
a few gimlet holes to let in air. The girl had been so careful to put the quilt of her baby's bed into it, for me to lie
down on. However, I was terribly shaken and discomposed
in this journey, though it were but of half an hour. For
the horse went about forty feet at every step, and trotted
so high, that the agitation was equal to the rising and falling
of a ship in a great storm, but much more frequent: our
journey was somewhat farther than from London to St.
Alban's. My master alighted at an inn which he used to
frequent; and after consulting a while with the inn-keeper,

and making some necessary preparations, he hired the grultrud or crier to give notice through the town of a strange creature to be seen at the sign of the Green Eagle, not so big as a splacknuck (an animal in that country very finely shaped, about six feet long), and in every part of the body resembling an human creature, could speak several words, and perform an hundred diverting tricks.

I was placed upon a table in the largest room of the inn, which might be near three hundred feet square. My little nurse stood on a low stool close to the table, to take care of me, and direct what I should do. My master, to avoid a crowd, would suffer only thirty people at a time to see me. I walked about on the table as the girl commanded: she asked me questions, as far as she knew my understanding of the language reached, and I answered them as loud as I could. I turned about several times to the company, paid my humble respects, said they were welcome, and used some other speeches I had been taught. I took up a thimble filled with liquor, which Glumdalclitch had given me for a cup, and drank their health. I drew out my hanger, and flourished with it after the manner of fencers in England. My nurse gave me part of a straw, which I exercised as a pike, having learned the art in my youth. I was that day shown to twelve sets of company, and as often forced to go over again the same fopperies, till I was half dead with weariness and vexation. For those who had seen me made such wonderful reports, that the people were ready to break down the doors to come in. My master, for his own interest, would not suffer any one to touch me except my nurse; and, to prevent danger, benches were set round the table at such a distance as to put me out of everybody's reach. However, an unlucky school-boy aimed a hazel-nut directly at my head, which very narrowly missed me; otherwise, it came with so much violence that it would have infallibly knocked out my brains, for it was almost as large as a small pumpion; but I had the satisfaction to see the young rogue well beaten, and turned out of the room.

My master gave public notice, that he would show me again the next market-day, and in the meantime he prepared a more convenient vehicle for me, which he had reason enough to do; for I was so tired with my first journey, and with entertaining company for eight hours together, that I could hardly stand upon my legs, or speak a word. It was at least three days before I recovered my strength; and that I might have no rest at home, all the neighbouring gentlemen from a hundred miles round, hearing of my fame, came to see me at my master's own house. There could not be fewer than thirty persons with their wives and children (for the country is very populous); and my master demanded the rate of a full room whenever he showed me at home, although it were only to a single family: so that for some time I had but little ease every day of the week (except Wednesday, which is their Sabbath) although I were not carried to the town.

My master, finding how profitable I was like to be, resolved to carry me to the most considerable cities of the kingdom. Having therefore provided himself with all things necessary for a long journey, and settled his affairs at home, he took leave of his wife, and upon the 17th of August 1703, about two months after my arrival, we set out for the metropolis, situated near the middle of that empire, and about three thousand miles distance from our house: my master made his daughter Glumdalclitch ride behind him. She carried me on her lap, in a box tied about her waist. The girl had lined it on all sides with the softest cloth she could get, well quilted underneath, furnished it with her baby's bed, provided me with linen and other necessaries, and made everything as convenient as she could. We had no other company but a boy of the house, who rode after us with the luggage.

My master's design was to show me in all the towns by the way, and to step out of the road for fifty or an hundred

GLUMDALCLITCH TEACHES GULLIVER TO READ

miles, to any village, or person of quality's house, where he might expect custom. We made easy journeys of not above seven or eight score miles a day; for Glumdalclitch, on purpose to spare me, complained she was tired with the trotting of the horse. She often took me out of my box, at my own desire, to give me air, and show me the country, but always held me fast by a leading-string. We passed over five or six rivers, many degrees broader and deeper than the Nile, or the Ganges; and there was hardly a rivulet so small as the Thames at London Bridge. We were ten weeks in our journey, and I was shown in eighteen large towns, besides many villages and private families.

On the 26th day of October, we arrived at the metropolis, called, in their language, Lorbrulgrud, or Pride of the Universe. My master took a lodging in the principal street of the city, not far from the royal palace, and put out bills in the usual form, containing an exact description of my person and parts. He hired a large room, between three and four hundred feet wide. He provided a table sixty feet in diameter, upon which I was to act my part, and pallisadoed it round three feet from the edge, and as many high, to prevent my falling over. I was shewn ten times a day, to the wonder and satisfaction of all people. I could now speak the language tolerably well, and perfectly understood every word that was spoken to me. Besides, I had learned their alphabet, and could make a shift to explain a sentence here and there; for Glumdalclitch had been my instructor while we were at home, and at leisure hours during our journey. She carried a little book in her pocket, not much larger than a Sanson's Atlas; it was a common treatise for the use of young girls, giving a short account of their religion; out of this she taught me my letters, and interpreted the words.

CHAPTER III

THE frequent labours I underwent, every day, made in few weeks a very considerable change in my health: the more my master got by me, the more insatiable he grew. I had quite lost my stomach, and was almost reduced to a skeleton. The farmer observed it, and, concluding I must soon die, resolved to make as good a hand of me as he could. While he was thus reasoning and resolving with himself, a slardral, or gentleman usher, came from Court, commanding my master to carry me immediately thither, for the diversion of the queen and her ladies. Some of the latter had already been to see me, and reported strange things of my beauty, behaviour, and good sense. Her Majesty, and those who attended her, were beyond measure delighted with my demeanour: I fell on my knees, and begged the honour of kissing her imperial foot; but this gracious princess held out her little finger towards me (after I was set on a table) which I embraced in both my arms, and put the tip of it, with the utmost respect, to my lips. She made me some general questions about my country, and my travels, which I answered as distinctly and in as few words as I could. She asked whether I would be content to live at Court. I bowed down to the board of the table, and humbly answered that I was my master's slave; but, if I were at my own disposal, I should be proud to devote my life to her Majesty's service. She then asked my master whether he were willing to sell me at a good price. He, who apprehended I could not live a month, was ready enough to part with me, and demanded a thousand pieces of gold, which were ordered him on the spot, each piece being about the bigness of eight hundred moidores; but,

allowing for the proportion of all things between that country
and Europe, and the high price of gold among them, was
hardly so great a sum as a thousand guineas would be in
England. I then said to the queen, since I was now her
Majesty's most humble creature and vassal, I must beg the
favour, that Glumdalclitch, who had always tended me
with so much care and kindness, and understood to do it
so well, might be admitted into her service, and continue to
be my nurse and instructor. Her Majesty agreed to my
petition, and easily got the farmer's consent, who was glad
enough to have his daughter preferred at Court; and the
poor girl herself was not able to hide her joy: my late
master withdrew, bidding me farewell, and saying he had
left me in a good service; to which I replied not a word,
only making him a slight bow.

The queen observed my coldness, and, when the farmer
was gone out of the apartment, asked me the reason. I
made bold to tell her Majesty that I owed no other obligation
to my late master, than his not dashing out the brains of a
poor harmless creature found by chance in his field; which
obligation was amply recompensed by the gain he had
made in showing me through half the kingdom, and the
price he had now sold me for. That the life I had since led,
was laborious enough to kill an animal of ten times my
strength. That my health was much impaired by the
continual drudgery of entertaining the rabble every hour
of the day, and that, if my master had not thought my life
in danger, her Majesty perhaps would not have got so cheap
a bargain. But as I was out of all fear of being ill-treated
under the protection of so great and good an Empress, the
ornament of nature, the darling of the world, the delight
of her subjects, the phœnix of the creation; so I hoped my
late master's apprehensions would appear to be groundless,
for I already found my spirits to revive by the influence of
her most august presence.

This was the sum of my speech, delivered with great

improprieties and hesitation; the latter part was altogether framed in the style peculiar to that people, whereof I learned some phrases from Glumdalclitch, while she was carrying me to Court.

The queen, giving great allowance for my defectiveness in speaking, was however surprised at so much wit and good sense in so diminutive an animal. She took me in her own hands, and carried me to the king, who was then retired to his cabinet. His Majesty, a prince of much gravity, and austere countenance, not well observing my shape at first view, asked the queen after a cold manner, how long it was since she grew fond of a splacknuck; for such it seems he took me to be, as I lay upon my breast in her Majesty's right hand. But this princess, who hath an infinite deal of wit and humour, set me gently on my feet upon the scrutoire, and commanded me to give his Majesty an account of myself, which I did in a very few words; and Glumdalclitch, who attended at the cabinet door, and could not endure I should be out of her sight, being admitted, confirmed all that had passed from my arrival at her father's house.

The king, although he be as learned a person as any in his dominions, and had been educated in the study of philosophy, and particularly mathematics, yet when he observed my shape exactly, and saw me walk erect, before I began to speak, conceived I might be a piece of clock-work (which is in that country arrived to a very great perfection) contrived by some ingenious artist. But when he heard my voice, and found what I delivered to be regular and rational, he could not conceal his astonishment. He was by no means satisfied with the relation I gave him of the manner I came into his kingdom, but thought it a story concerted between Glumdalclitch and her father, who had taught me a set of words to make me sell at a better price. Upon this imagination he put several other questions to me, and still received rational answers, no otherwise defective, than by a foreign accent, and an imperfect knowledge in the language, with some rustic phrases which I had learned at the farmer's house, and did not suit the polite style of a Court.

His Majesty sent for three great scholars who were then in their weekly waiting, according to the custom in that country. These gentlemen, after they had a while examined my shape with much nicety, were of different opinions concerning me. They all agreed that I could not be produced according to the regular laws of nature, because I was not framed with a capacity of preserving my life, either by swiftness, or climbing of trees, or digging holes in the earth. They observed by my teeth, which they viewed with great exactness, that I was a carnivorous animal; yet most quadrupeds being an overmatch for me, and field-mice, with some others, too nimble, they could not imagine how I should be able to support myself, unless I fed upon snails and other insects, which they offered, by many learned arguments, to evince that I could not possibly do. Others who observed my limbs to be perfect and finished, said that I had lived several years, as it was manifest from my beard, the stumps whereof they plainly discovered through a magnifying-glass. They would not allow me to be a dwarf, because my littleness was beyond all degrees of comparison; for the queen's favourite dwarf, the smallest ever known in that kingdom, was near thirty feet high. After much debate, they concluded unanimously that I was only *relplum scalcatch*, which is interpreted literally, *lusus naturæ;* a determination exactly agreeable to the modern philosophy of Europe, whose professors, disdaining the old evasion of occult causes, whereby the followers of Aristotle endeavoured in vain to disguise their ignorance, have invented this wonderful solution of all difficulties, to the unspeakable advancement of human knowledge.

After this decisive conclusion, I entreated to be heard a word or two. I applied myself to the king, and assured his Majesty that I came from a country which abounded with several millions of both sexes, and of my own stature; where the animals, trees, and houses were all in proportion, and where by consequence I might be as able to defend myself, and to find sustenance, as any of his Majesty's subjects could do here; which I took for a full answer to those gentlemen's arguments. To this they only replied with a smile of contempt, saying that the farmer had instructed me very well in my lesson.   The king, who had a much better understanding, dismissing his learned men, sent for the farmer, who by good fortune was not yet gone out of town: having therefore first examined him privately, and then confronted him with me and the young girl, his Majesty began to think that what we told him might possibly be true. He desired the queen to order that a particular care should be taken of me, and was of opinion that Glumdalclitch should still continue in her office of tending me, because he observed we had a great affection for each other. A convenient apartment was provided for her at court; she had a sort of governess appointed to take care of her education, a maid to dress her, and two other servants for menial offices; but the care of me was wholly appropriated to herself. The queen commanded her own cabinet-maker to contrive a box that might serve me for a bed-chamber, after the model that Glumdalclitch and I should agree upon. This man was a most ingenious artist, and, according to my directions, in three weeks finished for me a wooden chamber of sixteen feet square and twelve high, with sash-windows, a door, and two closets, like a London bed-chamber. The board that made the ceiling was to be lifted up and down by two hinges, to put in a bed ready furnished by her Majesty's upholsterer, which Glumdalclitch took out every day to air, made it with her own hands, and, letting it down at night, locked up the roof over me. A nice workman, who was famous for little curiosities, undertook to make me two chairs, with backs and frames of a substance not unlike ivory, and two tables, with a cabinet to put my things in. The room was quilted on all sides, as well as the floor and the ceiling, to prevent any accident from the carelessness of those who carried me, and to break the force of a jolt when I went in a coach. I desired a lock for my door, to prevent rats and mice from coming in: the smith, after several attempts, made the smallest that ever was seen among them, for I have known a larger at the gate of a gentleman's house in England. I made a shift to keep the key in a pocket of my own, fearing Glumdalclitch might lose it. The queen likewise ordered the thinnest silks that could be gotten to make me clothes, not much thicker than an English blanket, very cumbersome, till I was accustomed to them. They were after the fashion of the kingdom, partly resembling the Persian, and partly the Chinese, and are a very grave and decent habit.

The queen became so fond of my company that she could not dine without me. I had a table placed upon the same at which her Majesty ate, just at her left elbow, and a chair to sit on. Glumdalclitch stood on a stool on the floor, near my table, to assist and take care of me. I had an entire set of silver dishes and plates, and other necessaries, which, in proportion to those of the queen's, were not much bigger than what I have seen of the same kind in a London toy-shop for the furniture of a baby-house. These my little nurse kept in her pocket in a silver box, and gave me at meals as I wanted them, always cleaning them herself. No person dined with the queen but the two princesses royal, the elder sixteen years old, and the younger at that time thirteen and a month. Her Majesty used to put a bit of meat upon one of my dishes, out of which I carved for myself; and her diversion was to see me eat in miniature. For the queen (who had, indeed, but a weak stomach) took up at one mouthful as much as a dozen English farmers could eat at a meal, which, to me, was for some time a very nauseous sight. She would crunch the wing of a lark, bones and all, between her teeth, although it were nine times as large as that of a full-grown turkey; and put a bit of bread into her mouth as big as two twelve-penny loaves. She drank out of a golden cup, above a hogshead at a draught. Her knives were twice as long as a scythe, set straight upon the handle. The spoons, forks, and other instruments were all in the same proportion. I remember, when Glumdalclitch carried me out of curiosity to see some of the tables at Court, where ten or a dozen of these enormous knives and forks were lifted up together, I thought I had never, till then, beheld so terrible a sight.

It is the custom that every Wednesday (which, as I have before observed, was their Sabbath) the king and queen, with the royal issue of both sexes, dine together in the apartment of his Majesty, to whom I was now become a great favourite; and at these times my little chair and table were placed at his left hand, before one of the salt-cellars. This prince took a pleasure in conversing with me, enquiring into the manners, religion, laws, government, and learning of Europe; wherein I gave him the best account I was able. His apprehension was so clear, and his judgment so exact, that he made very wise reflections and observations upon all I said. But I confess, that after I had been a little too copious in talking of my own beloved country, of our trade, and wars by sea and land, of our schisms in religion, and parties in the State; the prejudices of his education prevailed so far, that he could not forbear taking me up in his right hand, and stroking me gently with the other, after an hearty fit of laughing, asked me whether I was a Whig or Tory. Then turning to his first minister, who waited behind him with a white staff, near as tall as the main-mast of the *Royal Sovereign*, he observed how contemptible a thing was human grandeur, which could be mimicked by such diminutive insects as I: " and yet," says he, " I dare engage, these creatures have their titles and distinctions of honour, they contrive little nests and burrows, that they call houses and cities; they make a figure in dress and equipage; they love, they fight, they dispute, they cheat, they betray." And thus he continued on, while my colour came and went several times, with indignation, to hear our noble country, the mistress of arts and arms, the scourge of France, the arbitress of Europe, the seat of virtue, piety, honour, and truth, the pride and envy of the world, so contemptuously treated.

But as I was not in a condition to resent injuries, so, upon mature thoughts, I began to doubt whether I was injured or no. For, after having been accustomed several months to the sight and converse of this people, and observed every object upon which I cast mine eyes to be of proportionable magnitude, the horror I had at first conceived, from their bulk and aspect, was so far worn off, that if I had then beheld a company of English lords and ladies in their finery and birthday clothes, acting their several parts in the most courtly manner, of strutting, and bowing, and prating; to say the truth, I should have been strongly tempted to laugh as much at them as the king and his grandees did at me. Neither, indeed, could I forbear smiling at myself, when the queen used to place me upon her hand towards a looking-glass, by which both our persons appeared before me in full view together; and there could nothing be more ridiculous than the comparison, so that I really began to imagine myself dwindled many degrees below my usual size.

Nothing angered and mortified me so much as the queen's dwarf, who, being of the lowest stature that was ever in that country (for I verily think he was not full thirty feet high) became insolent at seeing a creature so much beneath him, that he would always affect to swagger and look big as he passed by me in the queen's ante-chamber while I was standing on some table talking with the lords or ladies of the Court, and he seldom failed of a smart word or two upon my littleness, against which I could only revenge myself by calling him brother, challenging him to wrestle, and such repartees as are usual in the mouths of Court pages. One day, at dinner, this malicious little cub was so nettled with something I had said to him, that, raising himself upon the frame of her Majesty's chair, he took me up by the middle, as I was sitting down, not thinking any harm, and let me drop into a large silver bowl of cream, and then ran away as fast as he could. I fell over head and ears, and if I had not been a good swimmer, it might have gone very hard with me; for Glumdalclitch, in that instant, happened to be at the other end of the room, and the queen was in such a fright that she wanted presence of mind to assist me. But my little nurse ran to my relief, and took me out, after I had swallowed above a quart of cream. I was put to bed; however, I received no other damage than the loss of a suit of clothes, which was utterly spoiled. The dwarf was soundly whipped, and, as a further punishment, forced to drink up the bowl of cream into which he had thrown me; neither was he ever restored to favour: for, soon after, the queen bestowed him on a lady of high quality, so that I saw him no more, to my very great satisfaction; for I could not tell to what extremity such a malicious urchin might have carried his resentment.

He had before served me a scurvy trick, which set the queen a-laughing, although at the same time she was heartily vexed, and would have immediately cashiered him, if I had not been so generous as to intercede. Her Majesty had taken a marrow-bone upon her plate, and, after knocking out the marrow, placed the bone again in the dish erect, as it stood before; the dwarf, watching his opportunity, while Glumdalclitch was gone to the side-board, mounted the stool she stood on to take care of me at meals, took me up in both hands, and, squeezing my legs together, wedged them into the marrow-bone above my waist, where I stuck for some time, and made a very ridiculous figure. I believe it was near a minute before any one knew what was become of me; for I thought it below me to cry out. But, as princes seldom get their meat hot, my legs were not scalded, only my stockings and breeches in a sad condition. The dwarf, at my entreaty, had no other punishment than a sound whipping.

I was frequently rallied by the queen upon account of my fearfulness; and she used to ask me whether the people of my country were as great cowards as myself? The occasion was this: the kingdom is much pestered with flies in summer; and these odious insects, each of them as big as a Dunstable lark, hardly gave me any rest while I sat at dinner, with their continual humming and buzzing about mine ears. They would sometimes alight upon my victuals. Sometimes they would fix upon my nose or forehead, where they stung me to the quick, smelling very offensively, and I could easily trace that viscous matter, which, our naturalists tell us, enables those creatures to walk with their feet upwards upon a ceiling. I had much ado to defend myself against these detestable animals, and could not forbear starting when they came on my face. It was the common practice of the dwarf to catch a number of these insects in his hand, as schoolboys do among us, and let them out suddenly under my nose, on purpose to frighten me, and divert the queen. My remedy was to cut them in pieces with my knife, as they flew in the air, wherein my dexterity was much admired.

I remember one morning, when Glumdalclitch had set me in my box upon a window, as she usually did in the fair days to give me air (for I durst not venture to let the box be hung on a nail out of the window, as we do with cages in England) after I had lifted up one of my sashes, and sat down at my table to eat a piece of sweet cake for my breakfast, above twenty wasps, allured by the smell, came flying into the room, humming louder than the drones of as many bagpipes. Some of them seized my cake, and carried it piecemeal away; others flew about my head and face, confounding me with the noise, and putting me in the utmost terror of their stings. However, I had the courage

to rise and draw my hanger, and attack them in the air.
I dispatched four of them, but the rest got away, and I
presently shut my window. These insects were as large
as partridges; I took out their stings, found them an inch
and a half long, and as sharp as needles. I carefully preserved them all, and having since shown them with some
other curiosities, in several parts of Europe, upon my return
to England, I gave three of them to Gresham College, and
kept the fourth for myself.

CHAPTER IV

I NOW intend to give the reader a short description of this country, as far as I travelled in it, which was not above two thousand miles round Lorbrulgrud, the metropolis. For the queen, whom I always attended, never went farther when she accompanied the king in his progresses, and there staid till his Majesty returned from viewing his frontiers. The whole extent of this prince's dominions reacheth about six thousand miles in length, and from three to five in breadth; from whence I cannot but conclude that our geographers of Europe are in a great error, by supposing nothing but sea between Japan and California; for it was ever my opinion that there must be a balance of earth to counterpoise the great continent of Tartary; and therefore they ought to correct their maps and charts, by joining this vast tract of land to the north-west parts of America, wherein I shall be ready to lend them my assistance.

The kingdom is a peninsula, terminated to the north-east by a ridge of mountains thirty miles high, which are altogether impassable, by reason of the volcanoes upon the tops. Neither do the most learned know what sort of mortals inhabit beyond those mountains, or whether they be inhabited at all. On the three other sides it is bounded by the ocean. There is not one sea-port in the whole kingdom, and those parts of the coasts into which the rivers issue are so full of pointed rocks, and the sea generally so rough, that there is no venturing with the smallest of their boats, so that these people are wholly excluded from any commerce with the rest of the world. But the large rivers are full of vessels, and abound with excellent fish, for they seldom get any from the sea, because the sea-fish

are of the same size with those in Europe, and consequently
not worth catching; whereby it is manifest that Nature,
in the production of plants and animals of so extraordinary
a bulk, is wholly confined to this continent, of which I leave
the reasons to be determined by philosophers. However,
now and then they take a whale that happens to be dashed
against the rocks, which the common people feed on heartily.
These whales I have known so large that a man could hardly
carry one upon his shoulders; and sometimes for curiosity
they are brought in hampers to Lorbrulgrud. I saw one
of them in a dish at the king's table, which passed for a
rarity, but I did not observe he was fond of it, for I think,
indeed, the bigness disgusted him, although I have seen one
somewhat larger in Greenland.

The country is well inhabited, for it contains fifty-one
cities, near an hundred walled towns, and a great number of
villages. To satisfy my curious reader, it may be sufficient
to describe Lorbrulgrud. This city stands upon almost
two equal parts on each side the river that passes through.
It contains above eighty thousand houses, and about six
hundred thousand inhabitants. It is in length three glom-
glungs (which make about fifty-four English miles) and two
and a half in breadth, as I measured it myself in the royal
map made by the king's order, which was laid on the ground
on purpose for me, and extended an hundred feet; I paced
the diameter and circumference several times bare-foot, and
computing by the scale, measured it pretty exactly.

The king's palace is no regular edifice, but an heap of
building about seven miles round: the chief rooms are
generally two hundred and forty feet high, and broad and
long in proportion. A coach was allowed to Glumdalclitch
and me, wherein her governess frequently took her out to
see the town, or go among the shops; and I was always
of the party, carried in my box, although the girl at my
own desire would often take me out, and hold me in her hand,
that I might more conveniently view the houses and the

people, as we passed along the streets. I reckoned our
coach to be about a square of Westminster Hall, but not
altogether so high: however, I cannot be very exact. One
day the governess ordered our coachman to stop at several
shops, where the beggars watching their opportunity,
crowded to the sides of the coach, and gave me the most
horrible spectacles that ever an European eye beheld.

Beside the large box in which I was usually carried, the
queen ordered a smaller one to be made for me, of about
twelve feet square and ten high, for the convenience of
travelling, because the other was somewhat too large for
Glumdalclitch's lap, and cumbersome in the coach; it was
made by the same artist, whom I directed in the whole
contrivance. This travelling-closet was an exact square
with a window in the middle of three of the squares, and
each window was latticed with iron wire on the outside,
to prevent accidents in long journeys. On the fourth side,
which had no window, two strong staples were fixed, through
which the person that carried me, when I had a mind to be
on horseback, put in a leathern belt, and buckled it about
his waist. This was always the office of some grave, trusty
servant in whom I could confide, whether I attended the
king and queen in their progresses, or were disposed to see
the gardens, or pay a visit to some great lady or minister
of state in the Court, when Glumdalclitch happened to be
out of order: for I soon began to be known and esteemed
among the greatest officers, I suppose more upon account
of their Majesties' favour than any merit of my own. In
journeys, when I was weary of the coach, a servant on horseback would buckle my box, and place it on a cushion before
him; and there I had a full prospect of the country on three
sides from the three windows. I had in this closet a field-
bed and a hammock hung from the ceiling, two chairs and
a table, neatly screwed to the floor, to prevent being tossed
about by the agitation of the horse or the coach. And
having been long used to sea-voyages, those motions,

although sometimes very violent, did not much discompose
me.

Whenever I had a mind to see the town, it was always
in my travelling-closet, which Glumdalclitch held in her
lap in a kind of open sedan, after the fashion of the country,
borne by four men, and attended by two others in the
queen's livery. The people, who had often heard of me,
were very curious to crowd about the sedan, and the girl
was complaisant enough to make the bearers stop, and to
take me in her hand that I might be more conveniently
seen.

I was very desirous to see the chief temple, and particularly the tower belonging to it, which is reckoned the
highest in the kingdom. Accordingly one day my nurse
carried me thither, but I may truly say I came back disappointed; for the height is not above three thousand feet,
reckoning from the ground to the highest pinnacle top;
which allowing for the difference between the size of those
people and us in Europe, is no great matter for admiration,
nor at all equal in proportion (if I rightly remember) to
Salisbury Steeple. But, not to detract from a nation to
which during my life I shall acknowledge myself extremely
obliged, it must be allowed that whatever this famous tower
wants in height is amply made up in beauty and strength.
For the walls are near an hundred feet thick, built of hewn
stone, whereof each is about forty feet square, and adorned
on all sides with statues of gods and emperors cut in marble
larger than the life, placed in their several niches. I
measured a little finger which had fallen down from one of
the statues, and lay unperceived among some rubbish, and
found it exactly four feet and an inch in length. Glumdalclitch wrapped it up in her handkerchief, and carried it
home in her pocket to keep among other trinkets, of which
the girl was very fond, as children at her age usually are.

The king's kitchen is indeed a noble building, vaulted
at top, and about six hundred feet high. The great oven

is not so wide by ten paces as the cupola at St. Paul's: for I measured the latter on purpose after my return. But if I should describe the kitchen grate, the prodigious pots and kettles, the joints of meat turning on the spits, with many other particulars, perhaps I should be hardly believed; at least a severe critic would be apt to think I enlarged a little, as travellers are often suspected to do. To avoid which censure, I fear I have run too much into the other extreme, and that if this treatise should happen to be translated into the language of Brobdingnag (which is the general name of that kingdom) and transmitted thither, the king and his people would have reason to complain that I had done them an injury by a false and diminutive representation.

His Majesty seldom keeps above six hundred horses in his stables: they are generally from fifty-four to sixty feet high. But, when he goes abroad on solemn days, he is attended for state by a militia guard of five hundred horse, which indeed I thought was the most splendid sight that could be ever beheld, till I saw part of his army in battalia, whereof I shall find another occasion to speak.

CHAPTER V

I SHOULD have lived happy enough in that country if my littleness had not exposed me to several ridiculous and troublesome accidents: some of which I shall venture to relate. Glumdalclitch often carried me into the gardens of the Court in my smaller box, and would sometimes take me out of it and hold me in her hand, or set me down to walk. I remember, before the dwarf left the queen, he followed us one day into those gardens, and my nurse having set me down, he and I being close together near some dwarf apple trees, I must need shew my wit by a silly allusion between him and the trees, which happens to hold in their language, as it doth in ours. Whereupon, the malicious rogue watching his opportunity, when I was walking under one of them, shook it directly over my head, by which a dozen apples, each of them near as large as a Bristol barrel, came tumbling about my ears: one of them hit me on the back as I chanced to stoop, and knocked me down flat on my face; but I received no other hurt, and the dwarf was pardoned at my desire because I had given the provocation.

Another day Glumdalclitch left me on a smooth grass plot to divert myself, while she walked at some distance with her governess. In the meantime there suddenly fell such a violent shower of hail, that I was immediately, by the force of it, struck to the ground: and, when I was down, the hailstones gave me such cruel bangs all over the body, as if I had been pelted with tennis balls; however, I made a shift to creep on all four, and shelter myself by lying flat on my face, on the lee side of a border of lemon thyme, but so bruised from head to foot that I could not go abroad in ten days. Neither is this at all to be wondered at, because Nature in that country observing the same proportion through all her operations, a hailstone is near eighteen hundred times as large as one in Europe, which I can assert upon experience, having been so curious to weigh and measure them.

But a more dangerous accident happened to me in the same garden, when my little nurse, believing she had put me in a secure place, which I often entreated her to do, that I might enjoy my own thoughts, and having left my box at home to avoid the trouble of carrying it, went to another part of the garden with her governess and some ladies of her acquaintance. While she was absent and out of hearing, a small white spaniel belonging to one of the chief gardeners, having got by accident into the garden, happened to range near the place where I lay. The dog, following the scent, came directly up, and taking me in his mouth ran straight to his master, wagging his tail, and set me gently on the ground. By good fortune he had been so well taught that I was carried between his teeth without the least hurt, or even tearing my clothes. But the poor gardener, who knew me well, and had a great kindness for me, was in a terrible fright. He gently took me up in both his hands, and asked me how I did; but I was so amazed and out of breath that I could not speak a word. In few minutes I came to myself, and he carried me safe to my little nurse, who by this time had returned to the place where she left me, and was in cruel agonies when I did not appear nor answer when she called: she severely reprimanded the gardener on account of his dog. But the thing was hushed up and never known at Court; for the girl was afraid of the queen's anger, and truly as to myself, I thought it would not be for my reputation that such a story should go about.

This accident absolutely determined Glumdalclitch never to trust me abroad for the future out of her sight. I had been long afraid of this resolution, and therefore concealed from her some little unlucky adventures that happened

in those times when I was left by myself. Once a kite,
hovering over the garden, made a stoop at me, and if I had
not resolutely drawn my hanger and run under a thick
espalier, he would have certainly carried me away in his
talons. Another time, walking to the top of a fresh mole-
hill, I fell to my neck in the hole through which that animal
had cast up the earth, and coined some lie, not worth
remembering, to excuse myself for spoiling my clothes.
I likewise broke my right shin against the shell of a snail,
which I happened to stumble over as I was walking alone
and thinking on poor England.

I cannot tell whether I were more pleased or mortified
to observe in those solitary walks that the smaller birds
did not appear to be at all afraid of me, but would hop
about within a yard's distance, looking for worms and other
food with as much indifference and security as if no creature
at all were near them. I remember a thrush had the confidence to snatch out of my hand with his bill a piece of
cake that Glumdalclitch had just given me for my breakfast. When I attempted to catch any of these birds they
would boldly turn against me, endeavouring to pick my
fingers, which I durst not venture within their reach; and
then they would hop back unconcerned, to hunt for worms
or snails, as they did before. But one day I took a thick
cudgel, and threw it with all my strength so luckily at a
linnet that I knocked him down, and seizing him by the neck
with both my hands, ran with him in triumph to my nurse.
However, the bird, who had only been stunned, recovering
himself, gave me so many boxes with his wings on both
sides of my head and body, though I held him at arm's
length and was out of the reach of his claws, that I was
twenty times thinking to let him go. But I was soon
relieved by one of our servants, who wrung off the bird's
neck, and I had him next day for dinner by the queen's
command. This linnet, as near as I can remember, seemed
to be somewhat larger than an England swan.

One day a young gentleman, who was nephew to my nurse's governess, came and pressed them both to see an execution. It was of a man who had murdered one of that gentleman's intimate acquaintance. Glumdalclitch was prevailed on to be of the company, very much against her inclination, for she was naturally tender-hearted: and, as for myself, although I abhorred such kind of spectacles, yet my curiosity tempted me to see something that I thought must be extraordinary. The malefactor was fixed in a chair upon a scaffold, erected for that purpose, and his head cut off at one blow, with a sword of about forty feet long. The veins and arteries spouted up such a prodigious quantity of blood, and so high in the air, that the great *jet d'eau* at Versailles was not equal for the time it lasted; and the head, when it fell on the scaffold floor, gave such a bounce as made me start, although I were at least half an English mile distant.

The queen, who often used to hear me talk of my sea-voyages, and took all occasions to divert me when I was melancholy, asked me whether I understood how to handle a sail, or an oar, and whether a little exercise of rowing might not be convenient for my health? I answered, that I understood both very well: for, although my proper employment had been to be surgeon or doctor to the ship, yet often, upon a pinch, I was forced to work like a common mariner. But I could not see how this could be done in their country, where the smallest wherry was equal to a first-rate man-of-war among us, and such a boat as I could manage would never live in any of their rivers. Her Majesty said, if I would contrive a boat, her own joiner would make it, and she would provide a place for me to sail in. The fellow was an ingenious workman, and, by my instructions, in ten days finished a pleasure-boat, with all its tackling, able conveniently to hold eight Europeans. When it was finished, the queen was so delighted, that she ran with it in her lap to the king, who ordered it to be put in a cistern full of water, with me in it, by way of trial; where I could not manage my two sculls, or little oars, for want of room. But the queen had before contrived another project: she ordered the joiner to make a wooden trough of three hundred feet long, fifty broad, and eight deep; which being well pitched, to prevent leaking, was placed on the floor along the wall, in an outer room of the palace. It had a cock near the bottom, to let out the water when it began to grow stale, and two servants could easily fill it in half an hour. Here I often used to row for my own diversion, as well as that of the queen and her ladies, who thought themselves well entertained with my skill and agility. Sometimes I would put up my sail, and then my business was only to steer, while the ladies gave me a gale with their fans; and, when they were weary, some of the pages would blow my sail forward with their breath, while I showed my art by steering starboard or larboard, as I pleased. When I had done, Glumdalclitch always carried back my boat into her closet, and hung it on a nail to dry.

In this exercise I once met an accident which had liked to have cost me my life: for, one of the pages having put my boat into the trough, the governess who attended Glumdalclitch very officiously lifted me up to place me in the boat, but I happened to slip through her fingers, and should infallibly have fallen down forty feet upon the floor, if, by the luckiest chance in the world, I had not been stopped by a corking-pin that stuck in the good gentlewoman's stomacher; the head of the pin passed between my shirt and the waistband of my breeches, and thus I was held by the middle in the air, till Glumdalclitch ran to my relief.

Another time, one of the servants, whose office it was to fill my trough every third day with fresh water, was so careless, to let a huge frog (not perceiving it) slip out of his pail. The frog lay concealed till I was put into my boat, but then, seeing a resting-place, climbed up and made it lean so much on one side, that I was forced to balance it with all my weight on the other, to prevent overturning. When the frog was got in, it hopped at once half the length of the boat, and then over my head, backwards and forwards, daubing my face and clothes with its odious slime. The largeness of its features made it appear the most deformed animal that can be conceived. However, I desired Glumdalclitch to let me deal with it alone. I banged it a good while with one of my sculls, and at last forced it to leap out of the boat.

But the greatest danger I ever underwent, in that kingdom, was from a monkey, who belonged to one of the clerks of the kitchen. Glumdalclitch had locked me up in her closet, while she went somewhere upon business, or a visit. The weather being very warm, the closet-window was left open, as well as the windows and the doors of my bigger box, in which I usually lived, because of its largeness and conveniency. As I sat quietly meditating at my table, I heard something bounce in at the closet window, and skip about from one side to the other; whereat although I were much alarmed, yet I ventured to look out, but not stirring from my seat; and then I saw this frolicsome animal frisking and leaping up and down, till at last he came to my box, which he seemed to view with great pleasure and curiosity, peeping in at the door and every window. I retreated to the farther corner of my room, or box, but the monkey, looking in at every side, put me into such a fright, that I wanted presence of mind to conceal myself under the bed, as I might have easily done. After some time spent in peeping, grinning, and chattering, he at last espied me, and reaching one of his paws in at the door, as a cat does when she plays with a mouse, although I often shifted place to avoid him, he at length seized the lappet of my coat (which, being made of that country silk, was very thick and strong) and dragged me out. He took me up in his right fore-foot, and held me as a nurse does a child she is going to suckle, just as I have seen the same sort of creature do with a kitten in Europe; and when I offered to struggle, he squeezed me so hard, that I thought it more prudent to submit. I have good reason to believe that he took me for a young one of his own species, by his often stroking my face very gently with his other paw. In these diversions, he was interrupted by a noise at the closet door, as if somebody were opening it; whereupon he suddenly leaped up to the window, at which he had come in, and thence upon the leads and gutters, walking upon three legs, and holding me in the fourth, till he clambered up to a roof that was next to ours. I heard Glumdalclitch give a shriek at the moment he was carrying me out. The poor girl was almost distracted: that quarter of the palace was all in an uproar, the servants ran for ladders; the monkey was seen by hundreds in the court, sitting upon the ridge of a building, holding me like a baby in one of his fore-paws, and feeding me with the other, by cramming into my mouth some victuals he had squeezed out of the bag on one side of his chaps, and patting me when I would not eat; whereat many of the rabble below could not forbear laughing; neither do I think they justly ought to be blamed, for, without question, the sight was ridiculous enough to everybody but myself. Some of the people threw up stones, hoping to drive the monkey down; but this was strictly forbidden, or else, very probably, my brains had been dashed out.

The ladders were now applied, and mounted by several men, which the monkey observing, and finding himself almost encompassed; not being able to make speed enough with his three legs, let me drop on a ridge tile, and made his escape. Here I sat for some time, five hundred yards from the ground, expecting every moment to be blown down by the wind, or to fall by my own giddiness, and come tumbling over and over from the ridge to the eaves: but an honest lad, one of my nurse's footmen, climbed up, and, putting me into his breeches pocket, brought me down safe.

I was almost choked with the filthy stuff the monkey had crammed down my throat; but my dear little nurse picked it out of my mouth with a small needle, and then I fell a-vomiting, which gave me great relief. Yet I was so weak and bruised in the sides with the squeezes given me by this odious animal, that I was forced to keep my bed a fortnight. The king, queen, and all the Court, sent every day to enquire after my health, and her Majesty made me several visits during my sickness. The monkey was killed, and an order made that no such animal should be kept about the palace.

When I attended the king after my recovery, to return him thanks for his favours, he was pleased to rally me a good deal upon this adventure. He asked me what my thoughts and speculations were, while I lay in the monkey's paw; how I liked the victuals he gave me; his manner of feeding; and whether the fresh air on the roof had sharpened my stomach. He desired to know what I would have done upon such an occasion in my own country. I told his Majesty, that in Europe we had no monkeys, except such as were brought for curiosities from other places, and so small, that I could deal with a dozen of them together, if they presumed to attack me. And as for that monstrous animal with whom I was so lately engaged (it was, indeed, as large as an elephant) if my fears had suffered me to think so far as to make use of my hanger (looking fiercely, and clapping my hand upon the hilt as I spoke) when he poked his paw into my chamber, perhaps I should have given him such a wound, as would have made him glad to withdraw it with more haste than he put it in. This I delivered in a firm tone, like a person who was jealous lest his courage should be called in question. However, my speech produced nothing else besides a loud laughter, which all the respect due to his Majesty from those about him could not make them contain. This made me reflect, how vain an attempt it is for a man to endeavour doing himself honour among those who are out of all degree of equality or comparison with him. And yet I have seen the moral of my own behaviour very frequent in England since my return, where a little contemptible varlet without the least title to birth, person, wit, or common sense, shall presume to look with importance, and put himself upon a foot with the greatest persons of the kingdom.

I was every day furnishing the Court with some ridiculous story; and Glumdalclitch, although she loved me to excess, yet was arch enough to inform the queen, whenever I committed any folly that she thought would be diverting to her Majesty.

CHAPTER VI

I USED to attend the king's levee once or twice a week, and had often seen him under the barber's hand, which, indeed, was at first very terrible to behold: for the razor was almost twice as long as an ordinary scythe. His Majesty, according to the custom of the country, was only shaved twice a week. I once prevailed on the barber to give me some of the suds or lather, out of which I picked forty or fifty of the strongest stumps of hair. I then took a piece of fine wood, and cut it like the back of a comb, making several holes in it at equal distance, with as small a needle as I could get from Glumdalclitch. I fixed in the stumps so artificially, scraping and sloping them with my knife towards the points, that I made a very tolerable comb; which was a seasonable supply, my own being so much broken in the teeth that it was almost useless: neither did I know any artist in that country so nice and exact, as would undertake to make me another.

And this puts me in mind of an amusement wherein I spent many of my leisure hours. I desired the queen's woman to save for me the combings of her Majesty's hair, whereof in time I got a good quantity, and consulting with my friend the cabinet-maker, who had received general orders to do little jobs for me, I directed him to make two chair-frames, no larger than those I had in my box, and then to bore little holes with a fine awl round those parts where I designed the backs and seats; through these holes I wove the strongest hairs I could pick out, just after the manner of cane chairs in England. When they were finished, I made a present of them to her Majesty, who kept them in her cabinet, and used to shew them for curiosities, as, indeed, they were the wonder of every one that beheld them. The queen would have had me sit upon one of these chairs, but I absolutely refused to obey her, protesting I would rather die a thousand deaths, than place my body on those precious hairs that once adorned her Majesty's head. Of these hairs (as I had always a mechanical genius) I likewise made a neat little purse about five feet long, with her Majesty's name deciphered in gold letters, which I gave to Glumdalclitch, by the queen's consent. To say the truth, it was more for shew than use, being not of strength to bear the weight of the larger coins, and therefore she kept nothing in it but some little toys that girls are fond of.

The king, who delighted in music, had frequent concerts at Court, to which I was sometimes carried, and set in my box on a table to hear them: but the noise was so great, that I could hardly distinguish the tunes. I am confident, that all the drums and trumpets of a royal army, beating and sounding together just at your ears, could not equal it. My practice was to have my box removed from the places where the performers sat, as far as I could, then to shut the doors and windows of it, and draw the window curtains; after which I found their music not disagreeable.

I had learned in my youth to play a little upon the spinet. Glumdalclitch kept one in her chamber, and a master attended twice a week to teach her: I call it a spinet, because it somewhat resembled that instrument, and was played upon in the same manner. A fancy came into my head that I would entertain the king and queen with an English tune upon this instrument. But this appeared extremely difficult: for the spinet was near sixty feet long, each key being almost a foot wide, so that, with my arms extended, I could not reach to above five keys, and to press them down required a good smart stroke with my fist, which would be too great a labour, and to no purpose. The method I contrived was this: I prepared two round sticks about the bigness of common cudgels; they were thicker at one

end than the other, and I covered the thicker ends
with a piece of mouse's skin, that, by rapping on them, I
might neither damage the tops of the keys, nor interrupt
the sound. Before the spinet a bench was placed about
four feet below the keys, and I was put upon the bench.
I ran sideling upon it that way and this, as fast as I could,
banging the proper keys with my two sticks, and made a
shift to play a jig, to the great satisfaction of both their
Majesties: but it was the most violent exercise I ever
underwent, and yet I could not strike above sixteen keys,
nor, consequently, play the bass and treble together, as
other artists do; which was a great disadvantage to my
performance.

The king, who, as I before observed, was a prince of
excellent understanding, would frequently order that I
should be brought in my box, and set upon the table in his
closet: he would then command me to bring one of my
chairs out of the box, and sit down within three yards
distance upon the top of the cabinet, which brought me
almost to a level with his face. In this manner I had
several conversations with him. I one day took the freedom
to tell his Majesty, that the contempt he discovered towards
Europe, and the rest of the world, did not seem answerable
to those excellent qualities of mind he was master of. That
reason did not extend itself with the bulk of the body:
on the contrary, we observed in our country, that the tallest
persons were usually least provided with it. That, among
other animals, bees and ants had the reputation of more
industry, art, and sagacity, than many of the larger kinds;
and that, as inconsiderable as he took me to be, I hoped I
might live to do his Majesty some signal service. The king
heard me with attention, and began to conceive a much
better opinion of me than he had ever before. He desired
I would give him as exact an account of the government
of England as I possibly could; because, as fond as princes
commonly are of their own customs (for so he conjectured

of other monarchs by my former discourses) he should be glad to hear of anything that might deserve imitation.

Imagine with thyself, courteous reader, how often I then wished for the tongue of Demosthenes or Cicero, that might have enabled me to celebrate the praise of my own dear native country, in a style equal to its merits and felicity.

I began my discourse, by informing his Majesty, that our dominions consisted of two islands, which composed three mighty kingdoms under one sovereign, besides our plantations in America. I dwelt long upon the fertility of our soil, and the temperature of our climate. I then spoke at large upon the constitution of an English Parliament, partly made up of an illustrious body, called the House of Peers, persons of the noblest blood, and of the most ancient and ample patrimonies. I described that extraordinary care always taken of their education in arts and arms, to qualify them for being counsellors both to the king and kingdom; to have a share in the Legislature; to be members of the highest court of judicature, from whence there could be no appeal; and to be champions always ready for the defence of their prince and country, by their valour, conduct, and fidelity. That these were the ornament and bulwark of the kingdom, worthy followers of their most renowned ancestors, whose honour had been the reward of their virtue, from which their posterity were never once known to degenerate. To these were joined several holy persons, as part of that assembly, under the title of bishops, whose peculiar business it is to take care of religion, and of those who instruct the people therein. These were searched and sought out through the whole nation, by the prince and his wisest counsellors, among such of the priesthood as were most deservedly distinguished by the sanctity of their lives, and the depth of their erudition, who were, indeed, the spiritual fathers of the clergy and the people.

That the other part of the Parliament consisted of an assembly called the House of Commons, who were all

principal gentlemen, freely picked and culled out by the
people themselves, for their great abilities, and love of
their country, to represent the wisdom of the whole nation.
And these two bodies make up the most august assembly
in Europe, to whom, in conjunction with the prince, the
whole Legislature is committed.

I then descended to the courts of justice, over which
the judges, those venerable sages and interpreters of the
law, presided, for determining the disputed rights and properties of men, as well as for the punishment of vice, and
protection of innocence. I mentioned the prudent management of our Treasury, the valour and achievements of our
forces by sea and land. I computed the number of our
people, by reckoning how many millions there might be
of each religious sect, or political party among us. I did not
omit even our sports and pastimes, or any other particular
which I thought might redound to the honour of my country.
And I finished all with a brief historical account of affairs and
events in England, for about an hundred years past.

This conversation was not ended under five audiences,
each of several hours; and the king heard the whole with
great attention, frequently taking notes of what I spoke,
as well as memorandums of several questions he intended
to ask me.

When I had put an end to these long discourses, his
Majesty, in a sixth audience, consulting his notes, proposed
many doubts, queries, and objections upon every article.
He asked what methods were used to cultivate the minds
and bodies of our young nobility, and in what kind of
business they commonly spent the first and teachable part
of their lives. What course was taken to supply that
assembly when any noble family became extinct. What
qualifications were necessary in those who are to be created
new lords: whether the humour of the prince, a sum of
money to a court lady, or a prime minister, or a design
of strengthening a party opposite to the public interest,

ever happened to be motives in those advancements. What
share of knowledge these lords had in the laws of their
country, and how they came by it, so as to enable them
to decide the properties of their fellow-subjects in their
last resort. Whether they were always so free from avarice,
partialities, or want, that a bribe, or some other sinister
view, could have no place among them. Whether those holy
lords I spoke of, were always promoted to that rank upon
account of their knowledge in religious matters, and the
sanctity of their lives, had never been compliers with the
times, while they were common priests, or slavish prostitute
chaplains to some nobleman, whose opinions they continued
servilely to follow, after they were admitted into that
assembly.

He then desired to know what arts were practised in
electing those whom I called commoners: whether a
stranger, with a strong purse, might not influence the
vulgar voters to choose him before their own landlord, or
the most considerable gentleman in the neighbourhood.
How it came to pass, that people were so violently bent
upon getting into this assembly, which I allowed to be a
great trouble and expense, often to the ruin of their families,
without any salary or pension: because that appeared such
an exalted strain of virtue and public spirit, that his Majesty
seemed to doubt it might possibly not be always sincere:
and he desired to know whether such zealous gentlemen
could have any views of refunding themselves for the
charges and trouble they were at, by sacrificing the public
good to the designs of a weak and vicious prince, in conjunction with a corrupted ministry. He multiplied his
questions, and sifted me thoroughly upon every part of
this head, proposing numberless enquiries and objections,
which I think it not prudent or convenient to repeat.

Upon what I said in relation to our courts of justice,
his Majesty desired to be satisfied in several points: and
this I was the better able to do, having been formerly

almost ruined by a long suit in chancery, which was decreed
for me with costs. He asked what time was usually spent
in determining between right and wrong, and what degree
of expense. Whether advocates and orators had liberty
to plead in causes manifestly known to be unjust, vexatious,
or oppressive. Whether party in religion or politics were
observed to be of any weight in the scale of justice. Whether
those pleading orators were persons educated in the general
knowledge of equity, or only in provincial, national, and
other local customs. Whether they or their judges had any
part in penning those laws which they assumed the liberty of
interpreting and glossing upon at their pleasure. Whether
they had ever at different times pleaded for and against
the same cause, and cited precedents to prove contrary
opinions. Whether they were a rich or a poor corporation.
Whether they received any pecuniary reward for pleading
or delivering their opinions. And particularly, whether
they were ever admitted as members in the lower senate.

He fell next upon the management of our treasury and
said he thought my memory had failed me, because I
computed our taxes at about five or six millions a year, and,
when I came to mention the issues, he found they sometimes amounted to more than double; for the notes he had
taken were very particular in this point, because he hoped,
as he told me, that the knowledge of our conduct might be
useful to him, and he could not be deceived in his calculations: but, if what I told him were true, he was still at a
loss how a kingdom could run out of its estate like a private
person. He asked me who were our creditors, and where
we should find money to pay them. He wondered to hear me
talk of such chargeable and expensive wars; that certainly
we must be a quarrelsome people, or live among very bad
neighbours, and that our generals must needs be richer
than our kings. He asked what business we had out of our
own islands, unless upon the score of trade or treaty, or
to defend the coast with our fleet. Above all, he was amazed

to hear me talk of a mercenary standing army in the midst of peace, and among a free people. He said, if we were governed by our own consent in the persons of our representatives, he could not imagine of whom we were afraid, or against whom we were to fight; and would hear my opinion, whether a private man's house might not better be defended by himself, his children, and family, than by half a dozen rascals picked up at a venture in the streets, for small wages, who might get an hundred times more by cutting their throats.

He laughed at my odd kind of arithmetic (as he was pleased to call it) in reckoning the numbers of our people by a computation drawn from the several sects among us in religion and politics. He said he knew no reason why those who entertain opinions prejudicial to the public, should be obliged to change, or should not be obliged to conceal them. And as it was tyranny in any government to require the first, so it was weakness not to enforce the second: for a man may be allowed to keep poisons in his closet, but not to vend them about for cordials.

He observed that, among the diversions of our nobility and gentry, I had mentioned gaming. He desired to know at what age this entertainment was usually taken up, and when it was laid down; how much of their time it employed; whether it ever went so high as to affect their fortunes; whether mean vicious people, by their dexterity in that art, might not arrive at great riches, and sometimes keep our very nobles in dependence, as well as habituate them to vile companions, wholly take them from the improvement of their minds, and force them, by the losses they had received, to learn and practise that infamous dexterity upon others.

He was perfectly astonished with the historical account I gave him of our affairs during the last century, protesting it was only a heap of conspiracies, rebellions, murders, massacres, revolutions, banishments, the very worst effects that avarice, faction, hypocrisy, perfidiousness, cruelty, rage, madness, hatred, envy, lust, malice, or ambition, could produce.

His Majesty in another audience was at the pains to recapitulate the sum of all I had spoken; compared the questions he made with the answers I had given; then taking me into his hands, and stroking me gently, delivered himself in these words, which I shall never forget, nor the manner he spoke them in: " My little friend Grildrig, you have made a most admirable panegyric upon your country: you have clearly proved, that ignorance, idleness, and vice are the proper ingredients for qualifying a legislator; that laws are best explained, interpreted, and applied by those whose interest and abilities lie in perverting, confounding, and eluding them. I observe among you some lines of an institution which, in its original, might have been tolerable; but these half erased, and the rest wholly blurred and blotted by corruptions. It doth not appear from all you have said, how any one perfection is required toward the procurement of any one station among you; much less that men are ennobled on account of their virtue, that priests are advanced for their piety or learning, soldiers for their conduct or valour, judges for their integrity, senators for the love of their country, or counsellors for their wisdom. As for yourself (continued the king) who have spent the greatest part of your life in travelling, I am well disposed to hope you may hitherto have escaped many vices of your country. But, by what I have gathered from your own relation, and the answers I have with much pain wringed and extorted from you, I cannot but conclude the bulk of your natives to be the most pernicious race of little odious vermin that Nature ever suffered to crawl upon the surface of the earth."

CHAPTER VII

NOTHING but an extreme love of truth could have hindered me from concealing this part of my story. It was in vain to discover my resentments, which were always turned into ridicule; and I was forced to rest with patience, while my noble and most beloved country was so injuriously treated. I am heartily sorry as any of my readers can possibly be, that such an occasion was given; but this prince happened to be so curious and inquisitive upon every particular, that it could not consist either with gratitude or good manners, to refuse giving him what satisfaction I was able. Yet thus much I may be allowed to say in my own vindication, that I artfully eluded many of his questions, and gave to every point a more favourable turn, by many degrees, than the strictness of truth would allow. For I have always borne that laudable partiality to my own country, which Dionysius Halicarnassensis with so much justice recommends to an historian: I would hide the frailties and deformities of my political mother, and place her virtues and beauties in the most advantageous light. This was my sincere endeavour in those many discourses I had with that mighty monarch, although it unfortunately failed of success.

But great allowances should be given to a king who lives wholly secluded from the rest of the world, and must therefore be altogether unacquainted with the manners and customs that must prevail in other nations: the want of which knowledge will ever produce many prejudices, and a certain narrowness of thinking, from which we and the politer countries of Europe are wholly exempted. And it would be hard indeed if so remote a prince's notions of virtue and vice were to be offered as a standard for all mankind.

To confirm what I have now said, and further, to shew

the miserable effects of a confined education, I shall here insert a passage which will hardly obtain belief. In hopes to ingratiate myself farther into his Majesty's favour, I told him of an invention discovered between three and four hundred years ago, to make a certain powder, into an heap of which the smallest spark of fire falling, would kindle the whole in a moment, although it were as big as a mountain, and make it all fly up in the air together, with a noise and agitation greater than thunder. That a proper quantity of this powder rammed into an hollow tube of brass or iron, according to its bigness, would drive a ball of iron or lead with such violence and speed, as nothing was able to sustain its force. That the largest balls, thus discharged, would not only destroy whole ranks of an army at once, but batter the strongest walls to the ground, sink down ships, with a thousand men in each, to the bottom of the sea; and, when linked together by a chain, would cut through masts and rigging, divide hundreds of bodies in the middle, and lay all waste before them. That we often put this powder into large hollow balls of iron, and discharged them by an engine into some city we were besieging, which would rip up the pavements, tear the houses to pieces, burst and throw splinters on every side, dashing out the brains of all who came near. That I knew the ingredients very well, which were cheap and common; I understood the manner of compounding them, and could direct his workmen how to make those tubes of a size proportionable to all other things in his Majesty's kingdom, and the largest need not be above an hundred feet long; twenty or thirty of which tubes, charged with the proper quantity of powder and balls, would batter down the walls of the strongest town in his dominions in few hours, or destroy the whole metropolis, if ever it should pretend to dispute his absolute commands. This I humbly offered to his Majesty, as a small tribute of acknowledgment in return for so many marks that I had received of his royal favour and protection.

The king was struck with horror at the description I had given of those terrible engines, and the proposal I had made. He was amazed how so impotent and grovelling an insect as I (these were his expressions) could entertain such inhuman ideas, and in so familiar a manner, as to appear wholly unmoved at all the scenes of blood and desolation which I had painted as the common effects of those destructive machines, whereof, he said, some evil genius, enemy to mankind, must have been the first contriver. As for himself, he protested that, although few things delighted him so much as new discoveries in art or in Nature, yet he would rather lose half his kingdom than be privy to such a secret, which he commanded me, as I valued my life, never to mention any more.

A strange effect of narrow principles and short views! that a prince possessed of every quality which procures veneration, love, and esteem; of strong parts, great wisdom, and profound learning, endued with admirable talents for government, and almost adored by his subjects, should, from a nice unnecessary scruple, whereof in Europe we can have no conception, let slip an opportunity put into his hands, that would have made him absolute master of the lives, the liberties, and the fortunes of his people. Neither do I say this with the least intention to detract from the many virtues of that excellent king, whose character, I am sensible, will on this account be very much lessened, in the opinion of an English reader: but I take this defect among them to have risen from their ignorance, by not having hitherto reduced politics into a science, as the more acute wits of Europe have done. For I remember very well, in a discourse one day with the king, when I happened to say there were several thousand books among us written upon the art of government, it gave him (directly contrary to my intention) a very mean opinion of our understandings. He professed both to abominate and despise all mystery, refinement, and intrigue, either in a prince or a minister. He could not tell what I meant by secrets of state, where an enemy, or some rival nation, were not in the case. He confined the knowledge of governing within very narrow bounds, to common sense and reason, to justice and lenity, to the speedy determination of civil and criminal causes; with some other obvious topics, which are not worth considering. And he gave it for his opinion, that whoever could make two ears of corn, or two blades of grass, to grow upon a spot of ground where only one grew before, would deserve better of mankind, and do more essential service to his country, than the whole race of politicians put together.

The learning of this people is very defective, consisting only in morality, history, poetry, and mathematics, wherein they must be allowed to excel. But the last of these is wholly applied to what may be useful in life, to the improvement of agriculture, and all mechanical arts; so that among us it would be little esteemed. And as to ideas, entities, abstractions, and transcendentals, I could never drive the least conception into their heads.

No law of that country must exceed in words the number of letters in their alphabet, which consists only in two and twenty. But, indeed, few of them extend even to that length. They are expressed in the most plain and simple terms, wherein those people are not mercurial enough to discover above one interpretation: and to write a comment upon any law is a capital crime. As to the decision of civil causes, or proceedings against criminals, their precedents are so few, that they have little reason to boast of any extraordinary skill in them.

They have had the art of printing, as well as the Chinese, time out of mind; but their libraries are not very large; for that of the king's, which is reckoned the biggest, doth not amount to above a thousand volumes, placed in a gallery of twelve hundred feet long, from whence I had liberty to borrow what books I pleased. The queen's joiner had contrived, in one of Glumdalclitch's rooms, a kind of wooden machine, five and twenty feet high, formed like a standing ladder, the steps were each fifty feet long: it was, indeed, a moveable pair of stairs, the lowest end placed at ten feet distance from the wall of the chamber. The book I had a mind to read, was put up leaning against the wall: I first mounted to the upper step of the ladder, and, turning my face towards the book, began at the top of the page, and so walking to the right and left, about eight or ten paces, according to the length of the lines, till I had gotten a little below the level of mine eyes, and then descending gradually till I came to the bottom; after which, I mounted again, and began the other page in the same manner, and so turned over the leaf, which I could easily do with both my hands, for it was as thick and stiff as a paste-board, and, in the largest folios, not above eighteen or twenty feet long.

Their style is clear, masculine, and smooth, but not florid; for they avoid nothing more than multiplying unnecessary words, or using various expressions. I have perused many of their books, especially those in history and morality. Among the rest, I was much diverted with a little old treatise which always lay in Glumdalclitch's bedchamber, and belonged to her governess, a grave elderly gentlewoman, who dealt in writings of morality and devotion. The book treats of the weakness of human kind, and is in little esteem, except among the women and the vulgar. However, I was curious to see what an author of that country could say upon such a subject. This writer went through all the usual topics of European moralists, shewing how diminutive, contemptible, and helpless an animal was man in his own nature; how unable to defend himself from inclemencies of the air, or the fury of wild beasts; how much he was excelled by one creature in strength, by another in speed, by a third in foresight, by a fourth in industry. He added, that nature was degenerated in these latter declining ages of the world, and could now produce only small abortive births, in comparison of those in ancient times. He said, it was very reasonable to think, not only that the species of men were originally much larger, but also, that there must have been giants in former ages, which, as it is asserted by history and tradition, so it hath been confirmed by huge bones and skulls casually dug up in several parts of the kingdom, far exceeding the common dwindling race of man in our days. He argued that the very laws of Nature absolutely required we should have been made in the beginning of a size more large and robust, not so liable to destruction from every little accident of a tile falling from an house, or a stone cast from the hand of a boy, or being drowned in a little brook. From this way of reasoning, the author drew several moral applications useful in the conduct of life, but needless here to repeat. For my part, I could not avoid reflecting how universally this talent was spread, of drawing lectures in morality, or, indeed, rather matter of discontent and repining, from the quarrels we raise with Nature. And, I believe, upon a strict enquiry, those quarrels might be shewn as ill-grounded among us as they are among that people.

As to their military affairs, they boast that the king's army consists of an hundred and seventy-six thousand foot, and thirty-two thousand horse: if that may be called an army which is made up of tradesmen in the several cities, and farmers in the country, whose commanders are only the nobility and gentry, without pay or reward. They are, indeed, perfect enough in their exercises, and under very good discipline, wherein I saw no great merit; for how should it be otherwise, where every farmer is under the command of his own landlord, and every citizen under that of the principal men in his own city, chosen after the manner of Venice by ballot!

I have often seen the militia of Lorbrulgrud drawn out to exercise in a great field near the city, of twenty miles square. They were, in all, not above twenty-five thousand foot, and six thousand horse; but it was impossible for me to compute their number, considering the space of ground they took up. A cavalier, mounted on a large steed, might be about ninety feet high. I have seen this whole body of horse, upon a word of command, draw their swords at once, and brandish them in the air. Imagination can figure nothing so grand, so surprising, and so astonishing! It looked as if ten thousand flashes of lightning were darting at the same time from every quarter of the sky.

I was curious to know how this prince, to whose dominions there is no access from any other country, came to think of armies, or to teach his people the practice of military discipline. But I was soon informed, both by conversation, and reading their histories: for, in the course of many ages, they have been troubled with the same disease to which the whole race of mankind is subject; the nobility often contending for power, the people for liberty, and the king for absolute dominion. All which, however happily tempered by the laws of that kingdom, have been sometimes violated by each of the three parties, and have once, or more, occasioned civil wars, the last whereof was happily put an end to by this prince's grandfather in a general composition; and the militia, then settled with common consent, hath been ever since kept in the strictest duty.

CHAPTER VIII

I HAD always a strong impulse, that I should some time recover my liberty, though it was impossible to conjecture by what means, or to form any project with the least hope of succeeding. The ship in which I sailed was the first ever known to be driven within sight of that coast, and the king had given strict orders that, if at any time another appeared, it should be taken ashore, and, with all its crew and passengers, brought in a tumbril to Lorbrulgrud. He was strongly bent to get me a woman of my own size, by whom I might propagate the breed; but, I think, I should rather have died, than undergone the disgrace of leaving a posterity to be kept in cages like tame canary birds, and perhaps, in time, sold about the kingdom to persons of quality for curiosities. I was, indeed, treated with much kindness: I was the favourite of a great king and queen, and the delight of the whole Court; but it was upon such a foot as ill became the dignity of human kind. I could never forget those domestic pledges I had left behind me. I wanted to be among people with whom I could converse upon even terms, and walk about the streets and fields without being afraid of being trod to death, like a frog or a young puppy. But my deliverance came sooner than I expected, and, in a manner, not very common: the whole story and circumstances of which I shall faithfully relate.

I had now been two years in this country; and, about the beginning of the third, Glumdalclitch and I attended the king and queen in a progress to the south coast of the kingdom. I was carried, as usual, in my travelling box, which, as I have already described, was a very convenient closet of twelve feet wide. And I had ordered a hammock to be fixed, by silken ropes, from the four corners at the top, to break the jolts, when a servant carried me before him on horseback, as I sometimes desired, and would often sleep in my hammock while we were upon the road. On the roof of my closet, just over the middle of the hammock, I ordered the joiner to cut out a hole of a foot square, to give me air in hot weather, as I slept; which hole I shut, at pleasure, with a board that drew backwards and forwards through a groove.

When we came to our journey's end, the king thought proper to pass a few days at a palace he hath near Flanflasnic, a city within eighteen English miles of the sea-side. Glumdalclitch and I were much fatigued; I had gotten a small cold, but the poor girl was so ill as to be confined to her chamber. I longed to see the ocean, which must be the only scene of my escape, if ever it should happen. I pretended to be worse than I really was, and desired leave to take the fresh air of the sea, with a page I was very fond of, and who had sometimes been trusted with me. I shall never forget with what unwillingness Glumdalclitch consented, nor the strict charge she gave the page to be careful of me, bursting at the same time into a flood of tears, as if she had some foreboding of what was to happen. The boy took me out in my box about half an hour's walk from the palace towards the rocks on the sea-shore. I ordered him to set me down, and lifting up one of my sashes, cast many a wistful melancholy look towards the sea. I found myself not very well, and told the page that I had a mind to take a nap in my hammock, which I hoped would do me good. I got in, and the boy shut the window close down to keep out the cold. I soon fell asleep, and all I can conjecture is, that while I slept, the page, thinking no danger could happen, went among the rocks to look for birds' eggs, having before observed him from my window searching about, and picking up one or two in the clefts. Be that as it will, I found myself suddenly awaked with a violent pull

upon the ring which was fastened at the top of my box, for
the conveniency of carriage. I felt my box raised very high
in the air, and then borne forward with prodigious speed.
The first jolt had like to have shaken me out of my hammock, but afterwards the motion was easy enough. I called
out several times, as loud as I could raise my voice, but all
to no purpose. I looked towards my windows, and could
see nothing but the clouds and sky. I heard a noise over
my head like the clapping of wings, and then began to perceive the woful condition I was in, that some eagle had got
the ring of my box in his beak, with an intent to let it fall
on a rock like a tortoise in a shell, and then pick out my
body, and devour it. For the sagacity and smell of this
bird enabled him to discover his quarry at a great distance,
though better concealed than I could be within a two-inch
board.

In a little time I observed the noise and flutter of wings
to increase very fast, and my box was tossed up and down
like a sign post in a windy day. I heard several bangs or
buffets, as I thought, given to the eagle (for such I am
certain it must have been that held the ring of my box
in his beak) and then all on a sudden felt myself falling
perpendicularly down for above a minute, but with such
incredible swiftness that I almost lost my breath. My fall
was stopped by a terrible squash, that sounded louder to
my ears than the cataract of Niagara; after which I was
quite in the dark for another minute, and then my box
began to rise so high that I could see light from the tops of
the windows. I now perceived that I was fallen into the
sea. My box, by the weight of my body, the goods that
were in, and the broad plates of iron fixed for strength at
the four corners of the top and bottom, floated above five
feet deep in water. I did then, and do now suppose that
the eagle which flew away with my box was pursued by
two or three others, and forced to let me drop while he was
defending himself against the rest, who hoped to share in

the prey. The plates of iron fastened at the bottom of the box (for those were the strongest) preserved the balance while it fell, and hindered it from being broken on the surface of the water. Every joint of it was well grooved; and the door did not move on hinges, but up and down like a sash, which kept my closet so tight that very little water came in. I got with much difficulty out of my hammock, having first ventured to draw back the slip-board on the roof already mentioned, contrived on purpose to let in air, for want of which I found myself almost stifled.

How often did I then wish myself with my dear Glumdalclitch, from whom one single hour had so far divided me! And I may say, with truth, that in the midst of my own misfortunes I could not forbear lamenting my poor nurse, the grief she would suffer for my loss, the displeasure of the queen, and the ruin of her fortune. Perhaps many travellers have not been under greater difficulties and distress than I was at this juncture, expecting every moment to see my box dashed in pieces, or at least overset by the first violent blast, or a rising wave. A breach in one single pane of glass would have been immediate death; nor could anything have preserved the windows but the strong lattice-wires placed on the outside against accidents in travelling. I saw the water ooze in at several crannies, although the leaks were not considerable, and I endeavoured to stop them as well as I could. I was not able to lift up the roof of my closet, which otherwise I certainly should have done, and sat on the top of it, where I might, at least, preserve myself some hours longer than by being shut up, as I may call it, in the hold. Or, if I escaped these dangers for a day or two, what could I expect but a miserable death of cold and hunger! I was four hours under these circumstances, expecting and indeed wishing every moment to be my last.

I have already told the reader, that there were two strong staples fixed upon that side of my box which had no window, and into which the servant who used to carry me on horseback would put a leathern belt, and buckle it about his waist. Being in this disconsolate state, I heard or at least thought I heard some kind of grating noise on that side of my box where the staples were fixed, and soon after I began to fancy that the box was pulled or towed along in the sea; for I now and then felt a sort of tugging, which made the waves rise near the tops of my windows, leaving me almost in the dark. This gave me some faint hopes of relief; although I was not able to imagine how it could be brought about. I ventured to unscrew one of my chairs, which were always fastened to the floor; and having made a hard shift to screw it down again directly under the slipping-board that I had lately opened, I mounted on the chair, and, putting my mouth as near as I could to the hole, I called for help in a loud voice, and in all the languages I understood. I then fastened my handkerchief to a stick I usually carried, and, thrusting it up the hole, waved it several times in the air, that, if any boat or ship were near, the seamen might conjecture some unhappy mortal to be shut up in the box.

I found no effect from all I could do, but plainly perceived my closet to be moved along; and in the space of an hour, or better, that side of the box where the staples were, and had no window, struck against something that was hard. I apprehended it to be a rock, and found myself tossed more than ever. I plainly heard a noise upon the cover of my closet, like that of a cable, and the grating of it as it passed through the ring. I then found myself hoisted up by degrees, at least three feet higher than I was before. Whereupon I again thrust up my stick and handkerchief, calling for help till I was almost hoarse. In return to which, I heard a great shout repeated three times, giving me such transports of joy as are not to be conceived but by those who feel them. I now heard a trampling over my head, and somebody calling through the hole with a loud voice in the English tongue, if there be anybody below, let them speak. I answered, I was an Englishman, drawn by ill fortune into the greatest calamity that ever any creature underwent, and begged, by all that was moving, to be delivered out of the dungeon I was in. The voice replied, I was safe, for my box was fastened to their ship; and the carpenter should immediately come and saw a hole in the cover large enough to pull me out. I answered, that was needless, and would take up too much time, for there was no more to be done, but let one of the crew put his finger into the ring, and take the box out of the sea into the ship, and so into the captain's cabin. Some of them, upon hearing me talk so wildly, thought I was mad; others laughed; for, indeed, it never came into my head that I was now got among people of my own stature and strength. The carpenter came, and in few minutes sawed a passage about four feet square, then let down a small ladder, upon which I mounted, and from thence was taken into the ship in a very weak condition.

The sailors were all in amazement, and asked me a thousand questions, which I had no inclination to answer. I was equally confounded at the sight of so many pigmies, for such I took them to be, after having so long accustomed mine eyes to the monstrous objects I had left. But the captain, Mr. Thomas Wilcocks, an honest worthy Shropshire man, observing I was ready to faint, took me into his cabin, gave me a cordial to comfort me, and made me to turn in upon his own bed, advising me to take a little rest, of which I had great need. Before I went to sleep, I gave him to understand that I had valuable furniture in my box, too good to be lost; a fine hammock, an handsome field-bed, two chairs, a table, and a cabinet: that my closet was hung on all sides, or rather quilted, with silk and cotton: that, if he would let one of the crew bring my closet into his cabin, I would open it there before him, and shew him my goods. The captain, hearing me utter these absurdities, concluded I was raving; however (I suppose to pacify me) he promised to give order, as I desired, and going upon deck, sent some of his men down into my closet, from whence (as I afterwards found) they drew up all my goods, and stripped off the quilting; but the chairs, cabinet, and bedstead, being screwed to the floor, were much damaged by the ignorance of the seamen, who tore them up by force. Then they knocked off some of the boards for the use of the ship, and, when they had got all they had a mind for, let the hulk drop into the sea, which, by reason of many breaches made in the bottom and sides, sunk to rights. And, indeed, I was glad not to have been a spectator of the havoc they made; because I am confident it would have sensibly touched me, by bringing former passages into my mind which I had rather forget.

I slept some hours, but perpetually disturbed with dreams of the place I had left, and the dangers I had escaped. However, upon waking, I found myself much recovered. It was now about eight o'clock at night, and the captain ordered supper immediately, thinking I had already fasted too long. He entertained me with great kindness, observing me not to look wildly, or talk inconsistently; and, when we were left alone, desired I would give him a relation of my travels, and by what accident I came to be set adrift in that monstrous wooden chest. He said that about twelve o'clock at noon, as he was looking through his glass, he spied it at a distance, and thought it was a sail, which he had a mind to make, being not much out of his course, in hopes of buying some biscuit, his own beginning to fall short. That upon coming nearer, and finding his error, he sent out his long-boat to discover what I was; that his men came back in a fright, swearing they had seen a swimming house. That he laughed at their folly, and went himself in the boat, ordering his men to take a strong cable along with them. That, the weather being calm, he rowed round me several times, observed my

windows, and the wire-lattices that defended them. That
he discovered two staples upon one side, which was all of
boards, without any passage for light. He then commanded his men to row up to that side, and, fastening a
cable to one of the staples, ordered them to tow my chest
(as they called it) towards the ship. When it was there, he
gave directions to fasten another cable to the ring fixed in
the cover, and to raise up my chest with pulleys, which all
the sailors were not able to do above two or three feet. He
said they saw my stick and handkerchief thrust out of the
hole, and concluded that some unhappy man must be shut
up in the cavity. I asked whether he or the crew had seen
any prodigious bird in the air about the time he first discovered me? To which he answered that, discoursing this
matter with the sailors while I was asleep, one of them said
he had observed three eagles flying towards the north, but
remarked nothing of their being larger than the usual
size, which I suppose must be imputed to the great height
they were at; and he could not guess the reason of my
question.

I then asked the captain, how far he reckoned we might
be from land? He said, by the best computation he could
make, we were at least an hundred leagues. I assured him
that he must be mistaken by almost half, for I had not left
the country from whence I came above two hours before I
dropt into the sea. Whereupon he began again to think
that my brain was disturbed, of which he gave me a hint,
and advised me to go to bed in a cabin he had provided. I
assured him I was well refreshed with his good entertainment and company, and as much in my senses as ever I was
in my life. He then grew serious, and desired to ask me
freely whether I were not troubled in mind by the consciousness of some enormous crime, for which I was punished at
the command of some prince, by exposing me in that chest,
as great criminals, in other countries, have been forced to
sea in a leaky vessel without provisions: for although he

should be sorry to have taken so ill a man into his ship, yet he would engage his word to set me safe ashore in the first port where we arrived. He added that his suspicions were much increased by some very absurd speeches I had delivered at first to the sailors, and afterwards to himself, in relation to my closet or chest, as well as by my odd looks and behaviour while I was at supper.

I begged his patience to hear me tell my story, which I faithfully did, from the last time I left England to the moment he first discovered me. And as truth always forceth its way into rational minds, so this honest worthy gentleman, who had some tincture of learning, and very good sense, was immediately convinced of my candour and veracity. But, farther to confirm all I had said, I entreated him to give order that my cabinet should be brought, of which I had the key in my pocket (for he had already informed me how the seamen disposed of my closet). I opened it in his presence, and showed him the small collection of rarities I made in the country from whence I had been so strangely delivered. There was the comb I had contrived out of the stumps of the king's beard, and another of the same materials, but fixed into a paring of her Majesty's thumb-nail, which served for the back. There was a collection of needles and pins from a foot to half a yard long; four wasp-stings, like joiners' tacks; some combings of the queen's hair; a gold ring which one day she made me a present of in a most obliging manner, taking it from her little finger, and throwing it over my head like a collar. I desired the captain would please to accept this ring, in return of his civilities; which he absolutely refused. I showed him a corn that I had cut off with my own hand from a maid of honour's toe; it was about the bigness of a Kentish pippin, and grown so hard, that, when I returned to England, I got it hollowed into a cup, and set in silver. Lastly, I desired him to see the breeches I had then on, which were made of a mouse's skin.

I could force nothing on him but a footman's tooth, which I observed him to examine with great curiosity, and found he had a fancy for it. He received it with abundance of thanks, more than such a trifle could deserve. It was drawn by an unskilful surgeon, in a mistake, from one of Glumdalclitch's men, who was afflicted with the toothache, but it was as sound as any in his head. I got it cleaned, and put it into my cabinet. It was about a foot long, and four inches in diameter.

The captain was very well satisfied with this plain relation I had given him, and said he hoped, when we returned to England, I would oblige the world by putting it in paper, and making it public. My answer was, that I thought we were already over-stocked with books of travels: that nothing could now pass which was not extraordinary; wherein I doubted some authors less consulted truth, than their own vanity, or interest, or the diversion of ignorant readers. That my story could contain little besides common events, without those ornamental descriptions of strange plants, trees, birds, and other animals; or of the barbarous customs and idolatry of savage people, with which most writers abound. However, I thanked him for his good opinion, and promised to take the matter into my thoughts.

He said he wondered at one thing very much, which was to hear me speak so loud, asking me whether the king or queen of that country were thick of hearing. I told him, it was what I had been used to for above two years past; and that I admired as much at the voices of him and his men, who seemed to me only to whisper, and yet I could hear them well enough. But when I spoke in that country, it was like a man talking in the street to another looking out from the top of a steeple, unless when I was placed on a table, or held in any person's hand. I told him I had likewise observed another thing, that when I first got into the ship, and the sailors stood all about me, I thought they

were the most little contemptible creatures I had ever
beheld. For, indeed, while I was in that prince's country,
I could never endure to look in a glass, after my eyes had
been accustomed to such prodigious objects, because the
comparison gave me so despicable a conceit of myself. The
captain said that, while we were at supper, he observed me
to look at everything with a sort of wonder, and that I often
seemed hardly able to contain my laughter, which he knew
not well how to take, but imputed it to some disorder in my
brain. I answered, it was very true; and I wondered how
I could forbear, when I saw his dishes of the size of a silver
three-pence, a leg of pork hardly a mouthful, a cup not so
big as a nut-shell; and so I went on, describing the rest of
his household-stuff and provisions, after the same manner.
For, although the queen had ordered a little equipage of all
things necessary for me while I was in her service, yet my
ideas were wholly taken up with what I saw on every side of
me, and I winked at my own littleness, as people 'do at
their own faults. The captain understood my raillery
very well, and merrily replied with the old English proverb,
that he doubted my eyes were bigger than my belly, for he
did not observe my stomach so good, although I had fasted
all day; and, continuing in his mirth, protested he would
have gladly given an hundred pounds to have seen my
closet in the eagle's bill, and afterwards in its fall from so
great a height into the sea; which would certainly have
been a most astonishing object, worthy to have the description of it transmitted to future ages: and the comparison
of Phaeton was so obvious, that he could not forbear applying it, although I did not much admire the conceit.

The captain having been at Tonquin, was, in his return
to England, driven north-eastward, to the latitude of 44
degrees, and of longitude 143. But, meeting a trade-wind
two days after I came on board him, we sailed southward a
long time, and coasting New Holland, kept our course
west-south-west, and then south-south-west, till we doubled

the Cape of Good Hope. Our voyage was very prosperous, but I shall not trouble the reader with a journal of it. The captain called in at one or two ports, and sent in his long-boat for provisions and fresh water, but I never went out of the ship till we came into the Downs, which was on the third day of June, 1706, about nine months after my escape. I offered to leave my goods in security for pay-ment of my freight; but the captain protested he would not receive one farthing. We took kind leave of each other, and I made him promise he would come to see me at my house in Redriff. I hired a horse and guide for five shillings, which I borrowed of the captain.

As I was on the road, observing the littleness of the houses, the trees, the cattle, and the people, I began to think myself in Lilliput. I was afraid of trampling on every traveller I met, and often called aloud to have them stand out of the way, so that I had like to have gotten one or two broken heads for my impertinence.

When I came to my own house, for which I was forced to enquire, one of the servants opening the door, I bent down to go in (like a goose under a gate) for fear of striking my head. My wife ran out to embrace me, but I stooped lower than her knees, thinking she could otherwise never be able to reach my mouth. My daughter kneeled to ask my blessing, but I could not see her till she arose, having been so long used to stand with my head and eyes erect, to above sixty feet; and then I went to take her up with one hand by the waist. I looked down upon the servants, and one or two friends who were in the house, as if they had been pigmies, and I a giant. I told my wife she had been too thrifty, for I found she had starved herself and her daughter to nothing. In short, I behaved myself so unaccountably, that they were all of the captain's opinion when he first saw me, and concluded I had lost my wits. This I mention as an instance of the great power of habit and prejudice.

In a little time, I and my family and friends came to a right understanding, but my wife protested I should never go to sea any more; although my evil destiny so ordered, that she had not power to hinder me, as the reader may know hereafter. In the meantime, I here conclude the second part of my unfortunate voyages.

THE END OF THE SECOND PART

PART 3

CHAPTER I

I HAD not been at home above ten days, when Captain
William Robinson, a Cornish man, commander of the
Hope Well, a stout ship of three hundred tons, came to my
house. I had formerly been surgeon of another ship where
he was master, and a fourth part owner, in a voyage to the
Levant; he had always treated me more like a brother than an
inferior officer, and, hearing of my arrival, made me a visit,
as I apprehended, only out of friendship, for nothing passed
more than what is usual after long absences. But repeating
his visits often, expressing his joy to find me in good health,
asking whether I were now settled for life, adding, that he
intended a voyage to the East Indies, in two months; at
last he plainly invited me, though with some apologies, to
be surgeon of the ship; that I should have another surgeon
under me, besides our two mates; that my salary should
be double to the usual pay; and that having experienced
my knowledge in sea-affairs to be at least equal to his, he
would enter into any engagement to follow my advice as
much as if I had shared in the command.

He said so many other obliging things, and I knew him
to be so honest a man, that I could not reject his proposal;
the thirst I had of seeing the world, notwithstanding my
past misfortunes, continuing as violent as ever. The only

difficulty that remained was to persuade my wife, whose consent, however, I at last obtained, by the prospect of advantage she proposed to her children.

We set out the 5th day of August, 1706, and arrived at Fort St. George the 11th of April, 1707. We stayed there three weeks to refresh our crew, many of whom were sick. From thence we went to Tonquin, where the captain resolved to continue some time, because many of the goods he intended to buy were not ready, nor could he expect to be dispatched in several months. Therefore, in hopes to defray some of the charges he must be at, he bought a sloop, loaded it with several sorts of goods, wherewith the Tonquinese usually trade to the neighbouring islands, and putting fourteen men on board, whereof three were of the country, he appointed me master of the sloop, and gave me power to traffic, while he transacted his affairs at Tonquin.

We had not sailed above three days, when, a great storm arising, we were driven five days to the north-north-east, and then to the east; after which we had fair weather, but still with a pretty strong gale from the west. Upon the tenth day we were chased by two pirates, who soon overtook us; for my sloop was so deep loaden that she sailed very slow, neither were we in a condition to defend ourselves.

We were boarded about the same time by both the pirates, who entered furiously at the head of their men; but finding us all prostrate upon our faces (for so I gave order) they pinioned us with strong ropes, and, setting a guard upon us, went to search the sloop.

I observed among them a Dutchman, who seemed to be of some authority, though he was not commander of either ship. He knew us by our countenances to be Englishmen, and, jabbering to us in his own language, swore we should be tied back to back, and thrown into the sea. I spoke Dutch tolerably well; I told him who we were, and begged him, in consideration of our being Christians and Protestants of neighbouring countries, in strict alliance, that he would move the captains to take some pity on us. This inflamed his rage, he repeated his threatenings, and, turning to his companions, spoke with great vehemence, in the Japanese language, as I suppose, often using the word *Christianos*.

The largest of the two pirate ships was commanded by a Japanese captain, who spoke a little Dutch, but very imperfectly. He came up to me, and after several questions, which I answered in great humility, he said we should not die. I made the captain a very low bow, and, then turning to the Dutchman, said, I was sorry to find more mercy in a heathen, than in a brother Christian. But I had soon reason to repent those foolish words; for that malicious reprobate, having often endeavoured in vain to persuade both the captains that I might be thrown into the sea (which they would not yield to after the promise made me, that I should not die) however prevailed so far as to have a punishment inflicted on me, worse, in all human appearance, than death itself. My men were sent, by an equal division, into both the pirate ships, and my sloop new manned. As to myself, it was determined that I should be set a-drift, in a small canoe, with paddles and a sail, and four days' provisions, which last the Japanese captain was so kind to double out of his own stores, and would permit no man to search me. I got down into the canoe, while the Dutchman, standing upon the deck, loaded me with all the curses and injurious terms his language could afford.

About an hour before we saw the pirates, I had taken an observation, and found we were in the latitude of 46 N. and of longitude 183. When I was at some distance from the pirates, I discovered by my pocket-glass several islands to the south-east. I set up my sail, the wind being fair, with a design to reach the nearest of those islands, which I made a shift to do in about three hours. It was all rocky, however I got many birds' eggs, and, striking fire, I kindled some heath and dry sea-weed, by which I roasted my eggs.

I ate no other supper, being resolved to spare my provisions as much as I could. I passed the night under the shelter of a rock, strewing some heath under me, and slept pretty well.

The next day I sailed to another island, and thence to a third and fourth, sometimes using my sail, and sometimes my paddles. But, not to trouble the reader with a particular account of my distresses, let it suffice that, on the fifth day, I arrived at the last island in my sight, which lay south-south-east to the former.

This island was at a greater distance than I expected, and I did not reach it in less than five hours. I encompassed it almost round, before I could find a convenient place to land in, which was a small creek, about three times the wideness of my canoe. I found the island to be all rocky, only a little intermingled with tufts of grass and sweet-smelling herbs. I took out my small provisions, and after having refreshed myself, I secured the remainder in a cave, whereof there were great numbers. I gathered plenty of eggs upon the rocks, and got a quantity of dry sea-weed and parched grass, which I designed to kindle the next day, and roast my eggs as well as I could (for I had about me my flint, steel, match, and burning-glass). I lay all night in the cave where I had lodged my provisions. My bed was the same dry grass and sea-weed which I intended for fuel. I slept very little, for the disquiets of my mind prevailed over my weariness, and kept me awake. I considered how impossible it was to preserve my life in so desolate a place, and how miserable my end must be. Yet I found myself so listless and desponding, that I had not the heart to rise; and, before I could get spirits enough to creep out of my cave, the day was far advanced. I walked a while among the rocks; the sky was perfectly clear, and the sun so hot, that I was forced to turn my face from it: when, all on a sudden, it became obscure, as I thought, in a manner very different from what happens by the interposi-

tion of a cloud. I turned back, and perceived a vast
opaque body between me and the sun, moving forwards
towards the island: it seemed to be about two miles high,
and hid the sun six or seven minutes, but I did not observe
the air to be much colder, or the sky more darkened, than
if I had stood under the shade of a mountain. As it ap-
proached nearer over the place where I was, it appeared to
be a firm substance, the bottom flat, smooth, and shining
very bright from the reflection of the sea below. I stood
upon a height, about two hundred yards from the shore,
and saw this vast body descending almost to a parallel with
me, at less than an English mile distance. I took out my
pocket-perspective and could plainly discover numbers of
people moving up and down the sides of it, which appeared
to be sloping; but what those people were doing I was not
able to distinguish.

The natural love of life gave me some inward motions of
joy, and I was ready to entertain a hope that this adventure might some way or other help to deliver me from the
desolate place and condition I was in. But at the same
time the reader can hardly conceive my astonishment, to
behold an island in the air, inhabited by men, who were
able (as it should seem) to raise or sink, or put it into a
progressive motion, as they pleased. But, not being at
that time in a disposition to philosophise upon this phenomenon, I rather chose to observe what course the island
would take, because it seemed for a while to stand still.
Yet soon after it advanced nearer, and I could see the sides
of it, encompassed with several gradations of galleries and
stairs, at certain intervals, to descend from one to the other.
In the lowest gallery, I beheld some people fishing with
long angling rods, and others looking on. I waved my cap
(for my hat was long since worn out) and my handkerchief
towards the island; and, upon its nearer approach, I called
and shouted with the utmost strength of my voice; and
then, looking circumspectly, I beheld a crowd gathered to

that side which was most in my view. I found by their pointing towards me, and to each other, that they plainly discovered me, although they made no return to my shouting. But I could see four or five men running in great haste up the stairs to the top of the island, who then disappeared. I happened rightly to conjecture that these were sent for orders to some person in authority upon this occasion.

The number of people increased, and, in less than half an hour, the island was moved and raised in such a manner, that the lowest gallery appeared in a parallel of less than a hundred yards distance from the height where I stood. I then put myself into the most supplicating postures, and spoke in the humblest accent, but received no answer. Those who stood nearest over-against me seemed to be persons of distinction, as I supposed by their habit. They conferred earnestly with each other, looking often upon me. At length one of them called out in a clear, polite, smooth dialect, not unlike in sound to the Italian; and therefore I returned an answer in that language, hoping, at least, that the cadence might be more agreeable to his ears. Although neither of us understood the other, yet my meaning was easily known, for the people saw the distress I was in.

They made signs for me to come down from the rock, and go towards the shore, which I accordingly did; and, the flying island being raised to a convenient height, the verge directly over me, a chain was let down from the lowest gallery, with a seat fastened to the bottom, to which I fixed myself, and was drawn up by pulleys.

GULLIVER RELEASED FROM THE STRINGS

RAISES AND STRETCHES HIMSELF

Part I, Chapter I

THE EMPEROR OF LILLIPUT REVIEWS HIS TROOPS
Part I, Chapter III

GULLIVER SEIZES THE ENEMY'S FLEET
Part I, Chapter V

GULLIVER KISSES THE QUEEN OF BROBDINGNAGIA'S HAND
Part II, Chapter III

GULLIVERS COMBAT WITH THE WASPS
Part II, Chapter III

APPLES CAME TUMBLING ABOUT MY EARS

Part II, Chapter V

GULLIVER'S ENCOUNTER WITH THE FROG
Part II, Chapter V

TWO OF THOSE SAGES . . . LIKE PEDLARS AMONG US
Part III, Chapter V

CHAPTER II

AT my alighting, I was surrounded with a crowd of people; but those who stood nearest seemed to be of better quality. They beheld me with all the marks and circumstances of wonder, neither, indeed, was I much in their debt; having never, till then, seen a race of mortals so singular in their shapes, habits, and countenances. Their heads were all reclined either to the right or the left; one of their eyes turned inward, and the other directly up to the zenith. Their outward garments were adorned with the figures of suns, moons, and stars, interwoven with those of fiddles, flutes, harps, trumpets, guitars, harpsicords, and many other instruments of music, unknown to us in Europe. I observed, here and there, many in the habit of servants, with a blown bladder fastened like a flail to the end of a short stick, which they carried in their hands. In each bladder was a small quantity of dried pease, or little pebbles (as I was afterwards informed). With these bladders they now and then flapped the mouths and ears of those who stood near them, of which practice I could not then conceive the meaning; it seems, the minds of these people are so taken up with intense speculations, that they neither can speak, nor attend to the discourses of others, without being roused by some external taction upon the organs of speech and hearing; for which reason, those persons, who are able to afford it always keep a flapper (the original is *climenole*) in their family, as one of their domestics, nor ever walk abroad, or make visits, without him. And the business of this officer is, when two or three more persons are in company, gently to strike with his bladder the mouth of him who is to speak, and the right ear of him or them to whom the speaker addresseth himself. This flapper is likewise employed diligently to attend his master in his walks, and, upon occasion, to give him a soft flap on his eyes, because he is always so wrapped up in cogitation that he is in manifest danger of falling down every precipice, and bouncing his head against every post; and in the streets, of jostling others, or being jostled himself, into the kennel.

It was necessary to give the reader this information, without which he would be at the same loss with me, to understand the proceedings of these people, as they conducted me up the stairs to the top of the island, and from thence to the royal palace. While we were ascending, they forgot several times what they were about, and left me to myself, till their memories were again roused by their flappers; for they appeared altogether unmoved by the sight of my foreign habit and countenance, and by the shouts of the vulgar, whose thoughts and minds were more disengaged.

At last we entered the palace, and proceeded into the chamber of presence, where I saw the king seated on his throne, attended on each side by persons of prime quality. Before the throne was a large table filled with globes and spheres, and mathematical instruments of all kinds. His Majesty took not the least notice of us, although our entrance was not without sufficient noise, by the concourse of all persons belonging to the Court. But he was then deep in a problem, and we attended at least an hour before he could solve it. There stood by him, on each side, a young page, with flaps in their hands, and, when they saw he was at leisure, one of them gently struck his mouth, and the other his right ear; at which he started like one awaked on the sudden, and looking towards me, and the company I was in, recollected the occasion of our coming, whereof he had been informed before. He spoke some words, whereupon immediately a young man with a flap came up to my side, and flapped me gently on the right ear, but I made signs, as well as I could, that I had no occasion for such an instrument; which, as I afterwards found, gave his Majesty, and the whole Court, a very mean opinion of my understanding. The king, as far as I could conjecture, asked me several questions, and I addressed myself to him in all the languages I had. When it was found that I could neither understand nor be understood, I was conducted, by his order, to an apartment in his palace (this prince being distinguished above all his predecessors, for his hospitality to strangers), where two servants were appointed to attend me. My dinner was brought, and four persons of quality, whom I remembered to have seen very near the king's person, did me the honour to dine with me. We had two courses, of three dishes each. In the first course, there was a shoulder of mutton, cut into an equilateral triangle, a piece of beef into a rhomboid, and a pudding into a cycloid. The second course was two ducks, trussed up into the form of fiddles; sausages and puddings resembling flutes and hautboys, and a breast of veal in the shape of a harp. The servants cut our bread into cones, cylinders, parallelo-grams, and several other mathematical figures.

While we were at dinner, I made bold to ask the names of several things in their language, and those noble persons, by the assistance of their flappers, delighted to give me answers, hoping to raise my admiration of their great abili-ties, if I could be brought to converse with them. I was soon able to call for bread and drink, or whatever else I wanted.

After dinner my company withdrew, and a person was sent to me, by the king's order, attended by a flapper. He brought with him pen, ink, and paper, and three or four books, giving me to understand by signs, that he was sent to teach me the language. We sat together four hours, in which time I wrote down a great number of words in columns, with the translations over-against them; I like-wise made a shift to learn several short sentences. For my tutor would order one of my servants to fetch something, to turn about, to make a bow, to sit, or to stand, or walk, and the like. Then I took down the sentence in writing. He shewed me also, in one of his books, the figures of the sun, moon, and stars, the Zodiac, the tropics, and polar circles, together with the denominations of many figures of planes and solids. He gave me the names and descriptions of all the musical instruments, and the general terms of art in playing on each of them. After he had left me, I placed all my words, with their interpretations, in alphabetical order. And thus, in a few days, by the help of a very faithful memory, I got some insight into their language.

The word which I interpret the flying or floating island, is, in the original, *laputa*, whereof I could never learn the true etymology. *Lap*, in the old obsolete language, signifieth high, and *untuh*, a governor, from which they say, by corruption, was derived *laputa*, from *lapuntuh*. But I do not approve of this derivation, which seems to be a little strained. I ventured to offer to the learned among them a conjecture of my own, that *laputa* was *quasi lap outed ;* *lap* signifying properly the dancing of the sun-beams in the sea, and *outed*, a wing; which, however, I shall not obtrude, but submit to the judicious reader.

Those to whom the king had entrusted me, observing how ill I was clad, ordered a tailor to come next morning and take my measure for a suit of clothes. This operator did his office after a different manner from those of his trade in Europe. He first took my altitude by a quadrant, and then, with rule and compasses, described the dimensions and outlines of my whole body, all which he entered upon paper, and in six days brought my clothes very ill made, and quite out of shape, by happening to mistake a figure in the calculation. But my comfort was, that I observed such accidents very frequent, and little regarded.

During my confinement for want of clothes, and by an indisposition that held me some days longer, I much enlarged my dictionary; and, when I went next to Court, was able to understand many things the king spoke, and to return him some kind of answers. His Majesty had given orders that the island should move north-east and by east, to the vertical point over Lagado, the metropolis of the whole kingdom below upon the firm earth. It was about ninety leagues distant, and our voyage lasted four days and an half. I was not in the least sensible of the progressive motion made in the air by the island. On the second morning, about eleven o'clock, the king himself, in person, attended by his nobility, courtiers, and officers, having prepared all their musical instruments, played on them for three hours, without intermission, so that I was quite stunned with the noise; neither could I possibly guess the meaning, till my tutor informed me. He said that the people of their island had their ears adapted to hear the music of the spheres, which always played at certain periods, and the Court was now prepared to bear their part, in whatever instrument they most excelled.

In our journey towards Lagado, the capital city, his Majesty ordered that the island should stop over certain towns and villages, from whence he might receive the petitions of his subjects. And, to this purpose, several packthreads were let down, with small weights at the bottom. On these packthreads the people strung their petitions, which mounted up directly, like the scraps of paper fastened by school-boys at the end of the string that holds their kite. Sometimes we received wine and victuals from below, which were drawn up by pulleys.

The knowledge I had in mathematics gave me great assistance in acquiring their phraseology, which depended much upon that science and music; and in the latter I was not unskilled. Their ideas are perpetually conversant in lines and figures. If they would, for example, praise the beauty of a woman, or any other animal, they describe it by rhombs, circles, parallelograms, ellipses, and other geometrical terms, or by words of art drawn from music, needless here to repeat.   I observed, in the king's kitchen, all sorts of mathematical and musical instruments, after the figures of which they cut up the joints that were served to his Majesty's table.

Their houses are very ill built, the walls bevil, without one right-angle in any apartment; and this defect ariseth from the contempt they bear to practical geometry, which they despise as vulgar and mechanic, those instructions they give being too refined for the intellectuals of their workmen, which occasions perpetual mistakes.   And although they are dexterous enough upon a piece of paper in the management of the rule, the pencil, and the divider, yet, in the common actions and behaviour of life, I have not seen a more clumsy, awkward, and unhandy people, nor so slow and perplexed in their conceptions upon all other subjects, except those of mathematics and music.   They are very bad reasoners, and vehemently given to opposition, unless when they happen to be of the right opinion, which is seldom their case.   Imagination, fancy, and invention they are wholly strangers to, nor have any words in their language by which those ideas can be expressed; the whole compass of their thoughts and mind being shut up within the two forementioned sciences.

Most of them, and especially those who deal in the astronomical part, have great faith in judicial astrology, although they are ashamed to own it publicly.   But, what I chiefly admired, and thought altogether unaccountable, was the strong disposition I observed in them towards news and politics, perpetually enquiring into public affairs, giving their judgments in matters of state, and passionately disputing every inch of a party opinion.   I have, indeed, observed the same disposition among most of the mathematicians I have known in Europe, although I could never discover the least analogy between the two sciences; unless those people suppose, that because the smallest circle hath as many degrees as the largest, therefore the regulation and management of the world require no more abilities than the handling and turning of a globe: but I rather take this quality to spring from a very common infirmity of human nature, inclining us to be more curious and conceited in matters where we have least concern, and for which we are least adapted, either by study or Nature.

These people are under continual disquietudes, never enjoying a minute's peace of mind; and their disturbances proceed from causes which very little affect the rest of mortals. Their apprehensions arise from several changes they dread in the celestial bodies. For instance, that the earth, by the continual approaches of the sun towards it, must, in course of time, be absorbed, or swallowed up. That the face of the sun will by degrees be encrusted with its own effluvia, and give no more light to the world. That the earth very narrowly escaped a brush from the tail of the last comet, which would have infallibly reduced it to ashes; and that the next, which they have calculated for one and thirty years hence, will probably destroy us. For, if in its perihelion it should approach within a certain degree of the sun (as by their calculations they have reason to dread) it will conceive a degree of heat ten thousand times more intense than that of red hot glowing iron; and, in its absence from the sun, carry a blazing tail ten hundred thousand and fourteen miles long; through which, if the earth should pass at the distance of one hundred thousand miles from the nucleus, or main body of the comet, it must in its passage be set on fire, and reduced to ashes. That the sun, daily spending its rays without any nutriment to supply them, will at last be wholly consumed and annihilated; which must be attended with the destruction of this earth, and of all the planets that receive their light from it.

They are so perpetually alarmed with the apprehensions of these and the like impending dangers, that they can neither sleep quietly in their beds, nor have any relish for the common pleasures or amusements of life. When they meet an acquaintance in the morning, the first question is about the sun's health, how he looked at his setting and rising, and what hopes they have to avoid the stroke of the approaching comet. This conversation they are apt to run into with the same temper that boys discover, in delighting to hear terrible stories of spirits and hobgoblins, which they greedily listen to, and dare not go to bed for fear.

The wives and daughters lament their confinement to the island, although I think it the most delicious spot of ground in the world; and although they live here in the greatest plenty and magnificence, and are allowed to do whatever they please, they long to see the world, and take the diversions of the metropolis, which they are not allowed to do without a particular licence from the king; and this is not easy to be obtained, because the people of quality have found by frequent experience how hard it is to persuade their women to return from below.

In about a month's time, I had made a tolerable proficiency in their language, and was able to answer most of the king's questions, when I had the honour to attend him. His Majesty discovered not the least curiosity to enquire into the laws, government, history, religion, or manners of the countries where I had been, but confined his questions to the state of mathematics, and received the account I gave him with great contempt and indifference, though often roused by his flapper on each side.

CHAPTER III

I DESIRED leave of this prince to see the curiosities of the island, which he was graciously pleased to grant, and ordered my tutor to attend me. I chiefly wanted to know to what cause in art, or in Nature, it owed its several motions, whereof I will now give a philosophical account to the reader.

The flying or floating island is exactly circular, its diameter 7837 yards, or about four miles and a half, and consequently contains ten thousand acres. It is three hundred yards thick. The bottom, or under surface, which appears to those who view it from below, is one even regular plate of adamant, shooting up to the height of about two hundred yards. Above it lie the several minerals in their usual order, and over all is a coat of rich mould, ten or twelve feet deep. The declivity of the upper surface, from the circumference to the centre, is the natural cause why all the dews and rains which fall upon the island are conveyed in small rivulets towards the middle, where they are emptied into four large basins, each of about half a mile in circuit, and two hundred yards distant from the centre. From these basins, the water is continually exhaled by the sun in the daytime, which effectually prevents their overflowing. Besides, as it is in the power of the monarch to raise the island above the region of clouds and vapours, he can prevent the falling of dews and rains whenever he pleases. For the highest clouds cannot rise above two miles, as naturalists agree; at least they were never known to do so in that country.

At the centre of the island there is a chasm about fifty yards in diameter, from whence the astronomers descend into a large dome, which is therefore called Flandona Gagnole, or the Astronomer's Cave, situated at the depth of a hundred yards beneath the upper surface of the adamant. In this cave are twenty lamps continually burning, which, from the reflection of the adamant, cast a strong light into every part. The place is stored with great variety of sextants, quadrants, telescopes, astrolabes, and other astronomical instruments. But the greatest curiosity, upon which the fate of the island depends, is a loadstone of a prodigious size, in shape resembling a weaver's shuttle. It is in length six yards, and, in the thickest part, at least three yards over. This magnet is sustained by a very strong axle of adamant passing through its middle, upon which it plays, and is poised so exactly that the weakest hand can turn it. It is hooped round with a hollow cylinder of adamant, four feet deep, as many thick, and twelve yards in diameter, placed horizontally, and supported by eight adamantine feet, each six yards high. In the middle of the concave side there is a groove twelve inches deep, in which the extremities of the axle are lodged, and turned round as there is occasion.

The stone cannot be moved from its place by any force, because the hoop and its feet are one continued piece with that body of adamant which constitutes the bottom of the island.

By means of this loadstone the island is made to rise and fall, and move from one place to another. For, with respect to that part of the earth over which the monarch presides, the stone is endued at one of its sides with an attractive power, and at the other with a repulsive. Upon placing the magnet erect, with its attracting end towards the earth, the island descends; but, when the repelling extremity points downwards, the island mounts directly upwards. When the position of the stone is oblique, the motion of the island is so too. For in this magnet the forces always act in lines parallel to its direction.

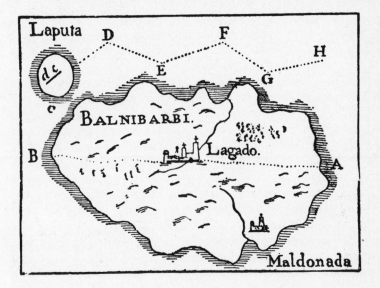

By this oblique motion the island is conveyed to different parts of the monarch's dominions.   To explain the manner of its progress, let *A B* represent a line drawn across the dominions of Balnibarbi, let the line *c d* represent the load-stone, of which let *d* be the repelling end, and *c* the attracting end, the island being over *C ;* let the stone be placed in the position *c d*, with its repelling end downwards; then the island will be driven up obliquely towards *D*.   When it has arrived at *D*, let the stone be turned upon its axle till its attracting end points towards *E*, and then the island will be carried obliquely towards *E ;* where, if the stone be again turned upon its axle, till it stands in the position *E F*, with its repelling point downward, the island will rise obliquely towards *F*, where, by directing the attracting end towards *G*, the island may be carried to *G*, and from *G* to *H*, by turning the stone, so as to make its repelling extremity point directly downward.   And thus, by changing the situation of the stone as often as there is occasion, the island is made to rise and fall by turns in an oblique direction, and by those alternate risings and fallings (the obliquity being not considerable) is conveyed from one part of the dominions to the other.

But it must be observed that this island cannot move beyond the extent of the dominions below, nor can it rise above the height of four miles.   For which the astronomers (who have written large systems concerning the stone) assign the following reason: that the magnetic virtue does not extend beyond the distance of four miles, and that the mineral which acts upon the stone in the bowels of the earth, and in the sea, about six leagues distant from the shore, is not diffused through the whole globe, but terminated with the limits of the king's dominions; and it was easy, from the great advantage of such a superior situation, for a prince to bring under his obedience whatever country lay within the attraction of that magnet.

When the stone is put parallel to the plane of the horizon, the island stands still; for, in that case, the extremities of it, being at equal distance from the earth, act with equal force, the one in drawing downwards, the other in pushing upwards, and consequently no motion can ensue.

This loadstone is under the care of certain astronomers, who, from time to time, give it such positions as the monarch directs.   They spend the greatest part of their lives in observing the celestial bodies, which they do by the assistance of glasses far excelling ours in goodness. For, although their largest telescopes do not exceed three feet, they magnify much more than those of a hundred yards among us, and, at the same time, shew the stars with greater clearness.   This advantage hath enabled them to extend their discoveries much farther than our astronomers in Europe; for they have made a catalogue of ten thousand fixed stars, whereas the largest of ours do not contain above one-third part of that number.   They have likewise discovered two lesser stars, or satellites, which revolve about

Mars, whereof the innermost is distant from the centre of
the primary planet exactly three of his diameters, and the
outermost five; the former revolves in the space of ten
hours, and the latter in twenty-one and a half; so that the
squares of their periodical times are very near in the same
proportion with the cubes of their distance from the centre
of Mars, which evidently shews them to be governed by the
same law of gravitation that influences the other heavenly
bodies.

They have observed ninety-three different comets, and
settled their periods with great exactness. If this be true
(and they affirm it with great confidence) it is much to be
wished that their observations were made public, whereby
the theory of comets, which at present is very lame and
defective, might be brought to the same perfection with
other parts of astronomy.

The king would be the most absolute prince in the
universe, if he could but prevail on a ministry to join with
him; but these having their estates below on the continent,
and considering that the office of a favourite hath a very
uncertain tenure, would never consent to enslaving their
country.

If any town should engage in rebellion or mutiny, fall
into violent factions, or refuse to pay the usual tribute, the
king hath two methods of reducing them to obedience
The first and the mildest course is by keeping the island
hovering over such a town, and the lands about it, whereby
he can deprive them of the benefit of the sun and the rain,
and consequently afflict the inhabitants with dearth and
diseases. And, if the crime deserve it, they are at the same
time pelted from above with great stones, against which
they have no defence but by creeping into cellars or caves,
while the roofs of their houses are beaten to pieces. But
if they still continue obstinate, or offer to raise insurrec-
tions, he proceeds to the last remedy, by letting the island
drop directly upon their heads, which makes a universal

destruction, both of houses and men.   However, this is an
extremity to which the prince is seldom driven, neither,
indeed, is he willing to put it in execution, nor dare his
ministers advise him to an action which, as it would render
them odious to the people, so it would be a great damage to
their own estates, which lie all below, for the island is the
king's demesne.

But there is still, indeed, a more weighty reason why
the kings of this country have been always averse from
executing so terrible an action, unless upon the utmost
necessity.   For, if the town intended to be destroyed should
have in it any tall rocks, as it generally falls out in the
larger cities, a situation probably chosen at first with a
view to prevent such a catastrophe; or if it abound in high
spires, or pillars of stone, a sudden fall might endanger the
bottom or under surface of the island, which, although it
consist, as I have said, of one entire adamant, two hundred
yards thick, might happen to crack by too great a shock,
or burst by approaching too near the fires from the houses
below, as the backs both of iron and stone will often do in
our chimneys.   Of all this the people are well apprised, and
understand how far to carry their obstinacy where their
liberty or property is concerned.   And the king, when he is
highest provoked, and most determined to press a city to
rubbish, orders the island to descend with great gentleness,
out of a pretence of tenderness to his people; but, indeed,
for fear of breaking the adamantine bottom; in which case,
it is the opinion of all their philosophers that the loadstone
could no longer hold it up, and the whole mass would fall
to the ground.

By a fundamental law of this realm, neither the king,
nor either of his two elder sons, are permitted to leave the
island, nor the queen, till she is past child-bearing.

CHAPTER IV

ALTHOUGH I cannot say that I was ill-treated in this island, yet, I must confess, I thought myself too much neglected, not without some degree of contempt. For neither prince nor people appeared to be curious in any part of knowledge, except mathematics and music, wherein I was far their inferior, and upon that account very little regarded.

On the other side, after having seen all the curiosities of the island, I was very desirous to leave it, being heartily weary of those people. They were, indeed, excellent in two sciences for which I have great esteem, and wherein I am not unversed, but at the same time so abstracted and involved in speculation, that I never met with such disagreeable companions. I conversed only with women, tradesmen, flappers, and Court pages during two months of my abode there; by which, at last, I rendered myself extremely contemptible; yet these were the only people from whom I could ever receive a reasonable answer.

I had obtained, by hard study, a good degree of knowledge in their language; I was weary of being confined to an island where I received so little countenance, and resolved to leave it with the first opportunity.

There was a great lord at Court, nearly related to the king, and, for that reason alone, used with respect. He was universally reckoned the most ignorant and stupid person among them. He had performed many eminent services for the crown, had great natural and acquired parts, adorned with integrity and honour, but so ill an ear for music, that his detractors reported he had been often known to beat time in the wrong place; neither could his

tutors, without extreme difficulty, teach him to demonstrate the most easy proposition in the mathematics. He
was pleased to show me many marks of favour, often did
me the honour of a visit, desired to be informed in the
affairs of Europe, the laws and customs, the manners and
learning of the several countries where I had travelled. He
listened to me with great attention, and made very wise
observations on all I spoke. He had two flappers
attending him for state, but never made use of them,
except at Court and in visits of ceremony, and would
always command them to withdraw when we were alone
together.

I entreated this illustrious person to intercede in my
behalf with his Majesty for leave to depart, which he accordingly did, as he was pleased to tell me, with regret;
for, indeed, he had made me several offers very advantageous, which, however, I refused with expressions of the
highest acknowledgment.

On the 16th day of February I took leave of his Majesty
and the Court. The king made me a present to the value of
about two hundred pounds English, and my protector, his
kinsman, as much more, together with a letter of recommendation to a friend of his in Lagado, the metropolis:
the island being then hovering over a mountain about two
miles from it, I was let down from the lowest gallery in the
same manner as I had been taken up.

The continent, as far as it is subject to the monarch of
the Flying Island, passes under the general name of Balnibarbi; and the metropolis, as I said before, is called Lagado.
I felt some little satisfaction in finding myself on firm
ground. I walked to the city without any concern, being
clad like one of the natives, and sufficiently instructed to
converse with them. I soon found out the person's house
to whom I was recommended, presented my letter from
his friend the grandee in the island, and was received with
much kindness. This great lord, whose name was Munodi,

ordered me an apartment in his own house, where I continued during my stay, and was entertained in a most hospitable manner.

The next morning after my arrival he took me in his chariot to see the town, which is about half the bigness of London, but the houses very strangely built, and most of them out of repair. The people in the streets walked fast, looked wild, their eyes fixed, and were generally in rags. We passed through one of the town gates, and went about three miles into the country, where I saw many labourers working with several sorts of tools in the ground, but was not able to conjecture what they were about; neither did I observe any expectation either of corn or grass, although the soil appeared to be excellent. I could not forbear admiring these odd appearances both in town and country; and I made bold to desire my conductor that he would be pleased to explain to me what could be meant by so many busy heads, hands, and faces, both in the streets and the fields, because I did not discover any good effects they produced; but, on the contrary, I never knew a soil so unhappily cultivated, houses so ill contrived and so ruinous, or a people whose countenances and habit expressed so much misery and want.

This Lord Munodi was a person of the first rank, and had been some years governor of Lagado; but, by a cabal of ministers, was discharged for insufficiency. However, the king treated him with tenderness, as a well-meaning man, but of a low, contemptible understanding.

When I gave that free censure of the country and its inhabitants, he made no further answer than by telling me that I had not been long enough among them to form a judgment, and that the different nations of the world had different customs; with other common topics to the same purpose. But, when we returned to his palace, he asked me how I liked the building, what absurdities I observed, and what quarrel I had with the dress or looks of his domestics.

This he might safely do, because everything about him was magnificent, regular, and polite. I answered that his Excellency's prudence, quality, and fortune had exempted him from those defects which folly and beggary had produced in others. He said, if I would go with him to his country house, about twenty miles distant, where his estate lay, there would be more leisure for this kind of conversation. I told his Excellency that I was entirely at his disposal; and accordingly we set out next morning.

During our journey he made me observe the several methods used by farmers in managing their lands, which, to me, were wholly unaccountable; for, except in some very few places, I could not discover one ear of corn, or blade of grass. But, in three hours travelling, the scene was wholly altered; we came into a most beautiful country; farmers' houses at small distances, neatly built, the fields enclosed, containing vineyards, corn-grounds, and meadows. Neither do I remember to have seen a more delightful prospect. His Excellency observed my countenance clear up; he told me, with a sigh, that there his estate began, and would continue the same till we should come to his house. That his countrymen ridiculed and despised him for managing his affairs no better, and for setting so ill an example to the kingdom, which, however, was followed by very few, such as were old and wilful and weak, like himself.

We came at length to the house, which was, indeed, a noble structure, built according to the best rules of ancient architecture. The fountains, gardens, walks, avenues, and groves, were all disposed with exact judgment and taste. I gave due praise to everything I saw, whereof his Excellency took not the least notice till after supper, when, there being no third companion, he told me with a very melancholy air, that he doubted he must throw down his houses in town and country, to rebuild them after the present mode, destroy all his plantations, and cast others into such a form as modern usage required; and give the same directions to all his tenants, unless he would submit to incur the censure of pride, singularity, affectation, ignorance, caprice, and, perhaps, increase his Majesty's displeasure. That the admiration I appeared to be under would cease, or diminish, when he had informed me of some particulars, which probably I never heard of at Court, the people there being too much taken up in their own speculations to have regard to what passed here below.

The sum of his discourse was to this effect: that, about forty years ago, certain persons went up to Laputa, either upon business or diversion, and after five months' continuance, came back with a very little smattering in mathematics, but full of volatile spirits, acquired in that airy region. That these persons, upon their return, began to dislike the management of everything below, and fell into schemes of putting all arts, sciences, languages, and mechanics upon a new foot. To this end they procured a royal patent for erecting an academy of projectors in Lagado; and the humour prevailed so strongly among the people that there is not a town of any consequence in the kingdom without such an academy. In these colleges, the professors contrive new rules and methods of agriculture and building, and new instruments and tools for all trades and manufactures, whereby, as they undertake, one man shall do the work of ten, a palace may be built in a week, of materials so durable as to last for ever, without repairing; all the fruits of the earth shall come to maturity at whatever season we think fit to choose, and increase an hundred fold more than they do at present; with innumerable other happy proposals. The only inconvenience is, that none of these projects are yet brought to perfection; and, in the meantime, the whole country lies miserably waste, the houses in ruins, and the people without food or clothes. By all which, instead of being discouraged, they are fifty times more violently bent upon prosecuting their schemes, driven equally on by hope and despair: that as for himself, being not of an enterprising spirit, he was content to go on in the old forms, to live in the houses his ancestors had built, and act as they did in every part of life, without innovation. That some few other persons of quality and gentry had done the same, but were looked on with an eye of contempt and ill-will, as enemies to art, ignorant, and ill commonwealth's men, preferring their own ease and sloth before the general improvement of their country.

His lordship added, that he would not by any further particulars prevent the pleasure I should certainly take in viewing the grand academy, whither he was resolved I should go. He only desired me to observe a ruined building upon the side of a mountain, about three miles distant, of which he gave me this account: that he had a very convenient mill within half a mile of his house, turned by a current from a large river, and sufficient for his own family, as well as a great number of his tenants. That, about seven years ago, a club of those projectors came to him, with proposals to destroy this mill, and build another on the side of that mountain, on the long ridge whereof a long canal must be cut for a repository of water, to be conveyed up by pipes and engines to supply the mill, because the wind and air upon a height agitated the water, and thereby made it fitter for motion; and because the water, descending down a declivity, would turn the mill with half the current of a river, whose course is more upon a level. He said that being then not very well with the Court, and pressed by many of his friends, he complied with the proposal; and, after employing an hundred men for two years, the work miscarried, the projectors went off, laying the blame entirely upon him, railing at him ever since, and putting others upon the same experiment, with equal assurance of success, as well as equal disappointment.

In a few days we came back to town, and his Excellency,

considering the bad character he had in the academy, would not go with me himself, but recommended me to a friend of his to bear me company thither. My lord was pleased to represent me as a great admirer of projects, and a person of much curiosity, and easy belief which, indeed, was not without truth; for I had myself been a sort of projector in my younger days.

CHAPTER V

THIS academy is not an entire single building, but a continuation of several houses on both sides of a street, which, growing waste, was purchased, and applied to that use. I was received very kindly by the warden, and went for many days to the academy. Every room hath in it one or more projectors; and, I believe, I could not be in fewer than five hundred rooms.

The first man I saw was of a meagre aspect, with sooty hands and face, his hair and beard long, ragged and singed in several places. His clothes, shirt, and skin were all of the same colour. He had been eight years upon a project for extracting sun-beams out of cucumbers, which were to be put into vials hermetically sealed, and let out to warm the air in raw inclement summers. He told me, he did not doubt, in eight years more, he should be able to supply the governor's gardens with sunshine at a reasonable rate; but he complained that his stock was low, and entreated me to give him something as an encouragement to ingenuity, especially since this had been a very dear season for cucumbers. I made him a small present, for my lord had furnished me with money on purpose, because he knew their practice of begging from all who go to see them.

I saw another at work to calcine ice into gunpowder, who likewise shewed me a treatise he had written concerning the malleability of fire, which he intended to publish.

There was a most ingenious architect, who had contrived a new method for building houses, by beginning at the roof, and working downwards to the foundation, which he justified to me, by the like practice of those two prudent insects, the bee and the spider.

There was a man born blind, who had several apprentices in his own condition: their employment was to mix colours for painters, which their master taught them to distinguish by feeling and smelling. It was, indeed, my misfortune to find them, at that time, not very perfect in their lessons, and the professor himself happened to be generally mistaken: this artist is much encouraged and esteemed by the whole fraternity.

In another apartment, I was highly pleased with a projector who had found a device of plowing the ground with hogs, to save the charges of ploughs, cattle, and labour. The method is this: in an acre of ground you bury, at six inches distance, and eight deep, a quantity of acorns, dates, chestnuts, and other mast, or vegetables, whereof these animals are fondest: then you drive six hundred, or more of them, into the field, where, in few days, they will root up the whole ground in search of their food, and make it fit for sowing; it is true, upon experiment, they found the charge and trouble very great, and they had little or no crop. However, it is not doubted that this invention may be capable of great improvement.

I went into another room, where the walls and ceiling were all hung round with cobwebs, except a narrow passage for the artist to go in and out. At my entrance, he called aloud to me not to disturb his webs. He lamented the fatal mistake the world had been so long in of using silkworms, while we had such plenty of domestic insects, who infinitely excelled the former, because they understood how to weave, as well as spin. And he proposed farther, that, by employing spiders, the charge of dying silks would be wholly saved; whereof I was fully convinced, when he shewed me a vast number of flies most beautifully coloured, wherewith he fed his spiders, assuring us that the webs would take a tincture from them; and, as he had them of all hues, he hoped to fit everybody's fancy, as soon as he could find proper food for the flies, of certain gums, oils, and other glutinous matter, to give a strength and consistence to the threads.

There was an astronomer, who had undertaken to place a sundial upon the great weather-cock on the town house, by adjusting the annual and diurnal motions of the earth and sun, so as to answer and coincide with all accidental turnings of the wind.

I visited many other apartments, but shall not trouble my reader with all the curiosities I observed, being studious of brevity.

I had hitherto seen only one side of the academy, the other being appropriated to the advancers of speculative learning, of whom I shall say something, when I have mentioned one illustrious person more, who is called among them the universal artist. He told us he had been thirty years employing his thoughts for the improvement of human life. He had two large rooms full of wonderful curiosities, and fifty men at work. Some were condensing air into a dry tangible substance, by extracting the nitre, and letting the aqueous or fluid particles percolate; others softening marble for pillows and pin-cushions; others petrifying the hoofs of a living horse, to preserve them from foundering. The artist himself was at that time busy upon two great designs; the first to sow land with chaff, wherein he affirmed the true seminal virtue to be contained, as he demonstrated by several experiments which I was not skilful enough to comprehend. The other was, by a certain composition of gums, minerals, and vegetables, outwardly applied, to prevent the growth of wool upon two young lambs; and he hoped, in a reasonable time, to propagate the breed of naked sheep all over the kingdom.

We crossed a walk to the other part of the academy, where, as I have already said, the projectors in speculative learning resided.

The first professor I saw was in a very large room, with forty pupils about him. After salutation, observing me to

look earnestly upon a frame which took up the greatest part
of both the length and breadth of the room, he said, perhaps
I might wonder to see him employed in a project for improving speculative knowledge by practical and mechanical
operations. But the world would soon be sensible of its
usefulness; and he flattered himself that a more noble
exalted thought never sprang in any other man's head.
Every one knew how laborious the usual method is of attain-
ing to arts and sciences; whereas, by his contrivance, the
most ignorant person, at a reasonable charge, and with a
little bodily labour may write books in philosophy, poetry,
politics, law, mathematics, and theology, without the least
assistance from genius or study. He then led me to the
frame, about the sides whereof all his pupils stood in ranks.
It was twenty feet square, placed in the middle of the
room. The superficies was composed of several bits of
wood, about the bigness of a die, but some larger than
others. They were all linked together by slender wires.
These bits of wood were covered on every square with paper
pasted on them; and on these papers were written all the
words of their language in their several moods, tenses, and
declensions; but without any order. The professor then
desired me to observe, for he was going to set his engine at
work. The pupils, at his command, took each of them hold
of an iron handle, whereof there were forty fixed round the
edges of the frame; and, giving them a sudden turn, the
whole disposition of the words was entirely changed. He
then commanded six and thirty of the lads to read the
several lines softly, as they appeared upon the frame; and,
where they found three or four words together that might
make part of a sentence, they dictated to the four remaining
boys who were scribes. This work was repeated three or
four times, and at every turn, the engine was so contrived,
that the words shifted into new places, as the square bits of
wood moved upside down.

Six hours a day the young students were employed in

this labour, and the professor shewed me several volumes in large folio already collected, of broken sentences, which he intended to piece together, and, out of those rich materials, to give the world a complete body of all arts and sciences; which, however, might be still improved, and much expedited, if the public would raise a fund for making and employing five hundred such frames in Lagado, and oblige the managers to contribute in common their several collections.

He assured me that this invention had employed all his thoughts from his youth; that he had emptied the whole vocabulary into his frame, and made the strictest computation of the general proportion there is in books between the numbers of particles, nouns, and verbs, and other parts of speech.

I made my humblest acknowledgment to this illustrious person for his great communicativeness; and promised, if ever I had the good fortune to return to my native country, that I would do him justice, as the sole inventor of this wonderful machine; the form and contrivance of which I desired leave to delineate upon paper.   I told him, although it were the custom of our learned in Europe to steal inventions from each other, who had thereby, at least, this advantage, that it became a controversy which was the right owner, yet I would take such caution, that he should have the honour entire, without a rival.

We next went to the school of languages, where three professors sat in consultation upon improving that of their own country.

The first project was to shorten discourse by cutting polysyllables into one, and leaving out verbs and participles; because, in reality, all things imaginable are but nouns.

The other project was a scheme for entirely abolishing all words whatsoever; and this was urged as a great advantage in point of health, as well as brevity.   For it is plain, that every word we speak is, in some degree, a diminu-

tion of our lungs by corrosion; and consequently con-
tributes to the shortening of our lives. An expedient was
therefore offered, that since words are only names for things,
it would be more convenient for all men to carry about them
such things as were necessary to express the particular
business they are to discourse on. And this invention
would certainly have taken place, to the great ease as well
as health of the subject, if the women, in conjunction with
the vulgar and illiterate, had not threatened to raise a
rebellion, unless they might be allowed the liberty to speak
with their tongues after the manner of their fore-fathers;
such constant irreconcilable enemies to science are the
common people. However, many of the most learned and
wise adhere to the new scheme of expressing themselves by
things; which hath only this inconvenience attending it,
that if a man's business be very great, and of various kinds,
he must be obliged, in proportion, to carry a greater bundle
of things upon his back, unless he can afford one or two
strong servants to attend him. I have often beheld two of
those sages almost sinking under the weight of their packs,
like pedlars among us; who, when they met in the streets,
would lay down their loads, open their sacks, and hold
conversation for an hour together; then put up their
implements, help each other resume their burthens, and
take their leave.

But, for short conversations, a man may carry implements in his pockets, and under his arms, enough to supply
him; and in his house he cannot be at a loss. Therefore
the room where company meet, who practise this art, is full
of all things ready at hand, requisite to furnish matter for
this kind of artificial converse.

Another great advantage, proposed by this invention,
was, that it would serve as an universal language, to be
understood in all civilised nations, whose goods and utensils
are generally of the same kind, or nearly resembling, so
that their uses might easily be comprehended. And thus

ambassadors would be qualified to treat with foreign princes, or ministers of state, to whose tongues they were utter strangers.

I was at the mathematical school, where the master taught his pupils after a method scarce imaginable to us in Europe. The proposition and demonstration were fairly written on a thin wafer, with ink composed of a cephalic tincture. This the student was to swallow upon a fasting stomach, and for three days following eat nothing but bread and water. As the wafer digested, the tincture mounted to his brain, bearing the proposition along with it. But the success had not hitherto been answerable, partly by some error in the quantum or composition, and partly by the perverseness of lads; to whom this bolus is so nauseous, that they generally steal aside, and discharge it upwards, before it can operate; neither have they been yet persuaded to use so long an abstinence as the prescription requires.

CHAPTER VI

In the school of political projectors, I was but ill entertained; the professors appearing, in my judgment, wholly
out of their senses; which is a scene that never fails to
make me melancholy. These unhappy people were proposing
schemes for persuading monarchs to choose favourites upon
the score of their wisdom, capacity, and virtue; of teaching
ministers to consult the public good; of rewarding merit,
great abilities, and eminent services; of instructing princes
to know their true interest, by placing it on the same
foundation with that of their people; of choosing for employments persons qualified to exercise them; with many
other wild impossible chimæras, that never entered before
into the heart of man to conceive; and confirmed in me the
old observation, that there is nothing so extravagant and
irrational which some philosophers have not maintained
for truth.

But, however, I shall so far do justice to this part of the
academy, as to acknowledge that all of them were not so
visionary. There was a most ingenious doctor, who seemed
to be perfectly versed in the whole nature and system of
government. This illustrious person had very usefully
employed his studies in finding out effectual remedies for
all diseases and corruptions to which the several kinds of
public administration are subject, by the vices or infirmities of those who govern, as well as by the licentiousness of
those who are to obey. For instance, whereas all writers
and reasoners have agreed that there is a strict universal
resemblance between the natural and the political body;
can there be anything more evident, than that the health of
both must be preserved, and the diseases cured by the same
prescriptions? It is allowed that senates and great councils

are often troubled with redundant, ebullient, and other
peccant humours; with many diseases of the head, and
more of the heart. This doctor therefore proposed, that,
upon the meeting of a senate, certain physicians should
attend at the three first days of their sitting, and, at the
close of each day's debate, feel the pulses of every senator;
after which, having maturely considered, and consulted
upon the nature of the several maladies, and the methods
of cure, they should on the fourth day return to the senate-
house, attended by their apothecaries stored with proper
medicines; and, according as these medicines should
operate, repeat, alter, or admit them at the next meeting.

This project could not be of any great expense to the
public, and would, in my poor opinion, be of much use for
the dispatch of business in those countries where senates
have any share in the legislative power; beget unanimity,
shorten debates, open a few mouths which are now closed,
and close many more which are now open; curb the petu-
lancy of the young, and correct the positiveness of the old,
rouse the stupid, and damp the pert.

Again: because it is a general complaint, that the
favourites of princes are troubled with short and weak
memories, the same doctor proposed, that whoever attended
a first minister, after having told his business with the
utmost brevity, and in the plainest words, should, at his
departure, give the said minister a tweak by the nose, or a
kick in the belly, or tread on his corns, or lug him thrice by
both ears, or run a pin into his breech, or pinch his arm
black and blue, to prevent forgetfulness; and at every
levee day, repeat the same operation, till the business were
done, or absolutely refused.

He likewise directed, that every senator in the great
council of a nation, after he had delivered his opinion, and
argued in the defence of it, should be obliged to give his vote
directly contrary; because, if that were done, the result
would infallibly terminate in the good of the public.

When parties in a state are violent, he offered a wonderful contrivance to reconcile them. The method is this: you take an hundred leaders of each party; you dispose them into couples of such whose heads are nearest of a size; then let two nice operators saw off the occiput of each couple at the same time, in such a manner that the brain may be equally divided. Let the occiputs thus cut off be interchanged, applying each to the head of his opposite party-man. It seems, indeed, to be a work that requireth some exactness, but the professor assured us that, if it were dexterously performed, the cure would be infallible. For he argued thus; that the two half brains being left to debate the matter between themselves, within the space of one skull, would soon come to a good understanding, and produce that moderation, as well as regularity of thinking, so much to be wished for in the heads of those who imagine they come into the world only to watch and govern its motion: and as to the difference of brains in quantity or quality, among those who are directors in faction, the doctor assured us, from his own knowledge, that it was a perfect trifle.

I heard a very warm debate between two professors, about the most commodious and effectual ways and means of raising money without grieving the subject. The first affirmed the justest method would be to lay a certain tax upon vices and folly; and the sum fixed upon every man to be rated after the fairest manner by a jury of his neighbours. The second was of an opinion directly contrary, to tax those qualities of body and mind for which men chiefly value themselves; the rate to be more or less according to the degrees of excelling: the decision whereof should be left entirely to their own breast. The highest tax was upon men who are the greatest favourites of the other sex, and the assessments according to the number and natures of the favours they have received; for which they are allowed to be their own vouchers. Wit, valour, and politeness were

likewise proposed to be largely taxed, and collected in the
same manner, by every person giving his own word for the
quantum of what he possessed. But as to honour, justice,
wisdom and learning, they should not be taxed at all;
because they are qualifications of so singular a kind that no
man will either allow them in his neighbour or value them
in himself.

The women were proposed to be taxed according to
their beauty, and skill in dressing; wherein they had the
same privilege with the men, to be determined by their own
judgment. But constancy, chastity, good sense, and good
nature were not rated, because they would not bear the
charge of collecting.

To keep senators in the interest of the crown, it was
proposed that the members should raffle for employments;
every man first taking an oath, and giving security that he
would vote for the Court, whether he won or no; after
which the losers had, in their turn, the liberty of raffling
upon the next vacancy. Thus hope and expectation would
be kept alive; none would complain of broken promises,
but impute their disappointments wholly to Fortune, whose
shoulders are broader and stronger than those of a ministry.

Another professor shewed me a large paper of instructions for discovering plots and conspiracies against the
government.

The whole discourse was written with great acuteness,
containing many observations both curious and useful for
politicians; but, as I conceived, not altogether complete.
This I ventured to tell the author, and offered, if he pleased,
to supply him with some additions. He received my proposition with more compliance than usual among writers,
especially those of the projecting species; professing he
would be glad to receive farther information.

I told him, that in the kingdom of Tribnia, by the
natives called Langden, where I had sojourned some time
in my travels, the bulk of the people consist, in a manner,

wholly of discoverers, witnesses, informers, accusers, prose-
cutors, evidences, swearers, together with their several
subservient and subaltern instruments, all under the
colours, the conduct, and pay of ministers of state, and their
deputies. The plots in that kingdom are usually the workmanship of those persons, who desire to raise their own
characters of profound politicians; to restore new vigour to
a crazy administration; to stifle or divert general discon-
tents; to fill their pockets with forfeitures; and raise or
sink the opinion of the public credit, as either shall best
answer their private advantage. It is first agreed and
settled among them, what suspected persons shall be
accused of a plot; then effectual care is taken to secure all
their letters and papers, and put the criminals in chains.
These papers are delivered to a set of artists, very dexterous
in finding out the mysterious meanings of words, syllables,
and letters: for instance, they can discover a flock of geese
to signify a senate; a lame dog, an invader; the plague, a
standing army; a buzzard, a prime minister; the gout, a
high priest; a gibbet, a secretary of state; a sieve, a court
lady; a broom, a revolution; a mouse-trap, an employment; a bottomless pit, a treasury; a sink, a court; a cap
and bells, a favourite; a broken reed, a court of justice;
an empty tun, a general ; a running sore, the administration.

Where this method fails, they have two others more
effectual, which the learned among them call acrostics and
anagrams. First, they can decipher all initial letters into
political meanings. Thus *N* shall signify a plot, *B* a regi-
ment of horse, *L* a fleet at sea: or, secondly, by transposing
the letters of the alphabet in any suspected paper, they can
lay open the deepest designs of a discontented party. So,
for example, if I should say in a letter to a friend, our
brother Tom has just got the piles, a skilful decipherer
would discover that the same letters which compose that
sentence, may be analysed in the following words: Resist,

——a plot is brought home——the tour.   And this is the anagrammatic method.

The professor made me great acknowledgments for communicating these observations, and promised to make honourable mention of me in his treatise.

I saw nothing in this country that could invite me to a longer continuance, and began to think of returning home to England.

CHAPTER VII

THE continent of which this kingdom is a part extends itself, as I have reason to believe, eastward to that unknown tract of America, westward of California, and north to the Pacific Ocean, which is not above a hundred and fifty miles from Lagado; where there is a good port, and much commerce with the great island of Luggnagg, situated to the north-west about 29 degrees north latitude, and 140 longitude. This island of Luggnagg stands south-eastwards of Japan, about an hundred leagues distant. There is a strict alliance between the Japanese emperor and the king of Luggnagg, which affords frequent opportunities of sailing from one island to the other. I determined therefore to direct my course this way, in order to my return to Europe. I hired two mules, with a guide, to shew me the way, and carry my small baggage. I took leave of my noble protector, who had shewn me so much favour, and made me a generous present at my departure.

My journey was without any accident or adventure worth relating. When I arrived at the port of Maldonada (for so it is called) there was no ship in the harbour bound for Luggnagg, nor like to be in some time. The town is about as large as Portsmouth. I soon fell into some acquaintance, and was very hospitably received. A gentleman of distinction said to me, that since the ships bound for Luggnagg could not be ready in less than a month, it might be no disagreeable amusement for me to take a trip to the little island of Glubbdubdrib, about five leagues off to the south-west. He offered himself and a friend to accompany me, and that I should be provided with a small convenient barque for the voyage.

Glubbdubdrib, as nearly as I can interpret the word, signifies the island of sorcerers or magicians. It is about one-third as large as the Isle of Wight, and extremely fruitful: it is governed by the head of a certain tribe, who are all magicians. This tribe marries only among each other, and the eldest, in succession, is prince or governor. He hath a noble palace, and a park of about three thousand acres, surrounded by a wall of hewn stone, twenty feet high. In this park are several small inclosures for cattle, corn, and gardening.

The governor and his family are served and attended by domestics of a kind somewhat unusual. By his skill in necromancy he hath a power of calling whom he pleaseth from the dead, and commanding their service for twenty-four hours, but no longer; nor can he call the same persons up again in less than three months, except upon very extraordinary occasions.

When we arrived at the island, which was about eleven in the morning, one of the gentlemen who accompanied me went to the governor, and desired admittance for a stranger, who came on purpose to have the honour of attending on his highness. This was immediately granted, and we all three entered the gate of the palace, between two rows of guards, armed and dressed after a very antique manner, and something in their countenances that made my flesh creep with a horror I cannot express. We passed through several apartments, between servants of the same sort, ranked on each side, as before, till we came to the chamber of presence, where, after three profound obeisances, and a few general questions, we were permitted to sit on three stools, near the lowest step of his highness's throne. He understood the language of Balnibarbi, although it were different from that of this island. He desired me to give him some account of my travels; and, to let me see that I should be treated without ceremony, he dismissed all his attendants with a turn of his finger, at which, to my great astonishment, they vanished in an instant, like visions in a dream, when we awake on a sudden. I could not recover myself in some time, till the governor assured me that I should receive no hurt; and observing my two companions to be under no concern, who had been often entertained in the same manner, I began to take courage, and related to his highness a short history of my several adventures; yet not without some hesitation, and frequently looking behind me, to the place where I had seen those domestic spectres. I had the honour to dine with the governor, where a new set of ghosts served up the meat, and waited at table. I now observed myself to be less terrified than I had been in the morning. I stayed till sun-set, but humbly desired his highness to excuse me for not accepting his invitation of lodging in the palace. My two friends and I lay at a private house in the town adjoining, which is the capital of this little island; and the next morning we returned to pay our duty to the governor, as he was pleased to command us.

After this manner we continued in the island for ten days, most part of every day with the governor, and at night in our lodging. I soon grew so familiarised to the sight of spirits, that, after the third or fourth time, they gave me no emotion at all; or, if I had any apprehensions left, my curiosity prevailed over them. For his highness the governor ordered me to call up whatever persons I would choose to name, and in whatever numbers, among all the dead, from the beginning of the world to this present time, and command them to answer any questions I should think fit to ask; with this condition, that my questions must be confined within the compass of the times they lived in. And one thing I might depend upon, that they would certainly tell me the truth, for lying was a talent of no use in the lower world.

I made my humble acknowledgments to his highness for so great a favour. We were in a chamber from whence there was a fair prospect into the park. And, because my first inclination was to be entertained with scenes of pomp and magnificence, I desired to see Alexander the Great, at the head of his army, just after the battle of Arbela, which, upon a motion of the governor's finger, immediately appeared in a large field under the window where we stood. Alexander was called up into the room: it was with great difficulty that I understood his Greek, and had but little of my own. He assured me, upon his honour, that he was not poisoned, but died of a fever by excessive drinking.

Next I saw Hannibal passing the Alps, who told me he had not a drop of vinegar in his camp.

I saw Cæsar and Pompey, at the head of their troops, just ready to engage. I saw the former in his last great triumph. I desired that the Senate of Rome might appear before me in one large chamber, and a modern representative in counterview, in another. The first seemed to be an assembly of heroes and demi-gods, the other a knot of pedlars, pick-pockets, highway-men, and bullies.

The governor, at my request, gave the sign for Cæsar and Brutus to advance towards us. I was struck with a profound veneration at the sight of Brutus, and could easily discover the most consummate virtue, the greatest intrepidity, and firmness of mind, the truest love of his country, and general benevolence for mankind, in every lineament of his countenance. I observed, with much pleasure, that these two persons were in good intelligence with each other; and Cæsar freely confessed to me, that the greatest actions of his own life were not equal, by many degrees, to the glory of taking it away. I had the honour to have much conversation with Brutus, and was told, that his ancestors Junius, Socrates, Epaminondas, Cato the younger, Sir Thomas More, and himself, were perpetually together: a sextumvirate to which all the ages of the world cannot add a seventh.

It would be tedious to trouble the reader with relating what vast numbers of illustrious persons were called up, to gratify that insatiable desire I had to see the world in every period of antiquity placed before me. I chiefly fed my eyes with beholding the destroyers of tyrants and usurpers, and the restorers of liberty to oppressed and injured nations. But it is impossible to express the satisfaction I received in my own mind, after such a manner as to make it a suitable entertainment to the reader.

CHAPTER VIII

HAVING a desire to see those ancients who were most renowned for wit and learning, I set apart one day on purpose. I proposed that Homer and Aristotle might appear at the head of all their commentators; but these were so numerous, that some hundreds were forced to attend in the court and outward rooms of the palace. I knew, and could distinguish those two heroes at first sight, not only from the crowd, but from each other. Homer was the taller and comelier person of the two, walked very erect for one of his age, and his eyes were the most quick and piercing I ever beheld. Aristotle stooped much, and made use of a staff. His visage was meagre, his hair lank and thin, and his voice hollow. I soon discovered that both of them were perfect strangers to the rest of the company, and had never seen or heard of them before. And I had a whisper from a ghost, who shall be nameless, that these commentators always kept in the most distant quarters from their principals in the lower world, through a consciousness of shame and guilt, because they had so horribly misrepresented the meaning of those authors to posterity. I introduced Didymus and Eustathius to Homer, and prevailed on him to treat them better than perhaps they deserved, for he soon found they wanted a genius to enter into the spirit of a poet. But Aristotle was out of all patience with the account I gave him of Scotus and Ramus, as I presented them to him, and he asked them whether the rest of the tribe were as great dunces as themselves.

I then desired the governor to call up Descartes and Gassendi, with whom I prevailed to explain their systems to Aristotle. This great philosopher freely acknowledged his own mistakes in natural philosophy, because he proceeded in many things upon conjecture, as all men must do; and he found that Gassendi, who had made the doctrine of Epicurus as palatable as he could, and the vortices of Descartes were equally exploded. He predicted the same fate to attraction, whereof the present learned are such zealous asserters. He said that new systems of nature were but new fashions, which would vary in every age; and even those who pretend to demonstrate them from mathematical principles would flourish but a short period of time, and be out of vogue when that was determined.

I spent five days in conversing with many others of the ancient learned. I saw most of the first Roman Emperors. I prevailed on the governor to call up Eliogabalus's cooks to dress us a dinner, but they could not show us much of their skill for want of materials. A helot of Agesilaus made us a dish of Spartan broth, but I was not able to get down a second spoonful.

The two gentlemen who conducted me to the island were pressed by their private affairs to return in three days, which I employed in seeing some of the modern dead, who had made the greatest figure for two or three hundred years past, in our own and other countries of Europe; and having been always a great admirer of old illustrious families, I desired the governor would call up a dozen or two of kings, with their ancestors, in order, for eight or nine generations. But my disappointment was grievous and unexpected: for, instead of a long train with royal diadems, I saw in one family two fiddlers, three spruce courtiers, and an Italian prelate; in another a barber, an abbot, and two cardinals. I have too great a veneration for crowned heads to dwell any longer on so nice a subject. But as to counts, marquesses, dukes, earls, and the like, I was not so scrupulous. And, I confess, it was not without some pleasure that I found myself able to trace the particular features by which certain families are distinguished up to their originals.   I could plainly discover from whence one family derives a long chin, why a second hath abounded with knaves for two generations, and fools for two more; why a third happened to be crack-brained, and a fourth to be sharpers.   Whence it came, what Polydore Virgil says of a certain great house, *Nec vir fortis, nec femina casta.*   How cruelty, falsehood, and cowardice grew to be characteristics by which certain families are distinguished as much as by their coat of arms.

Neither could I wonder at all this, when I saw such an interruption of lineages by pages, lacqueys, valets, coachmen, gamesters, fiddlers, players, captains, and pickpockets.

I was chiefly disgusted with modern history. For, having strictly examined all the persons of greatest name in the courts of princes for an hundred years past, I found how the world had been misled by prostitute writers, to ascribe the greatest exploits in war to cowards, the wisest counsel to fools, sincerity to flatterers, Roman virtue to betrayers of their country, piety to atheists, truth to informers: how many innocent and excellent persons had been condemned to death or banishment, by the practising of great ministers upon the corruption of judges and the malice of factions: how many villains had been exalted to the highest places of trust, power, dignity, and profit: how great a share in the motions and events of courts, councils, and senates might be challenged by parasites and buffoons. How low an opinion I had of human wisdom and integrity, when I was truly informed of the springs and motives of great enterprises and revolutions in the world, and of the contemptible accidents to which they owed their success!

Here I discovered the roguery and ignorance of those who pretend to write anecdotes, or secret history; who send so many kings to their graves with a cup of poison; will repeat the discourse between a prince and chief minister, where no witness was by; unlock the thoughts and cabinets of ambassadors and secretaries of state; and have the perpetual misfortune to be mistaken. Here I discovered the true causes of many great events that have surprised the world. A general confessed in my presence, that he got a victory, purely by the force of cowardice and ill conduct; and an admiral, that, for want of proper intelligence, he beat the enemy to whom he intended to betray the fleet. Three kings protested to me, that, in their whole reigns, they did never once prefer any person of merit, unless by mistake, or treachery of some minister in whom they confided: neither would they do it, if they were to live again; and they shewed with great strength of reason, that the royal throne could not be supported without corruption, because that positive, confident, restive temper which virtue infused into man, was a perpetual clog to public business.

I had the curiosity to inquire, in a particular manner, by what method great numbers had procured to themselves high titles of honour and prodigious estates; and I confined my inquiry to a very modern period: however, without grating upon present times, because I would be sure to give no offence even to foreigners (for I hope the reader need not be told, that I do not in the least intend my own country in what I say upon this occasion) a great number of persons concerned were called up, and, upon a very slight examination, discovered such a scene of infamy, that I cannot reflect upon it without some seriousness. Perjury, oppression, subornation, fraud, and the like infirmities were amongst the most excusable arts they had to mention, and for these I gave, as it was reasonable, due allowance. But when some confessed they owed their greatness and wealth to vice, others to the betraying their country or their prince; some to poisoning, more to the perverting of justice in order to destroy the innocent: I hope I may be pardoned, if these discoveries inclined me a little to abate of that profound veneration which I am naturally apt to pay to persons of high rank, who ought to be treated with the utmost respect due to their sublime dignity by us, their inferiors.

I had often read of some great services done to princes and states, and desired to see the persons by whom those services were performed. Upon inquiry, I was told that their names were to be found on no record, except a few of them, whom history hath represented as the vilest rogues and traitors. As to the rest, I had never once heard of them. They all appeared with dejected looks, and in the meanest habit, most of them telling me they died in poverty and disgrace, and the rest on a scaffold or a gibbet.

Among others, there was one person whose case appeared a little singular. He had a youth about eighteen years old standing by his side. He told me he had for many years been commander of a ship; and, in the sea fight at Actium, had the good fortune to break through the enemy's great line of battle, sink three of their capital ships, and take a fourth, which was the sole cause of Anthony's flight, and of the victory that ensued; that the youth standing by him, his only son, was killed in the action. He added, that upon the confidence of some merit, the war being at an end, he went to Rome, and solicited at the court of Augustus, to be preferred to a greater ship, whose commander had been killed; but, without any regard to his pretensions, it was given to a youth who had never seen the sea, the son of Libertina, who waited on one of the Emperor's mistresses. Returning back to his own vessel, he was charged with neglect of duty, and the ship given to a favourite page of Publicola, the vice-admiral; whereupon he retired to a poor farm, at a great distance from Rome, and there ended his life. I was so curious to know the truth of this story, that I desired Agrippa might be called, who was admiral in that fight. He appeared, and confirmed the whole account; but with much more advantage to the captain, whose modesty had extenuated or concealed a great part of his merit.

I was surprised to find corruption grown so high and so quick in that empire, by the force of luxury so lately introduced, which made me less wonder at many parallel cases in other countries, where vices of all kinds have reigned so much longer, and where the whole praise, as well as pillage, hath been engrossed by the chief commander, who, perhaps, had the least title to either.

As every person called up made exactly the same appearance he had done in the world, it gave me melancholy reflections to observe how much the race of human kind was degenerate among us, within these hundred years past.

I descended so low, as to desire that some English yeomen, of the old stamp, might be summoned to appear; once so famous for the simplicity of their manners, diet, and dress; for justice in their dealings; for their true spirit of liberty; for their valour and love of their country. Neither could I be wholly unmoved, after comparing the living with the dead, when I considered how all these pure native virtues were prostituted for a piece of money by their grandchildren, who, in selling their votes, and managing at elections, have acquired every vice and corruption that can possibly be learned in a court.

CHAPTER IX

THE day of our departure being come, I took leave of his highness, the governor of Glubbdubdribb, and returned with my two companions to Maldonada, where, after a fortnight's waiting, a ship was ready to sail for Luggnagg. The two gentlemen, and some others, were so generous and kind as to furnish me with provisions, and see me on board. I was a month in this voyage. We had one violent storm, and were under a necessity of steering westward, to get into the trade-wind, which holds for above sixty leagues. On the 21st of April, 1708, we sailed into the river of Clumegnig, which is a seaport town, at the south-east point of Luggnagg. We cast anchor within a league of the town, and made a signal for a pilot. Two of them came on board in less than half an hour, by whom we were guided between certain shoals and rocks, which are very dangerous in the passage, to a large basin, where a fleet may ride in safety, within a cable's length of the town wall.

Some of our sailors, whether out of treachery or inadvertence, had informed the pilots that I was a stranger and a great traveller; whereof these gave notice to a custom-house officer, by whom I was examined very strictly upon my landing. This officer spoke to me in the language of Balnibarbi, which, by the force of much commerce, is generally understood in that town, especially by seamen, and those employed in the customs. I gave him a short account of some particulars, and made my story as plausible and consistent as I could; but I thought it necessary to disguise my country, and call myself an Hollander, because my intentions were for Japan, and I knew the Dutch were the only Europeans permitted to enter into that kingdom.

I therefore told the officer, that having been shipwrecked on the coast of Balnibarbi, and cast on a rock, I was received up into Laputa, or the flying island (of which he had often heard) and was now endeavouring to get to Japan, from whence I might find a convenience of returning to my own country. The officer said, I must be confined till he could receive orders from Court, for which he would write immediately, and hoped to receive an answer in a fortnight. I was carried to a convenient lodging, with a sentry placed at the door; however, I had the liberty of a large garden, and was treated with humanity enough, being maintained all the time at the king's charge. I was invited by several persons, chiefly out of curiosity, because it was reported that I came from countries very remote, of which they had never heard.

I hired a young man who came in the same ship to be an interpreter; he was a native of Luggnagg, but had lived some years at Maldonada, and was a perfect master of both languages. By his assistance, I was able to hold a conversation with those who came to visit me; but this consisted only of their questions, and my answers.

The dispatch came from Court about the time we expected. It contained a warrant for conducting me and my retinue to Traldragdubb, or Trildrogdrib, for it is pronounced both ways, as near as I can remember, by a party of ten horse. All my retinue was that poor lad for an interpreter, whom I persuaded into my service, and, at my humble request, we had each of us a mule to ride on. A messenger was dispatched half a day's journey before us, to give the king notice of my approach, and to desire that his Majesty would please to appoint a day and hour, when it would be his gracious pleasure that I might have the honour to lick the dust before his foot-stool. This is the court style, and I found it to be more than matter of form. For, upon my admittance two days after my arrival, I was commanded to crawl on my belly, and lick the floor as I advanced; but, on account of my being a stranger, care was taken to have it made so clean that the dust was not offensive. However, this was a peculiar grace, not allowed to any but persons of the highest rank, when they desire an admittance. Nay, sometimes the floor is strewed with dust on purpose, when the person to be admitted happens to have powerful enemies at Court. And I have seen a great lord with his mouth so crammed, that, when he had crept to the proper distance from the throne, he was not able to speak a word. Neither is there any remedy; because it is capital for those who receive an audience, to spit or wipe their mouths in his Majesty's presence. There is, indeed, another custom, which I cannot altogether approve of: when the king hath a mind to put any of his nobles to death, in a gentle, indulgent manner, he commands the floor to be strewed with a certain brown powder, of a deadly composition, which, being licked up, infallibly kills him in twenty-four hours. But in justice to this prince's great clemency, and the care he hath of his subjects' lives (wherein it were much to be wished, that the monarchs of Europe would imitate him) it must be mentioned for his honour, that strict orders are given to have the infected parts of the floor well washed, after every such execution; which if his domestics neglect, they are in danger of incurring his royal displeasure. I myself heard him give directions that one of his pages should be whipped, whose turn it was to give notice about washing the floor after an execution, but maliciously had omitted it, by which neglect, a young lord of great hopes, coming to an audience, was unfortunately poisoned, although the king, at that time, had no design against his life. But this good prince was so gracious as to forgive the poor page his whipping, upon promise that he would do so no more, without special orders.

To return from this digression; when I had crept within four yards of the throne, I raised myself gently upon my knees, and then, striking my forehead seven times on the ground, I pronounced the following words, as they had been taught me the night before, *Ickpling gloffthrobb squut serumm blhiop mlashnalt zwin tnodbalkuffh slhiophad gurdlubh asht.* This is the compliment established by the laws of the land, for all persons admitted to the king's presence. It may be rendered into English thus: May your celestial Majesty outlive the sun eleven moons and a half. To this the king returned some answer, which although I could not understand, yet I replied as I had been directed: *Fluft drin yalerick dwuldom prastrad mirpush,* which properly signifies, My tongue is in the mouth of my friend; and by this expression was meant, that I desired leave to bring my interpreter; whereupon the young man already mentioned was accordingly introduced, by whose intervention I answered as many questions as his Majesty could put in above an hour. I spoke in the Balnibarbian tongue, and my interpreter delivered my meaning in that of Luggnagg.

The king was much delighted with my company, and ordered his *bliffmarklub,* or high chamberlain, to appoint a lodging in the Court for me and my interpreter, with a daily allowance for my table, and a large purse of gold for my common expenses.

I stayed three months in this country, out of perfect obedience to his Majesty, who was pleased highly to favour me, and made me very honourable offers. But I thought it more consistent with prudence and justice to pass the remainder of my days with my wife and family.

CHAPTER X

THE Luggnaggians are a polite and generous people, and although they are not without some share of that pride which is peculiar to all eastern countries, yet they shew themselves courteous to strangers, especially such as are countenanced by the Court. I had many acquaintances among persons of the best fashion, and being always attended by my interpreter, the conversation we had was not disagreeable.

One day, in much good company, I was asked by a person of quality, whether I had seen any of their struldbrugs, or immortals. I said I had not; and desired he would explain to me what he meant by such an appellation, applied to a mortal creature. He told me, that sometimes, though very rarely, a child happened to be born in a family with a red circular spot in the forehead, directly over the left eye-brow, which was an infallible mark that it should never die. The spot, as he described it, was about the compass of a silver three-pence, but in the course of time grew larger, and changed its colour; for at twelve years old it became green, so continued till five and twenty, then turned to a deep blue; at five and forty it grew coal black, and as large as an English shilling; but never admitted any farther alteration. He said these births were so rare, that he did not believe there could be above eleven hundred struldbrugs of both sexes in the whole kingdom, of which he computed about fifty in the metropolis, and, among the rest, a young girl born about three years ago: that these productions were not peculiar to any family, but a mere effect of chance; and the children of the struldbrugs themselves were equally mortal with the rest of the people.

I freely own myself to have been struck with inexpressible delight upon hearing this account: and the person who gave it me happening to understand the Balnibarbian language, which I spoke very well, I could not forbear breaking out into expressions, perhaps a little too extravagant. I cried out, as in a rapture: " Happy nation, where every child hath at least a chance of being immortal! Happy people, who enjoy so many living examples of ancient virtue, and have masters ready to instruct them in the wisdom of all former ages! But happiest beyond all comparison are those excellent struldbrugs, who, born exempt from that universal calamity of human nature, have their minds free and disengaged, without the weight and depression of spirits caused by the continual apprehension of death." I discovered my admiration that I had not observed any of these illustrious persons at Court; the black spot on the forehead being so remarkable a distinction, that I could not have easily overlooked it; and it was impossible that his Majesty, a most judicious prince, should not provide himself with a good number of such wise and able councillors. Yet perhaps the virtue of those reverend sages was too strict for the corrupt and libertine manners of a court. And we often find by experience, that young men are too opinionative and volatile to be guided by the sober dictates of their seniors. However, since the king was pleased to allow me access to his royal person, I was resolved, upon the very first occasion, to deliver my opinion to him on this matter freely, and at large, by the help of my interpreter; and whether he would please to take my advice or no, yet in one thing I was determined, that, his Majesty having frequently offered me an establishment in this country, I would with great thankfulness accept the favour, and pass my life here in the conversation of those superior beings, the struldbrugs, if they would please to admit me.

The gentleman to whom I addressed my discourse, because (as I have already observed) he spoke the language

of Balnibarbi, said to me with a sort of a smile, which
usually ariseth from pity to the ignorant, that he was glad
of any occasion to keep me among them, and desired my
permission to explain to the company what I had spoke.
He did so, and they talked together for some time in their
own language, whereof I understood not a syllable, neither
could I observe by their countenances what impression my
discourse had made on them. After a short silence, the
same person told me that his friends and mine (so he
thought fit to express himself) were very much pleased with
the judicious remarks I had made on the great happiness
and advantages of immortal life, and they were desirous to
know in a particular manner, what scheme of living I
should have formed to myself, if it had fallen to my lot to
have been born a struldbrug.

I answered, it was easy to be eloquent on so copious and
delightful a subject, especially to me, who have been often
apt to amuse myself with visions of what I should do, if I
were a king, a general, or a great lord: and, upon this very
case, I had frequently run over the whole system how I
should employ myself, and pass the time. if I were sure to
live for ever.

That, if it had been my good fortune to come into the
world a struldbrug, as soon as I could discover my own
happiness, by understanding the difference between life
and death, I would first resolve, by all arts and methods
whatsoever, to procure myself riches. In the pursuit of
which, by thrift and management, I might reasonably
expect, in about two hundred years, to be the wealthiest
man in the kingdom. In the second place, I would from
my earliest youth apply myself to the study of arts and
sciences, by which I should arrive in time to excel all others
in learning. Lastly, I would carefully record every action
and event of consequence that happened in the public,
impartially draw the characters of the several successions
of princes, and great ministers of state, with my own obser-

vations on every point. I would exactly set down the several changes in customs, language, fashions of dress, diet and diversions. By all which acquirements, I should be a living treasury of knowledge and wisdom, and certainly become the oracle of the nation.

I would never marry after threescore, but live in an hospitable manner, yet still on the saving side. I would entertain myself in forming and directing the minds of hopeful young men, by convincing them from my own remembrance, experience, and observation, fortified by numerous examples, of the usefulness of virtue in public and private life. But my choice and constant companions should be a set of my own immortal brotherhood, among whom I would elect a dozen from the most ancient, down to my own contemporaries. Where any of these wanted fortunes, I would provide them with convenient lodges round my own estate, and have some of them always at my table, only mingling a few of the most valuable among you mortals, whom length of time would harden me to lose, with little or no reluctance, and treat your posterity after the same manner; just as a man diverts himself with the annual succession of pinks and tulips in his garden, without regretting the loss of those which withered the preceding year.

These struldbrugs and I would mutually communicate our observations and memorials through the course of time; remark the several gradations by which corruption steals into the world, and oppose it in every step, by giving perpetual warning and instruction to mankind; which, added to the strong influence of our own example, would probably prevent that continual degeneracy of human nature, so justly complained of in all ages.

Add to all this, the pleasure of seeing the various revolutions of states and empires; the changes in the lower and upper world; ancient cities in ruins, and obscure villages become the seats of kings; famous rivers lessening into shallow brooks; the ocean leaving one coast dry, and over-whelming another; the discovery of many countries yet unknown; barbarity over-running the politest nations, and the most barbarous become civilised. I should then see the discovery of the longitude, the perpetual motion, the universal medicine, and many other great inventions brought to the utmost perfection.

What wonderful discoveries should we make in astro-nomy, by out-living and confirming our own predictions, by observing the progress and returns of comets, with the changes of motion in the sun, moon, and stars.

I enlarged upon many other topics, which the natural desire of endless life and sublunary happiness could easily furnish me with. When I had ended, and the sum of my discourse had been intrepreted, as before, to the rest of the company, there was a good deal of talk among them in the language of the country, not without some laughter at my expense. At last, the same gentleman who had been my interpreter said he was desired by the rest to set me right in a few mistakes, which I had fallen into through the common imbecility of human nature, and, upon that allowance, was less answerable for them. That this breed of struldbrugs was peculiar to their country, for there were no such people, either in Balnibarbi or Japan, where he had the honour to be ambassador from his Majesty, and found the natives in both those kingdoms very hard to believe that the fact was possible; and it appeared from my astonishment, when he first mentioned the matter to me, that I received it as a thing wholly new, and scarcely to be credited. That in the two kingdoms above mentioned, where, during his residence, he had conversed very much, he observed long life to be the universal desire and wish of mankind. That whoever had one foot in the grave, was sure to hold back the other as strongly as he could. That the oldest had still hopes of living one day longer, and looked on death as the greatest evil, from which Nature always prompted him to retreat; only in this island of Luggnagg the appetite for living was not so eager, from the continual example of the struldbrugs before their eyes.

That the system of living, contrived by me, was unreasonable and unjust, because it supposed a perpetuity of youth, health, and vigour, which no man could be so foolish to hope, however extravagant he may be in his wishes. That the question therefore was not whether a man would choose to.be always in the prime of youth, attended with prosperity and health; but how he would pass a perpetual life under all the usual disadvantages which old age brings along with it. For although few men will avow their desires of being immortal upon such hard conditions, yet in the two kingdoms before mentioned, of Balnibarbi and Japan, he observed that every man desired to put off death for some time longer, let it approach ever so late; and he rarely heard of any man who died willingly, except he were incited by the extremity of grief or torture. And he appealed to me, whether in those countries I had travelled, as well as my own, I had not observed the same general disposition.

After this preface, he gave me a particular account of the struldbrugs among them. He said they commonly acted like mortals, till about thirty years old, after which, by degrees, they grew melancholy and dejected, increasing in both till they came to fourscore. This he learned from their own confession; for otherwise, there not being above two or three of that species born in an age, they were too few to form a general observation by. When they came to fourscore years, which is reckoned the extremity of living in this country, they had not only all the follies and infirmities of other old men, but many more, which arose from the dreadful prospects of never dying. They were not only opinionative, peevish, covetous, morose, vain, talkative; but incapable of friendship, and dead to all natural affection, which never descended below their grandchildren. Envy and impotent desires are their prevailing passions. But those objects, against which their envy seems principally directed, are the vices of the younger sort, and the deaths of the old. By reflecting on the former, they find themselves cut off from all possibility of pleasure; and whenever they see a funeral, they lament and repine that others are gone to an harbour of rest, to which they themselves never can hope to arrive. They have no remembrance of anything but what they learned and observed in their youth and middle age, and even that is very imperfect. And, for the truth or particulars of any fact, it is safer to depend on common traditions than upon their best recollections. The least miserable among them appear to be those who turn to dotage, and entirely lose their memories; these meet with more pity and assistance, because they want many bad qualities, which abound in others.

If a struldbrug happen to marry one of his own kind, the marriage is dissolved, of course, by the courtesy of the kingdom, as soon as the younger of the two comes to be fourscore. For the law thinks it a reasonable indulgence, that those who are condemned, without any fault of their own, to a perpetual continuance in the world, should not have their misery doubled by the load of a wife.

As soon as they have completed the term of eighty years, they are looked on as dead in law; their heirs immediately succeed to their estates, only a small pittance is reserved for their support; and the poor ones are maintained at the public charge. After that period, they are held incapable of any employment of trust or profit, they cannot purchase lands, or take leases, neither are they allowed to be witnesses in any cause, either civil or criminal, not even for the decision of meers and bounds.

At ninety they lose their teeth and hair; they have at that age no distinction of taste, but eat and drink whatever they can get, without relish or appetite. The diseases

they were subject to still continue, without increasing or
diminishing. In talking, they forget the common appellation of things, and the names of persons, even of those
who are their nearest friends and relations. For the same
reason they never can amuse themselves with reading,
because their memory will not serve to carry them from the
beginning of a sentence to the end; and, by this defect, they
are deprived of the only entertainment whereof they might
otherwise be capable.

The language of this country being always upon the
flux, the struldbrugs of one age do not understand those
of another; neither are they able, after two hundred years,
to hold any conversation (farther than by a few general
words) with their neighbours, the mortals; and thus they
lie under the disadvantage of living like foreigners in their
own country.

This was the account given me of the struldbrugs, as
near as I can remember. I afterwards saw five or six of
different ages, the youngest not above two hundred years
old, who were brought to me at several times, by some of
my friends; but although they were told that I was a great
traveller, and had seen all the world, they had not the least
curiosity to ask me a question; only desired I would give
them *slumskudask*, or a token of remembrance; which is a
modest way of begging, to avoid the law that strictly
forbids it, because they are provided for by the public,
although, indeed, with a very scanty allowance.

They are despised and hated by all sorts of people;
when one of them is born, it is reckoned ominous, and their
birth is recorded very particularly; so that you may know
their age, by consulting the register; which, however, hath
not been kept above a thousand years past, or, at least,
hath been destroyed by time, or public disturbances. But
the usual way of computing how old they are, is, by asking
them what kings or great persons they can remember, and
then consulting history; for, infallibly, the last prince in

their mind did not begin his reign after they were fourscore years old.

They were the most mortifying sight I ever beheld; and the women more horrible than the men. Besides the usual deformities in extreme old age, they acquired an additional ghastliness, in proportion to their number of years, which is not to be described; and, among half a dozen, I soon distinguished which was the eldest, although there was not above a century or two between them.

The reader will easily believe that from what I have heard and seen, my keen appetite for perpetuity of life was much abated. I grew heartily ashamed of the pleasing visions I had formed; and thought no tyrant could invent a death into which I would not run with pleasure from such a life. The king heard of all that had passed between me and my friends upon this occasion, and rallied me very pleasantly; wishing I would send a couple of struldbrugs to my own country, to arm our people against the fear of death; but this, it seems, is forbidden by the fundamental laws of the kingdom, or else I should have been well content with the trouble and expense of transporting them.

I could not but agree that the laws of this kingdom, relating to the struldbrugs, were founded upon
the strongest reasons, and such as any other country
would be under the necessity of enacting in
the like circumstances. Otherwise, as avarice
is the necessary consequent of old age,
those immortals would in time become
proprietors of the whole nation,
and engross the civil power;
which, for want of abili-
ties to manage, must
end in the ruin
of the public.

CHAPTER XI

I THOUGHT this account of the strudlbrugs might be some entertainment to the reader, because it seems to be a little out of the common way; at least, I do not remember to have met the like in any book of travels that hath come to my hands: and, if I am deceived, my excuse must be, that it is necessary for travellers, who describe the same country, very often to agree in dwelling on the same particulars, without deserving the censure of having borrowed or transcribed from those who wrote before them.

There is, indeed, a perpetual commerce between this kingdom and the great empire of Japan; and it is very probable that the Japanese authors may have given some account of the struldbrugs; but my stay in Japan was so short, and I was so entirely a stranger to the language, that I was not qualified to make any inquiries. But I hope the Dutch, upon this notice, will be curious and able enough to supply my defects.

His Majesty having often pressed me to accept some employment in his Court, and finding me absolutely determined to return to my native country, was pleased to give me his licence to depart, and honoured me with a letter of recommendation, under his own hand, to the Emperor of Japan. He likewise presented me with four hundred and forty-four large pieces of gold (this nation delighting in even numbers) and a red diamond, which I sold in England for eleven hundred pounds.

On the 6th day of May 1709, I took a solemn leave of his Majesty, and all my friends. This prince was so gracious as to order a guard to conduct me to Glanguenstald, which is a royal port to the south-west part of the island. In six

days I found a vessel ready to carry me to Japan, and spent
fifteen days in the voyage.   We landed at a small port-
town called Xamoschi, situated on the south-east part of
Japan; the town lies on the western point, where there is
a narrow strait, leading northward into a long arm of the
sea, upon the north-west part of which, Yedo, the metropolis, stands.   At landing I shewed the custom-house
officers my letter from the King of Luggnagg to his Imperial
Majesty.   They knew the seal perfectly well, it was as
broad as the palm of my hand.   The impression was, a
king lifting up a lame beggar from the earth.   The magis-
trates of the town, hearing of my letter, received me as a
public minister;   they provided me with carriages and
servants, and bore my charges to Yedo, where I was admitted to an audience, and delivered my letter, which was
opened with great ceremony, and explained to the Emperor
by an interpreter, who gave me notice, by his Majesty's
order, that I should signify my request, and, whatever it
were, it should be granted, for the sake of his royal brother
of Luggnagg.   This interpreter was a person employed to
transact affairs with the Hollanders;   he soon conjectured
by my countenance that I was an European, and therefore
repeated his Majesty's commands in Low Dutch, which he
spoke perfectly well.   I answered (as I had before determined) that I was a Dutch merchant, shipwrecked in a very
remote country, from whence I had travelled by sea and
land to Luggnagg, and then took shipping for Japan, where
I knew my countrymen often traded, and with some of these
I hoped to get an opportunity of returning into Europe: I
therefore most humbly entreated his royal favour to give
order, that I should be conducted in safety to Nangasac:
to this I added another petition, that, for the sake of my
patron, the King of Luggnagg, his Majesty would condescend to excuse my performing the ceremony imposed on
my countrymen, of trampling upon the crucifix; because
I had been thrown into his kingdom by my misfortunes,

without any intention of trading. When this latter petition was interpreted to the Emperor, he seemed a little
surprised; and said, he believed I was the first of my
countrymen who ever made any scruple in this point; and
that he began to doubt whether I was a real Hollander, or
no; but rather suspected I must be a Christian. However,
for the reasons I had offered, but chiefly to gratify the King
of Luggnagg by an uncommon mark of his favour, he would
comply with the singularity of my humour; but the affair
must be managed with dexterity, and his officers should be
commanded to let me pass, as it were, by forgetfulness.
For he assured me, that if the secret should be discovered
by my countrymen, the Dutch, they would cut my throat
in the voyage. I returned my thanks, by the interpreter,
for so unusual a favour; and, some troops being at that
time on their march to Nangasac, the commanding officer
had orders to convey me safe thither, with particular instructions about the business of the crucifix.

On the 9th day of June 1709, I arrived at Nangasac,
after a very long and troublesome journey. I soon fell into
company of some Dutch sailors belonging to the *Amboyna*
of Amsterdam, a stout ship of 450 tons. I had lived long
in Holland, pursuing my studies at Leyden, and I spoke
Dutch well. The seamen soon knew from whence I came
last; they were curious to inquire into my voyages, and
course of life. I made up a story as short and probable as
I could, but concealed the greatest part. I knew many
persons in Holland; I was able to invent names for my
parents, whom I pretended to be obscure people in the
province of Gelderland. I would have given the captain
(one Theodorus Vangrult) what he pleased to ask for my
voyage to Holland; but, understanding I was a surgeon,
he was contented to take half the usual rate, on condition
that I would serve him in the way of my calling. Before
we took shipping, I was often asked by some of the crew,
whether I had performed the ceremony above-mentioned?

I evaded the question by general answers, that I had satisfied the Emperor, and Court, in all particulars. However, a malicious rogue of a skipper went to an officer, and, pointing to me, told him I had not yet trampled on the crucifix; but the other, who had received instructions to let me pass, gave the rascal twenty strokes on the shoulders with a bamboo; after which I was no more troubled with such questions.

Nothing happened worth mentioning in this voyage. We sailed with a fair wind to the Cape of Good Hope, where we stayed only to take in fresh water. On the 16th of April we arrived safely at Amsterdam, having lost only three men by sickness in the voyage, and a fourth who fell from the fore-mast into the sea, not far from the coast of Guinea. From Amsterdam, I soon after set sail for England, in a small vessel belonging to that city.

On the 10th of April 1710, we put in at the Downs. I landed next morning, and saw once more my native country, after an absence of five years and six months complete. I went straight to Redriff, where I arrived the same day at two in the afternoon, and found my wife and family in good health.

THE END OF THE THIRD PART

PART 4

CHAPTER I

I CONTINUED at home with my wife and children about five months, in a very happy condition, if I could have learned the lesson of knowing when I was well. I left my poor wife and accepted an advantageous offer made me, to be captain of the *Adventure*, a stout merchant-man, of 350 tons; for I understood navigation well, and being grown weary of a surgeon's employment at sea, which, however, I could exercise upon occasion, I took a skilful young man of that calling, one Robert Purefoy, into my ship. We set sail from Portsmouth upon the 2nd day of August 1710; on the 14th we met with Captain Pocock, of Bristol, at Teneriffe, who was going to the Bay of Campechy, to cut logwood. On the 16th he was parted from us by a storm; I heard, since my return, that his ship foundered, and none escaped but one cabin-boy. He was an honest man, and a good sailor, but a little too positive in his own opinions, which was the cause of his destruction, as it hath been of several others. For, if he had followed my advice, he might have been safe at home with his family at this time, as well as myself.

I had several men died in my ship of calentures, so that

I was forced to get recruits out of Barbadoes, and the
Leeward Islands, where I touched by the direction of the
merchants who employed me; which I had soon too much
cause to repent; for I found afterwards that most of them
had been buccaneers. I had fifty hands on board, and my
orders were that I should trade with the Indians, in the
South Sea, and make what discoveries I could. These
rogues whom I had picked up debauched my other men,
and they all formed a conspiracy to seize the ship, and
secure me; which they did one morning, rushing into my
cabin, and binding me hand and foot, threatening to throw
me overboard if I offered to stir. I told them I was their
prisoner, and would submit. This they made me swear to
do, and then they unbound me, only fastening one of my
legs with a chain near my bed, and placed a sentry at my
door with his piece charged, who was commanded to shoot
me dead, if I attempted my liberty. They sent me down
victuals and drink, and took the government of the ship
to themselves. Their design was to turn pirates, and
plunder the Spaniards, which they could not do till they
got more men. But first they resolved to sell the goods in
the ship, and then go to Madagascar for recruits, several
among them having died since my confinement. They
sailed many weeks and traded with the Indians; but I
knew not what course they took, being kept a close prisoner
in my cabin, and expecting nothing less than to be
murdered, as they often threatened me.

Upon the 9th day of May 1711, one James Welch came
down to my cabin, and said he had orders from the captain
to set me ashore. I expostulated with him, but in vain;
neither would he so much as tell me who their new captain
was. They forced me into the long boat, letting me put on
my best suit of clothes, which were as good as new, and a
small bundle of linen, but no arms, except my hanger;
and they were so civil as not to search my pockets, into
which I conveyed what money I had, with some other little

necessaries. They rowed about a league; and then set me down on a strand. I desired them to tell me what country it was. They all swore they knew no more than myself, but said that the captain (as they called him) was resolved, after they had sold the lading, to get rid of me in the first place where they could discover land. They pushed off immediately, advising me to make haste, for fear of being overtaken by the tide, and so bade me farewell.

In this desolate condition I advanced forward, and soon got upon firm ground, where I sat down on a bank to rest myself, and consider what I had best do. When I was a little refreshed, I went up into the country, resolving to deliver myself to the first savages I should meet, and purchase my life from them by some bracelets, glass rings, and other toys, which sailors usually provide themselves with in those voyages, and whereof I had some about me: the land was divided by long rows of trees, not regularly planted, but naturally growing; there was great plenty of grass, and several fields of oats. I walked very circumspectly, for fear of being surprised, or suddenly shot with an arrow from behind, or on either side. I fell into a beaten road, where I saw many tracks of human feet, and some of cows, but most of horses. At last I beheld several animals in a field, and one or two of the same kind sitting in trees. Their shape was very singular, and deformed, which a little discomposed me, so that I lay down behind a thicket to observe them better. Some of them, coming forward near the place where I lay, gave me an opportunity of distinctly marking their form. Their heads and breasts were covered with a thick hair, some frizzled, and others lank; they had beards like goats, and a long ridge of hair down their backs and the fore-parts of their legs and feet; but the rest of their bodies were bare, so that I might see their skins, which were of a brown buff colour. They had no tails, and were accustomed to sit as well as to lie down, and often stood on their hind feet. They climbed high trees as

nimbly as a squirrel, for they had strong extended claws
before and behind, terminating in sharp points, and hooked.
They would often spring and bound, and leap with prodigious agility. The females were not so large as the males;
they had long lank hair on their heads, but none on their
faces, nor anything more than a sort of down on the rest of
their bodies. The hair of both sexes was of several colours,
brown, red, black, and yellow. Upon the whole, I never
beheld, in all my travels, so disagreeable an animal, nor one
against which I naturally conceived so strong an antipathy.
So that thinking I had seen enough, full of contempt and
aversion, I got up, and pursued the beaten road, hoping
it might direct me to the cabin of some Indian. I had not
got far, when I met one of these creatures full in my way,
and coming up directly to me. The ugly monster, when
he saw me, distorted several ways every feature of his
visage, and stared as at an object he had never seen before;
then, approaching nearer, lifted up his fore-paw, whether
out of curiosity or mischief, I could not tell. But I drew
my hanger, and gave him a good blow with the flat side of
it, for I durst not strike with the edge, fearing the inhabitants might be provoked against me, if they should come
to know that I had killed or maimed any of their cattle.
When the beast felt the smart, he drew back, and roared so
loud, that a herd of at least forty came flocking about me
from the next field, howling and making odious faces; but
I ran to the body of a tree, and, leaning my back against
it, kept them off by waving my hanger.

In the midst of this distress, I observed them all to run
away on a sudden as fast as they could, at which I ventured
to leave the tree and pursue the road, wondering what it
was that could put them into this fright. But, looking on
my left hand, I saw a horse walking softly in the field;
which my persecutors having sooner discovered, was the
cause of their flight. The horse started a little when he
came near me, but soon recovering himself looked full in my

face, with manifest tokens of wonder: he viewed my hands
and feet, walking round me several times. I would have
pursued my journey, but he placed himself directly in the
way, yet looking with a very mild aspect, never offering
the least violence. We stood gazing at each other for
some time; at last I took the boldness to reach my hand
towards his neck, with a design to stroke it, using the
common style and whistle of jockeys, when they are going
to handle a strange horse. But this animal seemed to
receive my civilities with disdain, shook his head, and bent
his brows, softly raising up his right fore-foot to remove my
hand. Then he neighed three or four times, but in so
different a cadence, that I almost began to think he was
speaking to himself in some language of his own.

While he and I were thus employed, another horse
came up; who, applying himself to the first in a very formal
manner, they gently struck each other's right hoof before,
neighing several times by turns, and varying the sound,
which seemed to be almost articulate. They went some
paces off, as if it were to confer together, walking side by
side, backward and forward, like persons deliberating upon
some affair of weight, but often turning their eyes towards
me, as it were to watch that I might not escape. I was
amazed to see such actions and behaviour in brute beasts;
and concluded with myself, that if the inhabitants of this
country were endued with a proportionable degree of
reason, they must needs be the wisest people upon earth.
This thought gave me so much comfort, that I resolved to
go forward, until I could discover some house or village, or
meet with any of the natives; leaving the two horses to
discourse together as they pleased. But the first, who was
a dapple-grey, observing me to steal off, neighed after me
in so expressive a tone, that I fancied myself to understand
what he meant; whereupon I turned back, and came near
him, to expect his further commands, but concealing my
fear as much as I could; for I began to be in some pain how

this adventure might terminate; and the reader will easily believe I did not much like my present situation.

The two horses came up close to me, looking with great earnestness upon my face and hands. The grey steed rubbed my hat all round with his right fore-hoof, and discomposed it so much, that I was forced to adjust it better, by taking it off, and settling it again; whereat both he and his companion (who was a brown bay) appeared to be much surprised; the latter felt the lappet of my coat, and, finding it to hang loose about me, they both looked with signs of wonder. He stroked my right hand, seeming to admire the softness and colour; but he squeezed it so hard between his hoof and his pastern, that I was forced to roar; after which they both touched me with all possible tenderness. They were under great perplexity about my shoes and stockings, which they felt very often, neighing to each other, and using various gestures, not unlike those of a philosopher, when he would attempt to solve some new and difficult phenomenon.

Upon the whole, the behaviour of these animals was so orderly and rational, so acute and judicious, that I at last concluded they must needs be magicians, who had thus metamorphosed themselves upon some design, and seeing a stranger in the way, were resolved to divert themselves with him; or, perhaps, were really amazed at the sight of a man so very different in habit, feature, and complexion from those who might probably live in so remote a climate. Upon the strength of this reasoning, I ventured to address them in the following manner: "Gentlemen, if you be conjurers, as I have good cause to believe, you can understand any language; therefore, I make bold to let your worships know, that I am a poor distressed Englishman, driven by his misfortunes upon your coast, and I entreat one of you to let me ride upon his back, as if he were a real horse, to some house or village, where I can be relieved. In return of which favour, I will make you a present of this

knife and bracelet " (taking them out of my pocket). The
two creatures stood silent while I spoke, seeming to listen
with great attention; and, when I had ended, they neighed
frequently towards each other, as if they were engaged
in serious conversation. I plainly observed, that their
language expressed the passions very well, and the words
might with little pains be resolved into an alphabet, more
easily than the Chinese.

I could frequently distinguish the word Yahoo, which
was repeated by each of them several times; and, although
it was impossible for me to conjecture what it meant, yet,
while the two horses were busy in conversation, I endeavoured to practise this word upon my tongue; and, as
soon as they were silent, I boldly pronounced Yahoo, in a
loud voice, imitating, at the same time, as near as I could,
the neighing of a horse; at which they were both visibly
surprised, and the grey repeated the same word twice, as if
he meant to teach me the right accent, wherein I spoke
after him as well as I could, and found myself perceivably
to improve every time, though far from any degree of perfection. Then the bay tried me with a second word, much
harder to be pronounced; but, reducing it to the English
orthography, may be spelt thus, Houyhnhnm. I did not
succeed in this so well as the former; but, after two or
three farther trials, I had better fortune; and they both
appeared amazed at my capacity.

After some farther discourse, which I then conjectured
might relate to me, the two friends took their leaves, with
the same compliment of striking each other's hoof; and the
grey made me signs that I should walk before him; wherein
I thought it prudent to comply, till I could find a better
director. When I offered to slacken my pace, he would
cry *Hhuun, Hhuun ;* I guessed his meaning, and gave him
to understand, as well as I could, that I was weary, and
not able to walk faster; upon which he would stand a
while to let me rest.

CHAPTER II

HAVING travelled about three miles, we came to a long kind of building, made of timber, stuck in the ground, and wattled across; the roof was low, and covered with straw. I now began to be a little comforted; and took out some toys, which travellers usually carry for presents to the savage Indians of America, and other parts, in hopes the people of the house would be thereby encouraged to receive me kindly. The horse made me a sign to go in first; it was a large room with a smooth clay floor, and a rack and manger, extending the whole length on one side. There were three nags and two mares, not eating, but some of them sitting down upon their hams, which I very much wondered at; but wondered more to see the rest employed in domestic business. These seemed but ordinary cattle; however, this confirmed my first opinion, that a people who could so far civilise brute animals, must needs excel in wisdom all the nations of the world. The grey came in just after, and thereby prevented any ill treatment which the others might have given me. He neighed to them several times in a style of authority, and received answers.

Beyond this room there were three others, reaching the length of the house, to which you passed through the doors, opposite to each other, in the manner of a vista; we went through the second room towards the third; here the grey walked in first, beckoning me to attend; I waited in the second room, and got ready my presents for the master and mistress of the house: they were two knives, three bracelets of false pearl, a small looking-glass, and a bead necklace. The horse neighed three or four times, and I waited to hear some answers in a human voice, but I

observed no other returns than in the same dialect, only
one or two a little shriller than his. I began to think that
this house must belong to some person of great note among
them, because there appeared so much ceremony before I
could gain admittance. But that a man of quality should
be served all by horses, was beyond my comprehension. I
feared my brain was disturbed by my sufferings and misfortunes: I roused myself, and looked about me in the room
where I was left alone; this was furnished like the first,
only after a more elegant manner. I rubbed my eyes
often, but the same objects still occurred. I pinched my
arms and sides, to awake myself, hoping I might be in a
dream. I then absolutely concluded that all these appearances could be nothing else but necromancy and magic.
But I had no time to pursue these reflections; for the grey
horse came to the door, and made me a sign to follow him
into the third room; where I saw a very comely mare,
together with a colt and foal, sitting on their haunches,
upon mats of straw, not unartfu'ly made, and perfectly
neat and clean.

The mare, soon after my entrance, rose from her mat,
and coming up close, after having nicely observed my hands
and face, gave me a most contemptuous look; then, turning to the horse, I heard the word Yahoo often repeated
betwixt them; the meaning of which word I could not then
comprehend, although it were the first I had learned to
pronounce; but I was soon better informed, to my ever-
lasting mortification: for the horse beckoning to me with
his head, and repeating the word *Hhuun, Hhuun*, as he did
upon the road, which I understood was to attend him, led
me out into a kind of court, where was another building at
some distance from the house. Here we entered, and I
saw three of those detestable creatures whom I first met
after my landing, feeding upon roots, and the flesh of some
animals, which I afterwards found to be that of asses and
dogs, and now and then a cow dead by accident or disease.

They were all tied by the neck with strong withes, fastened
to a beam; they held their food between the claws of their
fore-feet, and tore it with their teeth.

The master horse ordered a sorrel nag, one of his
servants, to untie the largest of these animals, and take
him into the yard. The beast and I were brought close
together; and our countenances diligently compared, both
by master and servant, who thereupon repeated several
times the word Yahoo. My horror and astonishment are
not to be described, when I observed in this abominable
animal a perfect human figure; the face of it, indeed, was
flat and broad, the nose depressed, the lips large, and the
mouth wide: but these differences are common to all
savage nations, where the lineaments of the countenance
are distorted, by the natives suffering their infants to lie
grovelling on the earth, or by carrying them on their backs,
nuzzling with their face against the mother's shoulders.
The fore-feet of the Yahoo differed from my hands in
nothing else but the length of the nails, the coarseness and
brownness of the palms, and the hairiness on the backs.
There was the same resemblance between our feet, with the
same differences, which I knew very well, though the horses
did not, because of my shoes and stockings; the same in
every part of our bodies, except as to hairiness and colour,
which I have already described.

The great difficulty that seemed to stick with the two
horses was, to see the rest of my body so very different from
that of a Yahoo, for which I was obliged to my clothes,
whereof they had no conception: the sorrel nag offered me
a root, which he held (after their manner, as we shall describe in its proper place) between his hoof and pastern; I
took it in my hand, and, having smelt it, returned it to him
again as civilly as I could. He brought out of the Yahoo's
kennel a piece of ass's flesh, but it smelt so offensively, that
I turned from it with loathing; he then threw it to the
Yahoo, by whom it was greedily devoured. He afterwards

shewed me a wisp of hay, and a fetlock full of oats; but I shook my head, to signify that neither of these were food for me. And, indeed, I now apprehended that I must absolutely starve, if I did not get to some of my own species: for as to those filthy Yahoos, although there were few greater lovers of mankind, at that time, than myself, yet, I confess, I never saw any sensitive being so detestable on all accounts; and the more I came near them, the more hateful they grew, while I stayed in that country. This the master horse observed by my behaviour, and therefore sent the Yahoo back to his kennel. He then put his fore-hoof to his mouth, at which I was much surprised, although he did it with ease, and with a motion that appeared perfectly natural; and made other signs to know what I would eat; but I could not return him such an answer as he was able to apprehend; and, if he had understood me, I did not see how it was possible to contrive any way for finding myself nourishment. While we were thus engaged, I observed a cow passing by, whereupon I pointed to her, and expressed a desire to let me go and milk her. This had its effect; for he led me back into the house, and ordered a mare servant to open a room, where a good store of milk lay in earthen and wooden vessels, after a very orderly and cleanly manner. She gave me a large bowl full, of which I drank very heartily, and found myself well refreshed.

About noon, I saw coming towards the house a kind of vehicle, drawn, like a sledge, by four Yahoos. There was in it an old steed, who seemed to be of quality; he alighted with his hind-feet forward, having by accident got a hurt in his fore-foot. He came to dine with our horse, who received him with great civility. They dined in the best room, and had oats boiled in milk for the second course, which the old horse eat warm, but the rest cold. Their mangers were placed circular in the middle of the room, and divided into several partitions, round which they sat on their haunches upon bosses of straw. In the middle was a large rack, with angles answering to every partition of the manger; so that each horse and mare eat their own hay, and their own mash of oats and milk, with much decency and regularity. The behaviour of the young colt and foal appeared very modest; and that of the master and mistress extremely cheerful and complaisant to their guest. The grey ordered me to stand by him; and much discourse passed between him and his friend concerning me, as I found by the stranger's often looking on me, and the frequent repetition of the word Yahoo.

I happened to wear my gloves, which the master grey observing, seemed perplexed, discovering signs of wonder what I had done to my fore-feet; he put his hoof three or four times to them, as if he would signify, that I should reduce them to their former shape, which I presently did, pulling off both my gloves, and putting them into my pocket. This occasioned farther talk, and I saw the company was pleased with my behaviour, whereof I soon found the good effects. I was ordered to speak the few words I understood; and while they were at dinner, the master taught me the names for oats, milk, fire, water, and some others; which I could readily pronounce after him, having from my youth a great facility in learning languages.

When dinner was done, the master horse took me aside, and by signs and words, made me understand the concern that he was in, that I had nothing to eat. Oats, in their tongue, are called *hluunh*. This word I pronounced two or three times; for although I had refused them at first, yet, upon second thoughts, I considered that I could contrive to make of them a kind of bread, which might be sufficient, with milk, to keep me alive, till I could make my escape to some other country, and to creatures of my own species. The horse immediately ordered a white mare servant, of his family, to bring me a good quantity of oats, in a sort of wooden tray. These I heated before the fire, as well as I could, and rubbed them till the husks came off, which I made a shift to winnow from the grain; I ground and beat them between two stones, then took water, and made them into a paste or cake, which I toasted at the fire, and ate warm with milk. It was at first a very insipid diet, though common enough in many parts of Europe, but grew tolerable by time; and, having been often reduced to hard fare in my life, this was not the first experiment I had made, how easily nature is satisfied. And I cannot but observe, that I never had one hour's sickness while I stayed in this island. It is true, I sometimes made a shift to catch a rabbit, or bird, by springs made of Yahoo's hairs; and I often gathered wholesome herbs, which I boiled, or eat as salads with my bread; and now and then for a rarity I made a little butter, and drank the whey. I was at first at a great loss for salt; but custom soon reconciled me to the want of it; and I am confident that the frequent use of salt among us is an effect of luxury, and was first introduced only as a provocative to drink; except where it is necessary for preserving flesh in long voyages, or in places remote from great markets. For we observe no animal to be fond of it but man: and as to myself, when I left this country, it was a great while before I could endure the taste of it in anything that I ate.

This is enough to say upon the subject of my diet, wherewith other travellers fill their books, as if the readers were personally concerned, whether we fared well or ill. However, it was necessary to mention this matter, lest the world should think it impossible that I could find sustenance for three years in such a country, and among such inhabitants.

When it grew towards evening, the master horse ordered a place for me to lodge in; it was but six yards from the house, and separated from the stable of the Yahoos. Here I got some straw, and, covering myself with my own clothes, slept very sound. But I was in a short time better accommodated, as the reader shall know hereafter, when I come to treat more particularly about my way of living.

CHAPTER III

My principal endeavour was to learn the language, which my master (for so I shall henceforth call him) and his children, and every servant of his house were desirous to teach me. For they looked upon it as a prodigy, that a brute animal should discover such marks of a rational creature. I pointed to everything, and inquired the name of it, which I wrote down in my journal-book when I was alone, and corrected my bad accent by desiring those of the family to pronounce it often. In this employment a sorrel nag, one of the under servants, was ready to assist me.

In speaking, they pronounce through the nose and throat, and their language approaches nearest to the High-Dutch, or German, of any I know in Europe, but is much more graceful and significant. The Emperor Charles V. made almost the same observation, when he said, that, if he were to speak to his horse, it should be in High-Dutch.

The curiosity and impatience of my master were so great, that he spent many hours of his leisure to instruct me. He was convinced (as he afterwards told me) that I must be a Yahoo; but my teachableness, civility, and cleanliness astonished him; which were qualities altogether so opposite to those animals. He was most perplexed about my clothes, reasoning sometimes with himself, whether they were a part of my body; for I never pulled them off till the family were asleep, and got them on before they waked in the morning. My master was eager to learn from whence I came; how I acquired those appearances of reason, which I discovered in all my actions; and to know my story from my own mouth, which he hoped he should soon do, by the great proficiency I made in learning

and pronouncing their words and sentences. To help my
memory, I formed all I learned into the English alphabet,
and writ the words down, with the translations. This last,
after some time, I ventured to do in my master's presence.
It cost me much trouble to explain to him what I was
doing; for the inhabitants have not the least idea of books
or literature.

In about ten weeks' time, I was able to understand most
of his questions; and in three months could give him some
tolerable answers. He was extremely curious to know
from what part of the country I came, and how I was
taught to imitate a rational creature; because the Yahoos
(whom he saw I exactly resembled in my head, hands, and
face, that were only visible) with some appearance of
cunning, and the strongest disposition to mischief, were
observed to be the most unteachable of all brutes. I
answered, that I came over the sea, from a far place, with
many others of my own kind, in a great hollow vessel made
of the bodies of trees; that my companions forced me to
land on this coast, and then left me to shift for myself. It
was with some difficulty, and by the help of many signs,
that I brought him to understand me. He replied that I
must needs be mistaken, or that I said the thing which was
not (for they have no word in their language to express
lying or falsehood). He knew it was impossible that there
could be a country beyond the sea, or that a parcel of brutes
could move a wooden vessel whither they pleased upon
water. He was sure no Houyhnhnm alive could make
such a vessel, nor would trust Yahoos to manage it.

The word Houyhnhnm, in their tongue, signifies a horse,
and in its etymology, the perfection of nature. I told my
master that I was at a loss for expression, but would improve as fast as I could; and hoped in a short time I should
be able to tell him wonders: he was pleased to direct his
own mare, his colt, and foal, and the servants of the family,
to take all opportunities of instructing me; and every day,

for two or three hours, he was at the same pains himself. Several horses and mares of quality, in the neighbourhood, came often to our house, upon the report spread of a wonderful Yahoo, that could speak like a Houyhnhnm, and seemed, in his words and actions, to discover some glimmerings of reason. These delighted to converse with me; they put many questions, and received such answers as I was able to return. By all these advantages, I made so great a progress that, in five months from my arrival, I understood whatever was spoken, and could express myself tolerably well.

The Houyhnhnms who came to visit my master, out of a design of seeking and talking with me, could hardly believe me to be a right Yahoo, because my body had a different covering from others of my kind. They were astonished to observe me without the usual hair, or skin, except on my head, face and hands; but I discovered that secret to my master, upon an accident, which happened about a fortnight before.

I have already told the reader, that every night when the family were gone to bed, it was my custom to strip, and cover myself with my clothes: it happened one morning early, that my master sent for me, by the sorrel nag, who was his valet; when he came, I was fast asleep, my clothes fallen off on one side, and my shirt above my waist. I awaked at the noise he made, and observed him to deliver his message in some disorder; after which he went to my master, and in a great fright gave him a very confused account of what he had seen: this I presently discovered; for going as soon as I was dressed, to pay my attendance upon his honour, he asked me the meaning of what his servant had reported; that I was not the same thing when I slept, as I appeared to be at other times; that his valet assured him some part of me was white, some yellow, at least not so white, and some brown.

I had hitherto concealed the secret of my dress, in order

to distinguish myself, as much as possible, from that cursed race of Yahoos; but now I found it in vain to do so any longer. Besides, I considered that my clothes and shoes would soon wear out, which already were in a declining condition, and must be supplied by some contrivance from the hides of Yahoos, or other brutes; whereby the whole secret would be known: I therefore told my master that, in the country from whence I came, those of my kind always covered their bodies with the hairs of certain animals prepared by art, as well for decency, as to avoid the inclemencies of air both hot and cold; of which, as to my own person, I would give him immediate conviction, if he pleased to command me. Whereupon, I first unbuttoned my coat, and pulled it off. I did the same with my waistcoat; I drew off my shoes, stockings, and breeches.

My master observed the whole performance with great signs of curiosity and admiration. He took up all my clothes in his pastern, one piece after another, and examined them diligently; he stroked my body very gently, and looked round me several times, after which he said, it was plain I must be a perfect Yahoo; but that I differed very much from the rest of my species, in the softness, and whiteness, and smoothness of my skin, my want of hair in several parts of my body, the shape and shortness of my claws behind and before, and my affectation of walking continually on my two hinder feet. He desired to see no more; and gave me leave to put on my clothes again, for I was shuddering with cold.

I expressed my uneasiness at his giving me so often the appellation of Yahoo, an odious animal, for which I had so utter an hatred and contempt: I begged he would forbear applying that word to me, and make the same order in his family, and among his friends, whom he suffered to see me. I requested, likewise, that the secret of my having a false covering to my body might be known to none but himself, at least, so long as my present clothing should last; for as to what the sorrel nag, his valet, had observed, his honour might command him to conceal it.

All this my master very graciously consented to, and thus the secret was kept till my clothes began to wear out, which I was forced to supply by several contrivances, that shall hereafter be mentioned. In the meantime, he desired I would go on with my utmost diligence to learn their language, because he was more astonished at my capacity for speech and reason, than at the figure of my body, whether it were covered or no; adding, that he waited with some impatience to hear the wonders which I promised to tell him.

From thenceforward he doubled the pains he had been at to instruct me; he brought me into all company, and made them treat me with civility, because, as he told them privately, this would put me into good humour, and make me more diverting.

Every day, when I waited on him, besides the trouble he was at in teaching, he would ask me several questions concerning myself, which I answered as well as I could; and by these means he had already received some general ideas, though very imperfect. It would be tedious to relate the several steps by which I advanced to a more regular conversation: but the first account I gave of myself, in any order and length, was to this purpose:

That I came from a very far country, as I already had attempted to tell him, with about fifty more of my own species; that we travelled upon the seas in a great hollow vessel made of wood, and larger than his honour's house. I described the ship to him in the best terms I could, and explained, by the help of my handkerchief displayed, how it was driven forward by the wind. That, upon a quarrel among us, I was set on shore on this coast, where I walked forward, without knowing whither, till he delivered me from the persecution of those execrable Yahoos. He asked me who made the ship, and how it was possible that the

Houyhnhnms of my country would leave it to the management of brutes? My answer was, that I durst proceed no further in my relation unless he would give me his word and honour that he would not be offended, and then I would tell him the wonders I had so often promised. He agreed, and I went on, by assuring him that the ship was made by creatures like myself, who in all the countries I had travelled, as well as in my own, were the only governing, rational animals; and that, upon my arrival hither, I was as much astonished to see the Houyhnhnms act like rational beings, as he or his friends could be in finding some marks of reason in a creature he was pleased to call a Yahoo; to which I owned my resemblance in every part, but could not account for their degenerate and brutal nature. I said further, that if good fortune ever restored me to my native country, to relate my travels hither, as I resolved to do, everybody would believe that I said the thing which was not; that I invented the story out of my own head; and, with all possible respect to himself, his family, and friends, and under his promise of not being offended, our countrymen would hardly think it probable that a Houyhnhnm should be the presiding creature of a nation, and a Yahoo the brute.

CHAPTER IV

My master heard me with great appearances of uneasiness in his countenance; because doubting, or not believing, are so little known in this country, that the inhabitants cannot tell how to behave themselves under such circumstances. And I remember, in frequent discourses with my master concerning the nature of manhood in other parts of the world, having occasion to talk of lying, and false representation, it was with much difficulty that he comprehended what I meant; although he had otherwise a most acute judgment. For he argued thus: that the use of speech was to make us understand one another, and to receive information of facts; now, if any one said the thing that was not, these ends were defeated; because I cannot properly be said to understand him; and I am so far from receiving information that he leaves me worse than in ignorance, for I am led to believe a thing black when it is white, and short when it is long. And these were all the notions he had concerning that faculty of lying, so perfectly well understood, and so universally practised, among human creatures.

To return from this digression; when I asserted that the Yahoos were the only governing animals in my country, which, my master said, was altogether past his conception, he desired to know whether we had Houyhnhnms among us, and what was their employment. I told him, we had great numbers; that in summer they grazed in the fields and in winter were kept in houses, with hay and oats, where Yahoo servants were employed to rub their skins smooth, comb their manes, pick their feet, serve them with food, and make their beds. "I understand you well," said my master; " it is now very plain, from all you have spoken, that, whatever share of reason the Yahoos pretend to, the Houyhnhnms are your masters; I heartily wish our Yahoos would be so tractable." I begged his honour would please to excuse me from proceeding any further, because I was very certain that the account he expected from me would be highly displeasing. But he insisted in commanding me to let him know the best and the worst: I told him, he should be obeyed. I owned, that the Houyhnhnms among us, whom we called horses, were the most generous and comely animal we had; that they excelled in strength and swiftness; and when they belonged to persons of quality, employed in travelling, racing, or drawing chariots, they were treated with much kindness and care, till they fell into diseases, or became foundered in the feet; but then they were sold, and used to all kind of drudgery, till they died; after which their skins were stripped, and sold for what they were worth, and their bodies left to be devoured by dogs and birds of prey. But the common race of horses had not so good fortune, being kept by farmers and carriers, and other mean people, who put them to greater labour, and fed them worse. I described, as well as I could, our way of riding; the shape and use of a bridle, a saddle, a spur, and a whip; of harness and wheels. I added, that we fastened plates of a certain hard substance, called iron, at the bottom of their feet, to preserve their hoofs from being broken by the stony ways on which we often travelled.

My master, after some expressions of great indignation, wondered how we dared to venture upon a Houyhnhnm's back; for he was sure, that the weakest servant in his house would be able to shake off the strongest Yahoo; or by lying down, and rolling on his back, squeeze the brute to death. I answered, that our horses were trained up from three or four years old, to the several uses we intended them for; that, if any of them proved intolerably vicious, they were employed for carriages; that they were severely beaten, while they were young, for any mischievous tricks; that they were, indeed, sensible of rewards and punishments: but his honour would please to consider, that they had not the least tincture of reason, any more than the Yahoos in this country.

It put me to the pains of many circumlocutions to give my master a right idea of what I spoke; for their language doth not abound in variety of words, because their wants and passions are fewer than among us. But it is impossible to represent his noble resentment at our savage treatment of the Houyhnhnm race. He said, if it were possible there could be any country where Yahoos alone were endued with reason, they certainly must be the governing animal; because reason will in time always prevail against brutal strength. But, considering the frame of our bodies, and especially of mine, he thought no creature of equal bulk was so ill contrived for employing that reason in the common offices of life; whereupon, he desired to know whether those among whom I lived resembled me, or the Yahoos of his country. I assured him, that I was as well shaped as most of my age: but the younger, and the females, were much more soft and tender, and the skins of the latter, generally as white as milk. He said I differed, indeed, from other Yahoos, being much more cleanly, and not altogether so deformed; but in point of real advantage, he thought I differed for the worse. That my nails were of no use, either to my fore or hinder-feet; as to my fore-feet, he could not properly call them by that name, for he never observed me to walk upon them; that they were too soft to bear the ground; that I generally went with them uncovered, neither was the covering I sometimes wore on them of the same shape, or so strong as that on my feet behind. That I could not walk with any security, for, if either of my hinder-feet slipped, I must inevitably fall. He then began to find fault with other parts of my body; the flatness of my face, the prominence of my nose, mine eyes placed directly in front, so that I could not look on either side without turning my head; that I was not able to feed myself, without lifting one of my fore-feet to my mouth; and therefore Nature had placed those joints to answer that necessity. He knew not what could be the use of those several clefts and divisions in my feet behind; that these were too soft to bear the hardness and sharpness of stones, without a covering made from the skin of some other brute; that my whole body wanted a fence against heat and cold, which I was forced to put on and off every day with tedious-ness and trouble. And lastly, that he observed every animal in this country naturally to abhor the Yahoos, whom the weaker avoided, and the stronger drove from them. So that supposing us to have the gift of reason, he could not see how it were possible to cure that natural antipathy which every creature discovered against us; nor consequently, how we could tame and render them serviceable. However, he would (as he said) debate the matter no farther, because he was more desirous to know my own story, the country where I was born, and the several actions and events of my life before I came hither.

I assured him, how extremely desirous I was that he should be satisfied in every point; but I doubted much, whether it would be possible for me to explain myself on several subjects whereof his honour could have no concep-tion, because I saw nothing in his country to which I could resemble them. That, however, I would do my best, and strive to express myself by similitudes, humbly desiring his assistance when I wanted proper words; which he was pleased to promise me.

I said my birth was of honest parents, in an island called England, which was remote from this country, as many days' journey as the strongest of his honour's servants could travel in the annual course of the sun. That I was bred a surgeon, whose trade it is to cure wounds and hurts in the body, got by accident or violence. That my country was governed by a female man, called a queen. That I left it to get riches, whereby I might maintain myself and family when I should return. That, in my last voyage, I was commander of the ship, and had about fifty Yahoos under me, many of which died at sea, and I was forced to supply them by others, picked out from several nations. That our ship was twice in danger of being sunk; the first time by a great storm, and the second, by striking against a rock. Here my master interposed, by asking me how I could persuade strangers out of different countries to venture with me, after the losses I had sustained, and the hazards I had run. I said they were fellows of desperate fortunes, forced to fly from the places of their birth, on account of their poverty or their crimes. Some were undone by lawsuits; others spent all they had in drinking and gaming; others fled for treason; many for murder, theft, poisoning, robbery, perjury, forgery, coining false money, for flying from their colours, or deserting to the enemy; and most of them had broken prison; none of these durst return to their native countries for fear of being hanged, or of starving in a jail; and, therefore, were under a necessity of seeking a livelihood in other places.

During this discourse, my master was pleased to interrupt me several times; I had made use of many circumlocutions, in describing to him the nature of several crimes, for which most of our crew had been forced to fly their country. This labour took up several days' conversation, before he was able to comprehend me. He was wholly at a loss to know what could be the use or necessity of practising those vices. To clear up which, I endeavoured to give him some ideas of the desire of power and riches; of the terrible effects of lust, intemperance, malice and envy. All this I was forced to define and describe, by putting cases, and making suppositions. After which, like one whose imagination was struck with something never seen or heard of before, he would lift up his eyes with amazement and indignation.

Power, government, war, law, punishment, and a thousand
other things had no terms wherein that language could
express them; which made the difficulty almost insuperable
to give my master any conception of what I meant. But
being of an excellent understanding, much improved by
contemplation and converse, he at last arrived at a com-
petent knowledge of what human nature, in our parts of
the world, is capable to perform, and desired I would give
him some particular account of that land which we call
Europe, but especially of my own country.

CHAPTER V

THE reader may please to observe, that the following extract of many conversations I had with my master, contains a summary of the most material points, which were discoursed at several times, for above two years; his honour often desiring fuller satisfaction, as I farther improved in the Houyhnhnm tongue. I laid before him, as well as I could, the whole state of Europe; I discoursed of trade and manufactures, of arts and sciences; and the answers I gave to all the questions he made, as they arose upon several subjects, were a fund of conversation not to be exhausted. But I shall here only set down the substance of what passed between us concerning my own country, reducing it into order as well as I can, without any regard to time, or other circumstances, while I strictly adhere to truth. My only concern is, that I shall hardly be able to do justice to my master's arguments and expressions, which must needs suffer by my want of capacity, as well as by a translation into our barbarous English.

In obedience, therefore, to his honour's commands I related to him the revolution under the Prince of Orange; the long war with France entered into by the said Prince, and renewed by his successor the present Queen, wherein the greatest powers of Christendom were engaged, and which still continued: I computed, at his request, that about a million of Yahoos might have been killed in the whole progress of it; and, perhaps, a hundred or more cities taken, and five times as many ships burnt or sunk.

He asked me what were the usual causes or motives that made one country go to war with another. I answered, they

were innumerable; but I should only mention a few of
the chief. Sometimes the ambition of princes, who never
think they have land or people enough to govern; sometimes the corruption of ministers, who engage their master
in a war, in order to stifle or divert the clamour of the subjects
against their evil administration. Difference in opinion hath
cost many millions of lives: for instance, whether whistling
be a vice or virtue; whether it be better to kiss a post, or
throw it into the fire; what is the best colour for a coat,
whether black, white, red, or grey; and whether it should
be long or short, narrow or wide, dirty or clean, with many
more. Neither are any wars so furious and bloody, or of
so long continuance, as those occasioned by difference in
opinion, especially if it be in things indifferent.

Sometimes the quarrel between two princes is to decide
which of them shall dispossess a third of his dominions,
where neither of them pretend to any right. Sometimes
one prince quarrelleth with another, for fear the other should
quarrel with him. Sometimes a war is entered upon because
the enemy is too strong; and sometimes because he is too
weak. Sometimes our neighbours want the things which
we have, or have the things which we want; and we both
fight, till they take ours, or give us theirs. It is a very
justifiable cause of a war, to invade a country, after the
people have been wasted by famine, destroyed by pestilence,
or embroiled by factions among themselves. It is justifiable
to enter into war against our nearest ally, when one of his
towns lies convenient for us, or a territory of land that would
render our dominions round and complete. If a prince sends
forces into a nation, where the people are poor and ignorant,
he may lawfully put half of them to death, and make slaves
of the rest, in order to civilise and reduce them from their
barbarous way of living. It is a very kingly, honourable,
and frequent practice when one prince desires the assistance of another to secure him against an invasion, that the
assistant, when he hath driven out the invader, should seize

on the dominions himself, and kill, imprison, or banish the prince he came to relieve. Alliance by blood, or marriage, is a frequent cause of war between princes; and the nearer the kindred is, the greater is their disposition to quarrel: poor nations are hungry, and rich nations are proud; and pride and hunger will ever be at variance. For these reasons the trade of a soldier is held the most honourable of all others: because a soldier is a Yahoo hired to kill in cold blood as many of his own species, who had never offended him, as possibly he can.

There is, likewise, a kind of beggarly princes in Europe, not able to make war by themselves, who hire out their troops to richer nations, for so much a day to each man; of which they keep three-fourths to themselves, and it is the best part of their maintenance; such are those in Germany and other northern parts of Europe.

" What you have told me " (said my master) " upon the subject of war, does, indeed, discover most admirably the defects of that reason you pretend to: however, it is happy that the shame is greater than the danger; and that Nature hath left you utterly incapable of doing much mischief.

" For, your mouths lying flat with your faces, you can hardly bite each other to any purpose, unless by consent. Then as to the claws upon your feet before and behind, they are so short and tender, that one of our Yahoos would drive a dozen of yours before him. And, therefore, in recounting the numbers of those who have been killed in battle, I cannot but think that you have said the thing which is not."

I could not forbear shaking my head, and smiling a little at his ignorance. And, being no stranger to the art of war, I gave him a description of cannons, culverins, muskets, carbines, pistols, bullets, powder, swords, bayonets, battles, sieges, retreats, attacks, undermines, countermines, bombardments, sea-fights; ships sunk with a thousand men; twenty thousand killed on each side; dying groans, limbs flying in the air; smoke, noise, confusion, trampling to death under horses' feet; flight, pursuit, victory; fields strewed with carcases, left for food to dogs and wolves, and birds of prey; plundering, stripping, ravishing, burning, and destroying. And, to set forth the valour of my own dear countrymen, I assured him that I had seen them blow up a hundred enemies at once in a siege, and as many in a ship; and beheld the dead bodies come down in pieces from the clouds to the great diversion of the spectators.

I was going on to more particulars when my master commanded me silence. He said, whoever understood the nature of Yahoos might easily believe it possible for so vile an animal, to be capable of every action I had named, if their strength and cunning equalled their malice. But as my discourse had increased his abhorrence of the whole species, so he found it gave him a disturbance in his mind, to which he was wholly a stranger before. He thought his ears, being used to such abominable words, might, by degrees, admit them with less detestation. That although he hated the Yahoos of this country, yet he no more blamed them for their odious qualities, than he did a *gnnayh* (a bird of prey) for its cruelty, or a sharp stone for cutting his hoof. But when a creature, pretending to reason, could be capable of such enormities, he dreaded lest the corruption of that faculty might be worse than brutality itself. He seemed therefore confident that, instead of reason, we were only possessed of some quality fitted to increase our natural vices; as the reflection from a troubled stream returns the image of an ill-shapen body, not only larger, but more distorted.

He added, that he had heard too much upon the subject of war, both in this, and some former discourses. There was another point which a little perplexed him at present. I had informed him that some of our crew left their country on account of being ruined by law; that I had already explained the meaning of the word; but he was at a loss how it should come to pass that the law, which was intended for every man's preservation, should be any man's ruin. Therefore he desired to be further satisfied what I meant by law, and the dispensers thereof, according to the present practice in my own country; because he thought Nature and reason were sufficient guides for a reasonable animal, as we pretended to be, in showing us what we ought to do, and what to avoid.

I assured his honour that law was a science in which I had not much conversed, further than by employing advocates in vain, upon some injustices that had been done me; however, I would give him all the satisfaction I was able.

I said, there was a society of men among us, bred up from their youth in the art of proving by words multiplied for the purpose, that white is black, and black is white, according as they are paid. " To this society all the rest of the people are slaves. For example, if my neighbour hath a mind to my cow, he hires a lawyer to prove that he ought to have my cow from me. I must then hire another to defend my right, it being against all rules of law that any man should be allowed to speak for himself. Now, in this case, I, who am the right owner, lie under two disadvantages; first, my lawyer, being practised almost from his cradle in defending falsehood, is quite out of his element, when he would be an advocate for justice, which is an unnatural office he always attempts with great awkwardness, if not with ill-will. The second disadvantage is, that my lawyer must proceed with great caution, or else he will be reprimanded by the judges, and abhorred by his brethren, as one that would lessen the practice of the law. And therefore I have but two methods to preserve my cow. The first is to gain over my adversary's lawyer with a double fee; who will then betray his client, by insinuating that he hath justice on his side. The second way is for my lawyer to make my cause appear as unjust as he can, by allowing the cow to belong to my adversary;

and this, if it be skilfully done, will certainly bespeak the favour of the bench. Now, your honour is to know that these judges are persons appointed to decide all controversies of property, as well as for the trial of criminals, and picked out from the most dexterous lawyers, who are grown old or lazy, and having been biassed all their lives against truth and equity, are under such a fatal necessity of favouring fraud, perjury, and oppression, that I have known several of them refuse a large bribe from the side where justice lay, rather than injure the faculty by doing anything unbecoming their nature or their office.

" It is a maxim among these lawyers, that whatever hath been done before, may legally be done again; and therefore they take special care to record all the decisions formerly made against common justice, and the general reason of mankind. These, under the name of precedents, they produce as authorities, to justify the most iniquitous opinions, and the judges never fail of directing accordingly.

" In pleading, they studiously avoid entering into the merits of the cause; but are loud, violent, and tedious, in dwelling upon all circumstances which are not to the purpose. For instance, in the case already mentioned: they never desire to know what claim or title my adversary hath to my cow; but whether the said cow were red or black; her horns long or short; whether the field I graze her in be round or square; whether she was milked at home or abroad; what diseases she is subject to, and the like; after which they consult precedents, adjourn the cause from time to time, and in ten, twenty, or thirty years, come to an issue.

" It is likewise to be observed that this society hath a peculiar cant and jargon of their own, that no other mortal can understand, and wherein all their laws are written, which they take special care to multiply; whereby they have wholly confounded the very essence of truth and falsehood, of right and wrong; so that it will take thirty years to decide whether the field left me by my ancestors for six generations, belongs to me, or to a stranger three hundred miles off.

" In the trial of persons accused for crimes against the state, the method is much more short and commendable: the judge first sends to sound the disposition of those in power, after which he can easily hang or save a criminal, strictly preserving all due forms of law."

Here my master interposing, said it was a pity that creatures endowed with such prodigious abilities of mind as these lawyers, by the description I gave of them, must certainly be, were not rather encouraged to be instructors of others in wisdom and knowledge. In answer to which, I assured his honour that, in all points out of their own trade, they were usually the most ignorant and stupid generation among us, the most despicable in common conversation, avowed enemies to all knowledge and learning, and equally disposed to pervert the general reason of mankind in every other subject of discourse, as in that of their own profession.

CHAPTER VI

My master was yet wholly at a loss to understand what motives could incite this race of lawyers to perplex, disquiet, and weary themselves, and engage in a confederacy of injustice, merely for the sake of injuring their fellow-animals; neither could he comprehend what I meant in saying, they did it for hire. Whereupon I was at much pains to describe to him the use of money, the materials it was made of, and the value of the metals; that, when a Yahoo had got a great store of this precious substance, he was able to purchase whatever he had a mind to, the finest clothing, the noblest houses, great tracts of land, the most costly meats and drinks; and have his choice of the most beautiful females. Therefore, since money alone was able to perform all these feats, our Yahoos thought they could never have enough of it to spend, or to save, as they found themselves inclined, from their natural bent either to profusion or avarice. That the rich man enjoyed the fruit of the poor man's labour, and the latter were a thousand to one in proportion to the former. That the bulk of our people were forced to live miserably, by labouring every day for small wages, to make a few live plentifully. I enlarged myself much on these and many other particulars, to the same purpose, but his honour was still puzzled: for he went upon a supposition, that all animals had a title to their share in the productions of the earth; and especially those who presided over the rest. Therefore he desired I would let him know what these costly meats were, and how any of us happened to want them. Whereupon I enumerated as many sorts as came into my head, with the various methods of dressing them, which could not be done without sending vessels by sea to every part of the world, as well for liquors to drink, as for sauces, and innumerable other conveniences. I assured him, that this whole globe of earth must be at least three times gone round, before one of our better female Yahoos could get her breakfast, or a cup to put it in. He said, that must needs be a miserable country, which cannot furnish food for its own inhabitants. But what he chiefly wondered at, was how such vast tracts of ground as I described, should be wholly without fresh water, and the people put to the necessity of sending over the sea for drink. I replied, that England (the dear place of my nativity) was computed to produce three times the quantity of food, more than its inhabitants are able to consume, as well as liquors extracted from grain, or pressed out of the fruit of certain trees, which made excellent drink; and the same proportion in every other convenience of life. But in order to feed the luxury and intemperance of the males, and the vanity of the females, we sent away the greatest part of our necessary things to other countries, from whence, in return, we brought the materials of diseases, folly, and vice, to spend among ourselves. Hence it follows of necessity, that vast numbers of our people are compelled to seek their livelihood by begging, robbing, stealing, cheating, forswearing, flattering, suborning, forging, gaming, lying, fawning, hectoring, voting, scribbling, star-gazing, poisoning, canting, libelling, free-thinking, and the like occupations: every one of which terms I was at much pains to make him understand.

That wine was not imported among us from foreign countries, to supply the want of water, or other drinks, but because it was a sort of liquid which made us merry, by putting us out of our senses; diverted all melancholy thoughts, begat wild extravagant imaginations in the brain, raised our hopes, and banished our fears; suspended every office of reason for a time, and deprived us of the use of our limbs till we fell into a profound sleep; although it must be confessed, that we always awaked sick and dispirited;

and that the use of this liquor filled us with diseases, which made our lives uncomfortable and short.

But, beside all this, the bulk of our people supported themselves by furnishing the necessities or conveniences of life to the rich, and to each other. For instance, when I am at home, and dressed, as I ought to be, I carry on my body the workmanship of an hundred tradesmen; the building and furniture of my house employ as many more, and five times the number to adorn my wife.

I was going on to tell him of another sort of people, who get their livelihood by attending the sick, having upon some occasions informed his honour that many of my crew had died of diseases. But here it was with the utmost difficulty that I brought him to apprehend what I meant. He could easily conceive that a Houyhnhnm grew weak and heavy a few days before his death; or, by some accident, might hurt a limb. But that Nature, who works all things to perfection, should suffer any pains to breed in our bodies, he thought impossible, and desired to know the reason of so unaccountable an evil. I told him we fed on a thousand things, which operated contrary to each other; that we ate when we were not hungry, and drank without the provocation of thirst; that we sat whole nights drinking strong liquors without eating a bit, which disposed us to sloth, inflamed our bodies, and precipitated or prevented digestion. That it would be endless to give him a catalogue of all diseases incident to human bodies; for they could not be fewer than five or six hundred spread over every limb and joint; in short, every part, external and intestine, having diseases appropriated to each. To remedy which, there was a sort of people bred up among us, in the profession, or pretence, of curing the sick. And, because I had some skill in the faculty, I would, in gratitude to his honour, let him know the whole mystery and method by which they proceed.

But, besides real diseases, we are subject to many that

are only imaginary, for which the physicians have invented imaginary cures; these have their several names, and so have the drugs that are proper for them; and with these our female Yahoos are always infested.

One great excellency in this tribe is their skill at prognostics, wherein they seldom fail; their predictions in real diseases, when they rise to any degree of malignity, generally portending death, which is always in their power, when recovery is not: and therefore, upon any unexpected signs of amendment, after they have pronounced their sentence, rather than be accused as false prophets, they know how to approve their sagacity to the world by a seasonable dose.

They are likewise of special use to eldest sons, to great ministers of state, and often to princes.

I had formerly, upon occasion, discoursed with my master upon the nature of government in general, and particularly of our own excellent constitution, deservedly the wonder and envy of the whole world. But having here accidentally mentioned a minister of state, he commanded me, some time after, to inform him what species of Yahoo I particularly meant by that appellation.

I told him, that a first or chief minister of state, who was the person I intended to describe, was a creature wholly exempt from joy and grief, love and hatred, pity and anger; at least, makes use of no other passions, but a violent desire of wealth, power, and titles; that he applies his words to all uses, except to the indication of his mind; that he never tells the truth, but with an intent that you should take it for a lie; nor a lie, but with a design that you should take it for a truth; that those he speaks worst of, behind their backs, are in the surest way of preferment; and whenever he begins to praise you to others, or to yourself, you are from that day forlorn. The worst mark you can receive is a promise, especially when it is confirmed with an oath; after which, every wise man retires, and gives over all hopes.

There are three methods by which a man may rise to be

chief minister: the first is, by knowing how with prudence to dispose of a wife, a daughter, or a sister: the second, by betraying or undermining his predecessor: and the third is, by a furious zeal in public assemblies against the corruptions of the Court. But a wise prince would rather choose to employ those who practise the last of these methods: because such zealots prove always the most obsequious and subservient to the will and passions of their master. That these ministers, having all employments at their disposal, preserve themselves in power by bribing the majority of a senate or great council; and at last, by an expedient called an Act of Indemnity (whereof I described the nature to him) they secure themselves from after reckonings, and retire from the public, laden with the spoils of the nation.

The palace of the chief minister is a seminary to breed up others in his own trade: the pages, lacqueys, and porter, by imitating their master, become ministers of state in their several districts, and learn to excel in the three principal ingredients of insolence, lying, and bribery. Accordingly, they have a subaltern court paid to them by persons of the best rank; and sometimes, by the force of dexterity and impudence, arrive, through several gradations, to be successors to their lord.

One day, in discourse, my master, having heard me mention the nobility of my country, was pleased to make me a compliment, which I could not pretend to deserve: that he was sure I must have been born of some noble family, because I far exceeded, in shape, colour, and cleanliness, all the Yahoos of his nation, although I seemed to fail in strength and agility, which must be imputed to my different way of living from those other brutes; and, besides, I was not only endowed with the faculty of speech, but likewise with some rudiments of reason, to a degree that, with all his acquaintance, I passed for a prodigy.

He made me observe that, among the Houyhnhnms, the

white, the sorrel, and the iron grey were not so exactly shaped as the bay, the dapple grey, and the black; nor born with equal talents of the mind, or a capacity to improve them; and therefore continued always in the condition of servants, without ever aspiring to match out of their own race, which, in that country, would be reckoned monstrous and unnatural.

I made his honour my humble acknowledgments for the good opinion he was pleased to conceive of me; but assured him, at the same time, that my birth was of the lower sort, having been born of plain honest parents, who were just able to give me a tolerable education: that nobility among us was altogether a different thing from the idea he had of it; that our young noblemen are bred from their childhood in idleness and luxury; and when their fortunes are almost ruined, they marry some woman of mean birth, disagreeable person, and unsound constitution, merely for the sake of money, whom they hate and despise. That a weak diseased body, a meagre countenance, and sallow complexion are the true marks of noble blood; and a healthy robust appearance disgraceful in a man of quality. The imperfections of his mind run parallel with those of his body, being a composition of spleen, dulness, ignorance, caprice, sensuality, and pride.

Without the consent of this illustrious body, no law can be made, repealed, or altered; and these have the decisions of all our possessions, without appeal.

CHAPTER VII

THE reader may be disposed to wonder how I could prevail on myself to give so free a representation of my own species, among a race of mortals who are already too apt to conceive the vilest opinion of human kind, from that entire congruity betwixt me and their Yahoos. But I must freely confess that the many virtues of those excellent quadrupeds, placed in opposite view to human corruptions, had so far opened my eyes, and enlarged my understanding, that I began to view the actions and passions of man in a very different light, and to think the honour of my own kind not worth managing; which, besides, it was impossible for me to do before a person of so acute a judgment as my master, who daily convinced me of a thousand faults in myself, whereof I had not the least perception before, and which, among us, would never be numbered even among human infirmities. I had likewise learned, from his example, an utter detestation of all falsehood or disguise; and truth appeared so amiable to me, that I determined upon sacrificing everything to it.

Let me deal so candidly with the reader as to confess that there was yet a much stronger motive for the freedom I took in my representation of things. I had not been a year in this country before I contracted such a love and veneration for the inhabitants, that I entered on a firm resolution never to return to human kind, but to pass the rest of my life among these admirable Houyhnhnms, in the contemplation and practice of every virtue; where I could have no example or incitement to vice. But it was decreed by fortune, my perpetual enemy, that so great a felicity should not fall to my share. However, it is now some comfort to reflect that, in what I said of my countrymen, I extenuated their faults as much as I durst, before so strict an examiner; and, upon every article, gave as favourable a turn as the matter would bear. For, indeed, who is there alive that would not be swayed by his bias and partiality to the place of his birth?

I have related the substance of several conversations I had with my master during the greatest part of the time I had the honour to be in his service; but have, indeed, for brevity sake, omitted much more than is here set down.

When I had answered all his questions, and his curiosity seemed to be fully satisfied, he sent for me one morning early, and commanding me to sit down at some distance (an honour which he had never before conferred on me), he said, he had been very seriously considering my whole story, as far as it related both to myself and my country; that he looked upon us as a sort of animals, to whose share, by what accident he could not conjecture, some small pittance of reason had fallen, whereof we made no other use than, by its assistance, to aggravate our natural corruptions, and to acquire new ones which nature had not given us: that we disarmed ourselves of the few abilities she had bestowed; had been very successful in multiplying our original wants, and seemed to spend our whole lives in vain endeavours to supply them by our own inventions. That as to myself, it was manifest I had neither the strength or agility of a common Yahoo; that I walked infirmly on my hinder feet; had found out a contrivance to make my claws of no use or defence, and to remove the hair from my chin, which was intended as a shelter from the sun and the weather. Lastly, that I could neither run with speed, nor climb trees like my brethren (as he called them) the Yahoos in this country.

That our institutions of government and law were plainly owing to our gross defects in reason, and by consequence, in virtue; because reason alone is sufficient to govern a rational creature; which was therefore a character we had no pretence to challenge, even from the account I had given of my own people; although he manifestly perceived, that in order to favour them, I had concealed many particulars, and often said the thing which was not.

He was the more confirmed in this opinion, because he observed, that as I agreed in every feature of my body with other Yahoos, except where it was to my real disadvantage, in point of strength, speed, and activity, the shortness of my claws, and some other particulars, where Nature had no part; so, from the representation I had given him of our lives, our manners, and our actions, he found as near a resemblance in the disposition of our minds. He said, the Yahoos were known to hate one another, more than they did any different species of animals; and the reason, usually assigned, was the odiousness of their own shapes, which all could see in the rest, but not in themselves. He had therefore begun to think it not unwise in us to cover our bodies, and, by that invention, conceal many of our own deformities from each other, which would else be hardly supportable. But he now found he had been mistaken, and that the dissensions of those brutes, in his country, were owing to the same cause with ours, as I had described them. "For if" (said he) "you throw among five Yahoos as much food as would be sufficient for fifty, they will, instead of eating peaceably, fall together by the ears, each single one impatient to have all to itself;" and therefore a servant was usually employed to stand by, while they were feeding abroad, and those kept at home were tied at a distance from each other; that if a cow died of age or accident, before a Houyhnhnm could secure it for his own Yahoos, those in the neighbourhood would come in herds to seize it, and then would ensue such a battle as I had described, with terrible wounds made by their claws on both sides, although they seldom were able to kill one another, for want of such convenient instruments of death as we had invented. At other times, the like battles have been fought between the Yahoos of several neighbourhoods, without any visible cause: those of one district watching all opportunities to surprise the next, before they are prepared. But, if they find their project hath miscarried, they return home, and, for want of enemies, engage in what I call a civil war among themselves.

That, in some fields of his country, there are certain shining stones of several colours, whereof the Yahoos are violently fond; and when part of these stones is fixed in the earth, as it sometimes happeneth, they will dig with their claws for whole days to get them out, then carry them away, and hide them by heaps in their kennels; but still looking round with great caution, for fear their comrades should find out their treasure. My master said, he could never discover the reason of this unnatural appetite, or how these stones could be of any use to a Yahoo; but now he believed it might proceed from the same principle of avarice, which I had ascribed to mankind: that he had once, by way of experiment, privately removed a heap of these stones from the place where one of his Yahoos had buried it; whereupon, the sordid animal missing his treasure, by his loud lamenting brought the whole herd to the place, there miserably howled, then fell to biting and tearing the rest; began to pine away, would neither eat, nor sleep, nor work, till he ordered a servant privately to convey the stones into the same hole, and hide them as before; which when his Yahoo had found, he presently recovered his spirits and good humour, but took care to remove them to a better hiding-place, and hath ever since been a very serviceable brute.

My master further assured me, which I also observed myself, that, in the fields where the shining stones abound, the fiercest and most frequent battles are fought, occasioned by perpetual inroads of the neighbouring Yahoos.

He said, it was common, when two Yahoos discovered such a stone in a field, and were contending which of them should be the proprietor, a third would take the advantage, and carry it away from them both; which my master would needs contend to have some kind of resemblance with our suits at law; wherein I thought it for our credit not to undeceive him; since the decision he mentioned was much more equitable than many decrees among us: because the plaintiff and defendant there lost nothing beside the stone they contended for, whereas our courts of equity would never have dismissed the cause, while either of them had anything left.

My master, continuing his discourse, said, there was nothing that rendered the Yahoos more odious, than their undistinguishing appetite to devour everything that came in their way, whether herbs, roots, berries, the corrupted flesh of animals, or all mingled together: and it was peculiar in their temper, that they were fonder of what they could get by rapine or stealth, at a greater distance, than much better food provided for them at home.

There was also a kind of root, very juicy, but somewhat rare and difficult to be found, which the Yahoos fought for with much eagerness, and would suck it with great delight; it produced in them the same effects that wine hath upon us. It would make them sometimes hug, and sometimes tear one another; they would howl and grin, and chatter, and reel, and tumble, and then fall asleep in the mud.

I did, indeed, observe that the Yahoos were the only animals in this country subject to any diseases; which, however, were much fewer than horses have among us, and contracted not by any ill treatment they meet with, but by the nastiness and greediness of that sordid brute. Neither has their language any more than a general appellation for those maladies, which is borrowed from the name of the beast, and called *Hnea-Yahoo*, or the Yahoo's-evil.

As to learning, government, arts, manufactures, and the like, my master confessed he could find little or no resemblance between the Yahoos of that country and those in ours. For he only meant to observe what parity there was in our natures. He had heard, indeed, some curious Houyhnhnms

observe, that, in most herds, there was a sort of ruling
Yahoo (as, among us, there is generally some leading or
principal stag in a park) who was always more deformed in
body, and mischievous in disposition, than any of the rest.
That this leader had usually a favourite as like himself as
he could get. This favourite is hated by the whole herd,
and therefore, to protect himself, keeps always near the
person of his leader. He usually continues in office till a
worse can be found; but, the very moment he is discarded,
his successor at the head of all the Yahoos in that district,
young and old, male and female, come in a body, and attack
him. But how far this might be applicable to our Courts
and favourites, and ministers of state, my master said I
could best determine.

I durst make no return to this malicious insinuation,
which debased human understanding below the sagacity of
a common hound, who has judgment enough to distinguish
and follow the cry of the ablest dog in the pack, without
being ever mistaken.

My master told me, that a thing he wondered at in the
Yahoos, was their strange disposition to nastiness and dirt;
whereas there appears to be a natural love of cleanliness in
all other animals. As to the two former accusations, I was
glad to let them pass without any reply, because I had not
a word to offer upon them in defence of my species, which
otherwise I certainly had done from my own inclinations.
But I could have easily vindicated human kind from the
imputation of singularity upon the last article, if there
had been any swine in that country (as unluckily for me
there was not) which, although it may be a sweeter quad-
ruped than a Yahoo, cannot, I humbly conceive in justice,
pretend to more cleanliness; and so his honour himself must
have owned, if he had seen their filthy way of feeding, and
their custom of wallowing and sleeping in the mud.

My master likewise mentioned another quality which his
servants had discovered in several Yahoos, and to him was

wholly unaccountable. He said, a fancy would sometimes take a Yahoo, to retire into a corner, to lie down, and howl and groan, and spurn away all that came near him, although he were young and fat, wanted neither food nor water; nor did the servants imagine what could possibly ail him. And the only remedy they found was, to set him to hard work, after which he would infallibly come to himself. To this I was silent, out of partiality to my own kind; yet here I could plainly discover the true seeds of spleen, which only seizeth on the lazy, the luxurious, and the rich; who, if they were forced to undergo the same regimen, I would undertake for the cure.

CHAPTER VIII

As I ought to have understood human nature much better than I supposed it possible for my master to do, so it was easy to apply the character he gave of the Yahoos to myself and my countrymen; and I believed I could yet make further discoveries from my own observation. I therefore often begged his favour to let me go among the herds of Yahoos in the neighbourhood, to which he always very graciously consented, being perfectly convinced that the hatred I bore those brutes would never suffer me to be corrupted by them; and his honour ordered one of his servants, a strong sorrel nag, very honest and good-natured, to be my guard, without whose protection I durst not undertake such adventures. For I have already told the reader how much I was pestered by those odious animals upon my first arrival. And I afterwards failed very narrowly three or four times of falling into their clutches, when I happened to stray at any distance without my hanger. And I have reason to believe they had some imagination that I was of their own species, which I often assisted myself, by stripping up my sleeves, and showing my naked arms and breast in their sight, when my protector was with me. At which times they would approach as near as they durst, and imitate my actions after the manner of monkeys, but ever with great signs of hatred; as a tame jack-daw, with cap and stockings, is always persecuted by the wild ones, when he happens to be got among them.

They are prodigiously nimble from their infancy; however, I once caught a young male of three years old, and endeavoured, by all marks of tenderness, to make it quiet; but the little imp fell a-squalling, and scratching, and biting, with such violence, that I was forced to let it go; and it was high time, for a whole troop of old ones came about us at the noise, but finding the cub was safe (for away it ran) and my sorrel nag being by, they durst not venture near us. I observed the young animal's flesh to smell very rank, and the stink was somewhat between a weasel and a fox, but much more disagreeable.

By what I could discover, the Yahoos appear to be the most unteachable of all animals; their capacities never reaching higher than to draw or carry burthens. Yet I am of opinion this defect ariseth chiefly from a perverse, restive disposition. For they are cunning, malicious, treacherous, and revengeful. They are strong and hardy, but of a cowardly spirit, and by consequence, insolent, abject, and cruel. It is observed, that the red haired of both sexes are more mischievous than the rest, whom yet they much exceed in strength and activity.

The Houyhnhnms keep the Yahoos for present use in huts not far from the house; but the rest are sent abroad to certain fields, where they dig up roots, eat several kinds of herbs, and search about for carrion, or sometimes catch weasels and luhimuhs (a sort of wild rat) which they greedily devour. Nature hath taught them to dig holes with their nails on the side of a rising ground, wherein they lie by themselves; only the kennels of the females are larger, sufficient to hold two or three cubs.

They swim from their infancy like frogs, and are able to continue long under water, where they often take fish, which the females carry home to their young.

Having lived three years in this country, the reader, I suppose, will expect that I should, like other travellers, give him some account of the manners and customs of its inhabitants, which it was, indeed, my principal study to learn.

As these noble Houyhnhnms are endowed by nature with a general disposition to all virtues, and have no conceptions or ideas of what is evil in a rational creature; so their grand maxim is, to cultivate reason, and to be wholly governed by it. Neither is reason, among them, a point problematical as with us, where men can argue with plausibility on both sides of a question, but strikes you with immediate conviction; as it must needs do, where it is not mingled, obscured, or discoloured by passion and interest. I remember it was with extreme difficulty that I could bring my master to understand the meaning of the word opinion, or how a point could be disputable; because reason taught us to affirm or deny only where we are certain; and, beyond our knowledge, we cannot do either. So that controversies, wranglings, disputes, and positiveness, in false or dubious propositions, are evils unknown among the Houyhnhnms. In the like manner, when I used to explain to him our several systems of natural philosophy, he would laugh, that a creature, pretending to reason, should value itself upon the knowledge of other people's conjectures, and in things where that knowledge, if it were certain, could be of no use. Wherein he agreed entirely with the sentiments of Socrates, as Plato delivers them; which I mention as the highest honour I can do that prince of philosophers. I have often since reflected, what destruction such a doctrine would make in the libraries of Europe; and how many paths to fame would be then shut up in the learned world.

Friendship and benevolence are the two principal virtues among the Houyhnhnms; and these not confined to particular objects, but universal to the whole race. For a stranger, from the remotest part, is equally treated with the nearest neighbour; and, wherever he goes, looks upon himself as at home. They preserve decency and civility in the highest degrees, but are altogether ignorant of ceremony. They have no fondness for their colts or foals, but the care they take in educating them proceeds entirely from the dictates of reason. And I observed my master to show the same affection to his neighbour's issue that he had for his own. They will have it, that Nature teaches them to love the whole species, and it is reason only that maketh a distinction of persons, where there is a superior degree of virtue.

In their marriages, they are exactly careful to choose such colours as will not make any disagreeable mixture in the breed. Strength is chiefly valued in the male, and comeliness in the female; not upon the account of love, but to preserve the race from degenerating; for where a female happens to excel in strength, a consort is chosen with regard to comeliness. Courtship, love, presents, jointures, settlements, have no place in their thoughts, or terms whereby to express them in their language. The young couple meet and are joined, merely because it is the determination of their parents and friends: it is what they see done every day, and they look upon it as one of the necessary actions of a reasonable being. But the violation of marriage, or any other unchastity, was never heard of: and the married pair pass their lives with the same friendship, and mutual benevolence, that they bear to all others of the same species, who come in their way; without jealousy, fondness, quarreling, or discontent.

In educating the youth of both sexes, their method is admirable, and highly deserves our imitation. These are not suffered to take a grain of oats, except upon certain days, till eighteen years old; nor milk but very rarely; and in summer they graze two hours in the morning, and as many in the evening, which their parents likewise observe; but the servants are not allowed above half that time, and a great part of their grass is brought home, which they eat at the most convenient hours, when they can be best spared from work.

Temperance, industry, exercise, and cleanliness, are the lessons equally enjoined to the young ones of both sexes; and my master thought it monstrous in us to give the females a different kind of education from the males, except in some articles of domestic management; whereby, as he truly observed, one half of our natives were good for nothing but bringing children into the world: and to trust the care of our children to such useless animals, he said, was yet a greater instance of brutality.

But the Houyhnhnms train up their youth to strength, speed, and hardiness, by exercising them in running races up and down steep hills, and over hard stony grounds, and when they are all in a sweat, they are ordered to leap over head and ears into a pond or river. Four times a year, the youth of a certain district meet to shew their proficiency in running, and leaping, and other feats of strength and agility; where the victor is rewarded with a song in his or her praise. On this festival, the servants drive a herd of Yahoos into the field, laden with hay, and oats, and milk, for a repast to the Houyhnhnms; after which these brutes are immediately driven back again, for fear of being noisome to the assembly.

Every fourth year, at the Vernal Equinox, there is a representative council of the whole nation, which meets in a plain about twenty miles from our house, and continues about five or six days. Here they enquire into the state and condition of the several districts; whether they abound or be deficient in hay or oats, or cows or Yahoos. And wherever there is any want (which is but seldom) it is immediately supplied by unanimous consent and contribution. Here likewise the regulation of children is settled: as for instance, if a Houyhnhnm hath two males, he chan- geth one of them with another that hath two females.

CHAPTER IX

ONE of these grand assemblies was held in my time, about
three months before my departure, whither my master
went, as the representative of our district. In this council
was resumed their old debate, and, indeed, the only debate
which ever happened in that country; whereof my master,
after his return, gave me a very particular account.

The question to be debated was, whether the Yahoos
should be exterminated from the face of the earth? One
of the members for the affirmative offered several arguments of great strength and weight; alleging, that as the
Yahoos were the most filthy, noisome, and deformed animal
which Nature ever produced, so they were the most restive
and indocible, mischievous and malicious: they would
privately suck the teats of the Houyhnhnms' cows; kill
and devour their cats, trample down their oats and grass, if
they were not continually watched, and commit a thousand
other extravagances. He took notice of a general tradition
that Yahoos had not been always in that country; but
that, many ages ago, two of these brutes appeared together
upon a mountain; whether produced by the heat of the
sun upon corrupted mud and slime, or from the ooze and
froth of the sea, was never known. Their brood, in a short
time, grew so numerous as to overrun and infest the whole
nation. That the Houyhnhnms, to get rid of this evil,
made a general hunting, and at last enclosed the whole
herd; and, destroying the elder, every Houyhnhnm kept
two young ones in a kennel, and brought them to such a
degree of tameness as an animal, so savage by nature, can
be capable of acquiring; using them for draught and
carriage. That there seemed to be much truth in this tradition, and that those creatures could not be *Ylnhniamshy*
(or aborigines of the land) because of the violent hatred the

Houyhnhnms, as well as all other animals, bore them; which, although their evil disposition sufficiently deserved, could never have arrived at so high a degree if they had been aborigines, or else they would have long since been rooted out. That the inhabitants, taking a fancy to use the service of the Yahoos, had very imprudently neglected to cultivate the breed of asses, which were a comely animal, easily kept, more tame and orderly, without any offensive smell, strong enough for labour, although they yield to the other in agility of body! and, if their braying be no agreeable sound, it is far preferable to the horrible howlings of the Yahoos. Several others declared their sentiments to the same purpose, when my master proposed an expedient to the assembly, whereof he had, indeed, borrowed the hint from me. He approved of the tradition mentioned by the honourable member who spoke before; and affirmed that the two Yahoos, said to be the first seen among them, had been driven thither over the sea; that coming to land, and being forsaken by their companions, they retired to the mountains, and, degenerating by degrees, became, in process of time, much more savage than those of their own species in the country from whence these two originals came. The reason of this assertion was, that he had now in his possession a certain wonderful Yahoo (meaning myself) which most of them had heard of, and many of them had seen. He then related to them how he first found me; that my body was all covered with an artificial composure of the skins and hairs of other animals: that I spoke in a language of my own, and had thoroughly learned theirs: that I had related to him the accidents which brought me thither: that, when he saw me without my covering, I was an exact Yahoo in every part, only of a whiter colour, less hairy, and with shorter claws. He added, how I had endeavoured to persuade him that, in my own and other countries, the Yahoos acted as the governing, rational animal, and held the Houyhnhnms in servitude: that he observed in me all the qualities of a Yahoo, only a little more civilised by some tincture of reason; which, however, was in a degree as far inferior to the Houyhnhnm race, as the Yahoos of their country were to me.

This was all my master thought fit to tell me at that time of what passed in the Grand Council. But he was pleased to conceal one particular, which related personally to myself, whereof I soon felt the unhappy effect, as the reader will know in its proper place, and from whence I date all the succeeding misfortunes of my life.

The Houyhnhnms have no letters, and consequently their knowledge is all traditional. But there happening few events of any moment among a people so well united, naturally disposed to every virtue, wholly governed by reason and cut off from all commerce with other nations, the historical part is easily preserved without burthening their memories. I have already observed that they are subject to no diseases, and therefore can have no need of physicians. However, they have excellent medicines composed of herbs, to cure accidental bruises and cuts in the pastern, or frog of the foot, by sharp stones, as well as other maims and hurts in the several parts of the body.

They calculate the year by the revolution of the sun and the moon, but use no subdivisions into weeks. They are well enough acquainted with the motions of those two luminaries, and understand the nature of eclipses; and this is the utmost progress of their astronomy.

In poetry, they must be allowed to excel all other mortals; wherein the justness of their similes, and the minuteness as well as exactness of their descriptions are, indeed, inimitable. Their verses abound very much in both of these; and usually contain either some exalted notions of friendship and benevolence, or the praises of those who were victors in races and other bodily exercises. Their buildings, although very rude and simple, are not inconvenient, but well contrived to defend them from all injuries of cold and heat. They have a kind of tree, which, at forty years old, loosens in the root, and falls with the first storm; it grows very straight, and being pointed like stakes, with a sharp stone (for the Houyhnhnms know not the use of iron), they stick them erect in the ground about ten inches asunder, and then weave in oat-straw, or sometimes wattles, betwixt them. The roof is made after the same manner, and so are the doors.

The Houyhnhnms use the hollow part, between the pastern and the hoof, of their forefeet, as we do our hands, and this with greater dexterity than I could at first imagine. I have seen a white mare of our family thread a needle (which I lent her on purpose) with that joint. They milk their cows, reap their oats, and do all the work which requires hands in the same manner. They have a kind of hard flints, which, by grinding against other stones, they form into instruments that serve instead of wedges, axes, and hammers. With tools made of these flints they likewise cut their hay, and reap their oats, which there grow naturally in several fields: the Yahoos draw home the sheaves in carriages, and the servants tread them in certain covered huts, to get out the grain, which is kept in stores. They make a rude kind of earthen and wooden vessels, and bake the former in the sun.

If they can avoid casualties, they die only of old age, and are buried in the obscurest places that can be found, their friends and relations expressing neither joy nor grief at their departure; nor does the dying person discover the least regret that he is leaving the world, any more than if he were upon returning home from a visit to one of his neighbours. I remember my master having once made an appointment with a friend and his family to come to his house upon some affair of importance: on the day fixed the mistress and her two children came very late; she made two excuses, first for her husband, who, as she said, happened that very morning to *lhnuwnh*. The word is strongly expressive in their language, but not easily rendered into English; it signifies, to retire to his first mother. Her excuse for not coming sooner was, that her husband dying late in the morning, she was a good while consulting her servants about a convenient place where his body should be laid; and, I observed, she behaved herself at our house as cheerfully as the rest: she died about three months after.

They live generally to seventy, or seventy-five years, very seldom to four-score: some weeks before their death, they feel a gradual decay; but without pain. During this time, they are much visited by their friends, because they cannot go abroad with their usual ease and satisfaction. However, about ten days before their death, which they seldom fail in computing, they return the visits that have been made them, by those who are nearest in the neighbourhood, being carried in a convenient sledge, drawn by Yahoos; which vehicle they use, not only upon this occasion, but when they grow old, upon long journeys, or when they are lamed by any accident. And, therefore, when the dying Houyhnhnms return those visits, they take a solemn leave of their friends, as if they were going to some remote part of the country, where they designed to pass the rest of their lives.

I know not whether it may be worth observing, that the Houyhnhnms have no word in their language to express any thing that is evil, except what they borrow from the deformities or ill qualities of the Yahoos. Thus they denote the folly of a servant, an omission of a child, a stone that cuts their feet, a continuance of foul or unseasonable weather, and the like, by adding to each the epithet of Yahoo. For instance, *Hhnm Yahoo*, *Whnaholm Yahoo*, *Ynlhmndwihlma Yahoo*, and an ill-contrived house, *Ynholmhnmrohlnw Yahoo*.

I could with great pleasure enlarge farther upon the manners and virtues of this excellent people; but, intending in a short time to publish a volume by itself expressly upon that subject, I refer the reader thither; and, in the meantime, proceed to relate my own sad catastrophe.

CHAPTER X

I HAD settled my little economy to my own heart's content. My master had ordered a room to be made for me after their manner, about six yards from the house; the sides and floors of which I plastered with clay, and covered with rush-mats of my own contriving; I had beaten hemp, which there grows wild, and made of it a sort of ticking; this I filled with the feathers of several birds I had taken with springes made of Yahoo's hairs, and were excellent food. I had worked two chairs with my knife, the sorrel nag helping me in the grosser and more laborious part. When my clothes were worn to rags, I made myself others with the skins of rabbits, and of a certain beautiful animal about the same size, called *Nnuhnoh*, the skin of which is covered with a fine down. Of these I also made very tolerable stockings. I soled my shoes with wood which I cut from a tree, and fitted to the upper leather; and when this was worn out I supplied it with the skins of Yahoos, dried in the sun. I often got honey out of hollow trees, which I mingled with water, or ate with my bread. No man could more verify the truth of these two maxims, that Nature is very easily satisfied; and that necessity is the mother of invention. I enjoyed perfect health of body, and tranquillity of mind; I did not feel the treachery or inconstancy of a friend, nor the injuries of a secret or open enemy. I had no occasion of bribing or flattering, to procure the favour of any great man, or of his minion. I wanted no fence against fraud or oppression; here was neither physician to destroy my body, nor lawyer to ruin my fortune; no informer to watch my words and actions, or forge accusations against me for hire: here were no gibers, censurers, back-biters, pick-pockets, highway-

men, house-breakers, attorneys, buffoons, gamesters, politicians, wits, splenetics, tedious talkers, controvertists,
murderers, robbers, virtuosos; no leaders or followers of
party and faction; no encouragers to vice, by seducement
or examples; no dungeon, axes, gibbets, whipping-posts,
or pillories; no cheating shopkeepers or mechanics; no
pride, vanity, or affectation; no fops, bullies, drunkards; no
ranting, expensive wives; no stupid, proud pedants; no
importunate, over-bearing, quarrelsome, noisy, roaring,
empty, conceited, swearing companions; no scoundrels,
raised from the dust, for the sake of their vices, or nobility
thrown into it, on account of their virtues; no lords, fiddlers,
judges, or dancing-masters.

I had the favour of being admitted to several Houyhnhnms, who came to visit or dine with my master; where
his honour graciously suffered me to wait in the room, and
listen to their discourse. Both he and his company would
often condescend to ask me questions and receive my answers.
I had also sometimes the honour of attending my master
in his visits to others. I never presumed to speak, except
in answer to a question; and then I did it with inward
regret, because it was a loss of so much time for improving
myself: but I was infinitely delighted with the station of an
humble auditor in such conversations, where nothing passed
but what was useful, expressed in the fewest and most
significant words; where (as I have already said) the greatest
decency was observed, without the least degree of ceremony;
where no person spoke, without being pleased himself, and
pleasing his companions; where there was no interruption,
tediousness, heat, or difference of sentiments. They have
a notion that, when people are met together, a short silence
doth much improve conversation: this I found to be true;
for, during those little intermissions of talk, new ideas
would arise in their thoughts, which very much enlivened
the discourse. Their subjects are generally on friendship
and benevolence, or order and economy; sometimes upon

the visible operations of Nature, or ancient traditions; upon the bounds and limits of virtue; upon the unerring rules of reason, or upon some determinations, to be taken at the next great assembly; and often upon the various excellences of poetry. I may add, without vanity, that my presence often gave them sufficient matter for discourse, because it afforded my master an occasion of letting his friends into the history of me and my country, upon which they were all pleased to descant in a manner not very advantageous to human kind; and, for that reason, I shall not repeat what they said: only I may be allowed to observe, that his honour, to my great admiration, appeared to understand the nature of Yahoos much better than myself. He went through all our vices and follies, and discovered many which I had never mentioned to him, by only supposing what qualities a Yahoo of their country, with a small proportion of reason, might be capable of exerting; and concluded, with too much probability, how vile, as well as miserable, such a creature must be.

I freely confess, that all the little knowledge I have, of any value, was acquired by the lectures I received from my master, and from hearing the discourses of him and his friends; to which I should be prouder to listen, than to dictate to the greatest and wisest assembly in Europe. I admired the strength, comeliness, and speed of the inhabitants; and such a constellation of virtues, in such amiable persons, produced in me the highest veneration. At first, indeed, I did not feel that natural awe which the Yahoos, and all other animals, bear towards them; but it grew upon me by degrees, much sooner than I imagined, and was mingled with a respectful love and gratitude, that they would condescend to distinguish me from the rest of my species.

When I thought of my family, my friends, my countrymen, or the human race in general, I considered them as they really were, Yahoos in shape and disposition, perhaps

GULLIVER HAS THE HONOUR OF BEING QUESTIONED
BY HIS MASTER'S GUESTS

a little more civilised, and qualified with the gift of speech;
but making no other use of reason than to improve and
multiply those vices, whereof their brethren in this country
had only the share that nature allotted them. When I
happened to behold the reflection of my own form in a
lake or a fountain, I turned away my face in horror and
detestation of myself; and could better endure the sight
of a common Yahoo than of my own person. By conversing with the Houyhnhnms, and looking upon them
with delight, I fell to imitate their gait and gesture, which
is now grown into an habit; and my friends often tell me
in a blunt way, that I trot like a horse; which, however,
I take for a great compliment: neither shall I disown, that,
in speaking, I am apt to fall into the voice and manner of
the Houyhnhnms, and hear myself ridiculed on that account,
without the least mortification.

In the midst of all this happiness, and when I looked
upon myself to be fully settled for life, my master sent for
me one morning, a little earlier than his usual hour. I
observed by his countenance that he was in some perplexity,
and at a loss how to begin what he had to speak. After
a short silence, he told me, he did not know how I would take
what he was going to say; that in the last general assembly,
when the affair of the Yahoos was entered upon, the representatives had taken offence at his keeping a Yahoo (meaning
myself) in his family, more like a Houyhnhnm than a brute
animal. That he was known frequently to converse with
me, as if he could receive some advantage or pleasure in
my company: that such a practice was not agreeable to
reason or nature, or a thing ever heard of before among
them. The assembly did therefore exhort him either to
employ me like the rest of my species, or command me to
swim back to the place from whence I came. That the first
of these expedients was utterly rejected by all the Houyhnhnms who had ever seen me at his house or their own;
for they alleged that, because I had some rudiments of

reason, added to the natural pravity of those animals, it was to be feared I might be able to seduce them into the woody and mountainous parts of the country, and bring them in troops by night to destroy the Houyhnhnms' cattle, as being naturally of the ravenous kind, and averse from labour.

My master added, that he was daily pressed by the Houyhnhnms of the neighbourhood to have the assembly's exhortation executed, which he could not put off much longer. He doubted it would be impossible for me to swim to another country; and therefore wished I would contrive some sort of vehicle resembling those I had described to him, that might carry me on the sea; in which work I should have the assistance of his own servants, as well as those of his neighbours. He concluded, that, for his own part, he could have been content to keep me in his service as long as I lived; because he found I had cured myself of some bad habits and dispositions, by endeavouring, as far as my inferior nature was capable, to imitate the Houyhnhnms.

I should here observe to the reader, that a decree of the general assembly, in this country, is expressed by the word *Hnhloayn*, which signifies an exhortation, as near as I can render it: for they have no conception how a rational creature can be compelled, but only advised or exhorted; because no persons can disobey reason, without giving up his claim to be a rational creature.

I was struck with the utmost grief and despair at my master's discourse; and, being unable to support the agonies I was under, I fell into a swoon at his feet: when I came to myself, he told me that he concluded I had been dead (for these people are subject to no such imbecilities of nature). I answered in a faint voice, that death would have been too great an happiness; that although I could not blame the assembly's exhortation, or the urgency of his friends, yet, in my weak and corrupt judgment, I thought it might consist with reason to have been less rigorous. That I could not swim a league, and, probably, the nearest land to theirs might be distant above an hundred: that many materials, necessary for making a small vessel to carry me off, were wholly wanting in this country, which, however, I would attempt, in obedience and gratitude to his honour, although I concluded the thing to be impossible, and therefore looked on myself as already devoted to destruction. That the certain prospect of an unnatural death was the least of my evils: for, supposing I should escape with life by some strange adventure, how could I think with temper, of passing my days among Yahoos, and relapsing into my old corruptions, for want of examples to lead and keep me within the paths of virtue. That I knew, too well, upon what solid reasons all the determinations of the wise Houyhnhnms were founded, not to be shaken by arguments of mine, a miserable Yahoo; and therefore, after presenting him with my humble thanks for the offer of his servants' assistance in making a vessel, and desiring a reasonable time for so difficult a work, I told him I would endeavour to preserve a wretched being; and, if ever I returned to England, was not without hopes of being useful to my own species, by celebrating the praises of the renowned Houyhnhnms, and proposing their virtues to the imitation of mankind.

My master, in a few words, made me a very gracious reply; allowed me the space of two months to finish my boat; and ordered the sorrel nag, my fellow-servant (for so at this distance I may presume to call him) to follow my instructions, because I told my master that his help would be sufficient, and I knew he had a tenderness for me.

In his company, my first business was to go to that part of the coast where my rebellious crew had ordered me to be set on shore. I got upon a height, and, looking on every side into the sea, fancied I saw a small island, towards the north-east: I took out my pocket-glass, and could then clearly distinguish it about five leagues off, as I computed; but it appeared to the sorrel nag to be only a blue cloud:

for, as he had no conception of any country beside his own, so he could not be as expert in distinguishing remote objects at sea as we who so much converse in that element.

After I had discovered this island, I considered no further; but resolved it should, if possible, be the first place of my banishment, leaving the consequence to fortune.

I returned home, and consulting with the sorrel nag, we went into a copse at some distance, where I with my knife, and he with a sharp flint fastened very artificially, after their manner, to a wooden handle, cut down several oak wattles, about the thickness of a walking staff, and some larger pieces. But I shall not trouble the reader with a particular description of my own mechanics; let it suffice to say, that in six weeks' time, with the help of the sorrel nag, who performed the parts that required most labour, I finished a sort of Indian canoe, but much larger, covering it with the skins of Yahoos, well stitched together with hempen threads of my own making. My sail was likewise composed of the skins of the same animal; but I made use of the youngest I could get, the older being too tough and thick; and I likewise provided myself with four paddles. I laid in a stock of boiled flesh, of rabbits and fowls; and took with me two vessels, one filled with milk, and the other with water.

I tried my canoe in a large pond, near my master's house, and then corrected in it what was amiss; stopping all the chinks with Yahoos' tallow, till I found it staunch, and able to bear me and my freight. And when it was as complete as I could possibly make it, I had it drawn on a carriage, very gently, by Yahoos, to the seaside, under the conduct of the sorrel nag and another servant.

When all was ready, and the day came for my departure, I took leave of my master and lady, and the whole family, my eyes flowing with tears, and my heart quite sunk with grief. But his honour, out of curiosity, and perhaps (if I may speak it without vanity) partly out of kindness, was determined to see me in my canoe; and got several of

his neighbouring friends to accompany him. I was forced
to wait above an hour for the tide, and then observing the
wind very fortunately bearing towards the island to which
I intended to steer my course, I took a second leave of my
master: but as I was going to prostrate myself to kiss his
hoof, he did me the honour to raise it gently to my mouth.
I am not ignorant how much I have been censured for
mentioning this last particular. For my detractors are
pleased to think it improbable, that so illustrious a person
should descend to give so great a mark of distinction to a
creature so inferior as I. Neither have I forgot how
apt some travellers are to boast of extraordinary favours
they have received. But if these censurers were better
acquainted with the noble and courteous disposition of
the Houyhnhnms, they would soon change their opinion.

I paid my respects to the rest of the Houyhnhnms in his
honour's company; then, getting into my canoe, I pushed
off from shore.

CHAPTER XI

I BEGAN this desperate voyage on February 15, 1714-15, at nine o'clock in the morning. The wind was very favourable; however, I made use, at first, only of my paddles; but considering I should soon be weary, and that the wind might probably chop about, I ventured to set up my little sail; and thus, with the help of the tide, I went at the rate of a league and a half an hour, as near as I could guess. My master and his friends continued on the shore till I was almost out of sight; and I often heard the sorrel nag (who always loved me) crying out, *Hnuy illa nyha majah Yahoo*, Take care of thyself, gentle Yahoo.

My design was, if possible, to discover some small island uninhabited, yet sufficient with my labour to furnish me with the necessaries of life, which I would have thought a greater happiness than to be first minister in the politest Court of Europe; so horrible was the idea I conceived of returning to live in the society and under the government of Yahoos. For, in such a solitude as I desired, I could, at least, enjoy my own thoughts, and reflect with delight on the virtues of those inimitable Houyhnhnms, without any opportunity of degenerating into the vices and corruptions of my own species.

The reader may remember what I related when my crew conspired against me, and confined me to my cabin. How I continued there several weeks, without knowing what course we took; and when I was put ashore in the long-boat, how the sailors told me with oaths, whether true or false, that they knew not in what part of the world we were. However, I did then believe us to be about ten degrees southward of the Cape of Good Hope, or about forty-five degrees southern latitude, as I gathered from some general words I overheard among them, being, I supposed, to the south-east in their intended voyage to Madagascar. And, although this were but little better than conjecture, yet I resolved to steer my course eastward, hoping to reach the south-west coast of New Holland, and perhaps some such island as I desired, lying westward of it. The wind was full west, and, by six in the evening I computed I had gone eastward at least eighteen leagues; when I spied a very small island about half a league off, which I soon reached. It was nothing but a rock with one creek, naturally arched by the force of tempests. Here I put in my canoe, and, climbing up a part of the rock, I could plainly discover land to the east, extending from south to north. I lay all night in my canoe; and, repeating my voyage early in the morning, I arrived in seven hours to the south-east point of New Holland. This confirmed me in the opinion I have long entertained, that the maps and charts place this country at least three degrees more to the east than it really is; which thought I communicated, many years ago, to my worthy friend, Mr. Herman Moll, and gave him my reasons for it, although he hath rather chosen to follow other authors.

I saw no inhabitants in the place where I landed, and, being unarmed, I was afraid of venturing far into the country. I found some shell-fish on the shore, and ate them raw, not daring to kindle a fire for fear of being discovered by the natives. I continued three days feeding on oysters and limpets, to save my own provisions; and I fortunately found a brook of excellent water, which gave me great relief.

On the fourth day, venturing out early a little too far, I saw twenty or thirty natives upon a height, not above five hundred yards from me. They were stark naked, men, women, and children, round a fire, as I could discover by the smoke. One of them spied me, and gave notice to the

rest; five of them advanced towards me, leaving the women
and children at the fire. I made what haste I could to the
shore, and, getting into my canoe, shoved off. The savages,
observing me retreat, ran after me, and, before I could
get far enough into the sea, discharged an arrow, which
wounded me deeply on the inside of my left knee (I shall
carry the mark to my grave). I apprehended the arrow
might be poisoned, and paddling out of the reach of their
darts (being a calm day) I made a shift to suck the wound,
and dress it as I could.

I was at a loss what to do, for I durst not return to the
same landing-place, but stood to the north, and was forced
to paddle; for the wind, though very gentle, was against
me, blowing north-west. As I was looking about for a
secure landing-place, I saw a sail to the north-north-east,
which appearing every minute more visible, I was in some
doubt whether I should wait for them or no; but, at last,
my detestation of the Yahoo race prevailed; and, turning
my canoe, I sailed and paddled together to the south, and
got into the same creek from whence I set out in the morning, choosing rather to trust myself among these barbarians
than live with European Yahoos. I drew up my canoe as
close as I could to the shore, and hid myself behind a stone
by the little brook, which, as I have already said, was
excellent water.

The ship came within half a league of this creek, and
sent out her long-boat, with vessels to take in fresh water
(for the place, it seems, was very well known), but I did not
observe it, till the boat was almost on shore; and it was too
late to seek another hiding-place. The seamen, at their
landing, observed my canoe, and, rummaging it all over,
easily conjectured that the owner could not be far off.
Four of them, well armed, searched every cranny and lurk-
ing-hole, till at last they found me flat on my face behind
the stone They gazed awhile in admiration at my strange
uncouth dress; my coat made of skins, my wooden-soled

shoes, and my furred stockings; from whence, however, they concluded, I was not a native of the place, who all go naked. One of the seamen, in Portuguese, bid me rise, and asked who I was. I understood that language very well, and getting upon my feet, said, I was a poor Yahoo, banished from the Houyhnhnms, and desired they would please to let me depart. They admired to hear me answer them in their own tongue, and saw by my complexion I must be a European; but were at a loss to know what I meant by Yahoos, and Houyhnhnms, and at the same time fell a-laughing at my strange tone in speaking, which resembled the neighing of a horse. I trembled all the while betwixt fear and hatred: I again desired leave to depart, and was gently moving to my canoe, but they laid hold on me, desiring to know what country I was of? whence I came? with many other questions. I told them, I was born in England, from whence I came about five years ago, and then their country and ours were at peace. I therefore hoped they would not treat me as an enemy, since I meant them no harm, but was a poor Yahoo, seeking some desolate place where to pass the remainder of his unfortunate life.

When they began to talk, I thought I never heard or saw anything so unnatural; for it appeared to me as monstrous, as if a dog or a cow should speak in England, or a Yahoo in Houyhnhnmland. The honest Portuguese were equally amazed at my strange dress, and the odd manner of delivering my words, which, however, they understood very well. They spoke to me with great humanity, and said they were sure the captain would carry me gratis to Lisbon, from whence I might return to my own country; that two of the seamen would go back to the ship, inform the captain of what they had seen, and receive his orders; in the meantime, unless I would give my solemn oath not to fly, they would secure me by force. I thought it best to comply with their proposal. They were very curious to know my story, but I gave them very little satisfaction; and they all conjectured, that my misfortunes had impaired my reason. In two hours the boat, which went loaded with vessels of water, returned, with the captain's command, to fetch me on board. I fell on my knees to preserve my liberty; but all was in vain, and the men, having tied me with cords, heaved me into the boat, from whence I was taken into the ship, and from thence into the captain's cabin.

His name was Pedro de Mendez; he was a very courteous and generous person; he entreated me to give some account of myself, and desired to know what I would eat or drink; said I should be used as well as himself, and spoke so many obliging things, that I wondered to find such civilities from a Yahoo. However, I remained silent and sullen; I was ready to faint at the very smell of him and his men. At last I desired something to eat out of my own canoe; but he ordered me a chicken, and some excellent wine, and then directed that I should be put to bed in a very clean cabin. I would not undress myself, but lay on the bedclothes, and in half an hour stole out, when I thought the crew was at dinner, and getting to the side of the ship, was going to leap into the sea, and swim for my life, rather than continue among Yahoos. But one of the seamen prevented me, and, having informed the captain, I was chained to my cabin.

After dinner, Don Pedro came to me, and desired to know my reason for so desperate an attempt; assured me, he only meant to do me all the service he was able, and spoke so very movingly, that at last I descended to treat him like an animal which had some little portion of reason. I gave him a very short relation of my voyage; of the conspiracy against me by my own men; of the country where they set me on shore, and of my three years' residence there. All which he looked upon as if it were a dream or a vision, whereat I took great offence; for I had quite forgot the faculty of lying, so peculiar to Yahoos in all countries where they preside, and consequently the disposition of suspecting truth in others of their own species. I asked him whether it were the custom in his country to say the thing that was not? I assured him I had almost forgot what he meant by falsehood, and, if I had lived a thousand years in Houyhnhnmland, I should never have heard a lie from the meanest servant; that I was altogether indifferent whether he believed me or no; but however, in return for his favours, I would give so much allowance to the corruption of his nature, as to answer any objection he would please to make, and then he might easily discover the truth.

The captain, a wise man, after many endeavours to catch me tripping in some part of my story, at last began to have a better opinion of my veracity. But he added that, since I professed so inviolable an attachment to truth, I must give him my word and honour to bear him company in this voyage, without attempting anything against my life, or else he would continue me a prisoner till we arrived at Lisbon. I gave him the promise he required; but at the same time protested, that I would suffer the greatest hardships rather than return to live among Yahoos.

Our voyage passed without any considerable accident. In gratitude to the captain, I sometimes sat with him, at his earnest request, and strove to conceal my antipathy to human kind, although it often broke out; which he suffered to pass without observation. But, the greatest part of the day, I confined myself to my cabin, to avoid seeing any of the crew. The captain had often entreated me to strip myself of my savage dress, and offered to lend me the best suit of clothes he had. This I would not be prevailed on to accept, abhorring to cover myself with anything that had been on the back of a Yahoo. I only desired he would lend me two clean shirts, which having been washed since he wore them, I believed would not so much defile me.

These I changed every second day, and washed them myself.

We arrived at Lisbon, Nov. 5, 1715. At our landing the captain forced me to cover myself with his cloak, to prevent the rabble from crowding about me. I was conveyed to his own house; and, at my earnest request, he led me up to the highest room backwards. I conjured him to conceal from all persons what I had told him of the Houyhnhnms; because the least hint of such a story would not only draw numbers of people to see me, but probably put me in danger of being imprisoned, or burnt by the Inquisition. The captain persuaded me to accept a suit of clothes newly made, but I would not suffer the tailor to take my measure; however, Don Pedro being almost of my size, they fitted me well enough. He accoutred me with other necessaries, all new, which I aired for twenty-four hours, before I would use them.

The captain had no wife, nor above three servants, none of which were suffered to attend at meals; and his whole deportment was so obliging, added to a very good human understanding, that I really began to tolerate his company. He gained so far upon me, that I ventured to look out of the back window. By degrees, I was brought into another room, from whence I peeped into the street, but drew my head back in a fright. In a week's time he seduced me down to the door. I found my terror gradually lessened, but my hatred and contempt seemed to increase. I was at last bold enough to walk the street in his company, but kept my nose well stopped with rue, or sometimes with tobacco.

In ten days, Don Pedro, to whom I had given some account of my domestic affairs, put it upon me as a matter of honour and conscience, that I ought to return to my native country, and live at home with my wife and children. He told me there was an English ship in the port just ready to sail, and he would furnish me with all things necessary. It would be tedious to repeat his arguments and my contradictions. He said it was altogether impossible to find such a solitary island as I had desired to live in; but I might command in my own house, and pass my time in a manner as recluse as I pleased.

I complied at last, finding I could not do better. I left Lisbon the 24th day of November, in an English merchantman, but who was the master I never inquired. Don Pedro accompanied me to the ship, and lent me twenty pounds. He took kind leave of me, and embraced me at parting, which I bore as well as I could. During the last voyage I had no commerce with the master or any of his men; but, pretending I was sick, kept close in my cabin. On the 5th of December 1715 we cast anchor in the Downs about nine in the morning, and at three in the afternoon I got safe to my house at Rotherhithe.

My wife and family received me with great surprise and joy, because they concluded me certainly dead; but I must freely confess the sight of them filled me only with hatred, disgust, and contempt; and the more by reflecting on the near alliance I had to them. For, although since my unfortunate exile from the Houyhnhnm country, I had compelled myself to tolerate the sight of Yahoos, and to converse with Don Pedro de Mendez, yet my memory and imagination were perpetually filled with the virtues and ideas of those exalted Houyhnhnms.

As soon as I entered the house, my wife took me in her arms, and kissed me; at which, having not been used to the touch of that odious animal for so many years, I fell in a swoon for almost an hour. At the time I am writing, it is five years since my last return to England: during the first year, I could not endure my wife or children in my presence, the very smell of them was intolerable; much less could I suffer them to eat in the same room. To this hour they dare not presume to touch my bread, or drink out of the same cup; neither was I ever able to let one of them take me by the hand. The first money I laid out was to buy two young horses, which I kept in a good stable, and next to them the groom is my greatest favourite; for I feel my spirits revived by the smell he contracts in the stable. My horses understand me tolerably well; I converse with them at least four hours every day. They are strangers to bridle or saddle; they live in great amity with me, and friendship to each other.

CHAPTER XII

THUS, gentle reader, I have given thee a faithful history of my travels for sixteen years and above seven months; wherein I have not been so studious of ornament as truth. I could perhaps, like others, have astonished thee with strange improbable tales; but I rather chose to relate plain matter of fact, in the simplest manner and style; because my principal design was to inform, and not to amuse thee.

It is easy for us who travel into remote countries, which are seldom visited by Englishmen, or other Europeans, to form descriptions of wonderful animals, both at sea and land. Whereas a traveller's chief aim should be, to make men wiser and better, and to improve their minds by the bad, as well as good example, of what they deliver concerning foreign places.

I could heartily wish a law was enacted that every traveller, before he were permitted to publish his voyages, should be obliged to make oath before the Lord High Chancellor, that all he intended to print was absolutely true, to the best of his knowledge; for then the world would no longer be deceived, as it usually is; while some writers, to make their works pass the better upon the public, impose the grossest falsities on the unwary reader. I have perused several books of travels, with great delight, in my younger days; but, having since gone over most parts of the globe, and been able to contradict many fabulous accounts from my own observation, it hath given me a great disgust against this part of reading, and some indignation to see the credulity of mankind so impudently abused. Therefore, since my acquaintances were pleased to think my poor endeavours might not be unacceptable to my country, I imposed on myself, as a maxim never to be swerved from, that I would strictly adhere to truth; neither, indeed, can I be ever under the least temptation to vary from it, while I retain in my mind the lectures and example of my noble master, and the other illustrious Houyhnhnms, of whom I had so long the honour to be an humble hearer.

—— Nec si miserum Fortuna Sinonem
Finxit, vanum etiam, mendacemque improba finget.

I know very well, how little reputation is to be got by writings which require neither genius nor learning, nor, indeed, any other talent except a good memory, or an exact journal. I know likewise, that writers of travels, like dictionary-makers, are sunk into oblivion by the weight and bulk of those who come last, and therefore lie uppermost. And it is highly probable that such travellers who shall hereafter visit the countries described in this work of mine, may, by detecting my errors (if there be any) and adding many new discoveries of their own, jostle me out of vogue, and stand in my place, making the world forget that I was ever an author. This indeed would be too great a mortification, if I wrote for fame: but, as my sole intention was the public good, I cannot be altogether disappointed. For who can read of the virtues I have mentioned in the glorious Houyhnhnms, without being ashamed of his own vices, when he considers himself as the reasoning, governing animal of his country? I shall say nothing of those remote nations where Yahoos preside; amongst which the least corrupted are the Brobdingnagians, whose wise maxims, in morality and government, it would be our happiness to observe. But I forbear descanting farther, and rather leave the judicious reader to his own remarks and applications.

I am not a little pleased that this work of mine can possibly meet with no censurers: for what objections can be made against a writer who relates only plain facts that happened in such distant countries, where we have not the least interest, with respect either to trade or negotiations? I have carefully avoided every fault with which common writers of travels are often too justly charged. Besides, I meddle not the least with any party, but write without passion, prejudice, or ill-will against any man, or number of men, whatsoever. I write for the noblest end, to inform and instruct mankind, over whom I may, without breach of modesty, pretend to some superiority, from the advantages I received by conversing so long among the most accomplished Houyhnhnms. I write without any view towards profit or praise. I never suffer a word to pass that may look like reflection, or possibly give the least offence, even to those who are most ready to take it. So that I hope I may, with justice, pronounce myself an author perfectly blameless; against whom the tribes of answerers, considerers, observers, reflecters, detecters, remarkers, will never be able to find matter for exercising their talents.

I confess it was whispered to me, that I was bound in duty, as a subject of England, to have given in a memorial to a Secretary of State, at my first coming over; because, whatever lands are discovered by a subject belong to the crown. But I doubt whether our conquests, in the countries I treat of, would be as easy as those of Ferdinando Cortez over the naked Americans. The Lilliputians, I think, are hardly worth the charge of a fleet and army to reduce them; and I question whether it might be prudent or safe to attempt the Brobdingnagians, or whether an English army would be much at their ease with the flying island over their heads. The Houyhnhnms, indeed, appear not to be so well prepared for war, a science to which they are perfect strangers, and especially against missive weapons. However, supposing myself, to be a minister of state, I could never give my advice for invading them. Their prudence, unanimity, unacquaintedness with fear, and their love of their country, would amply supply all defects in the military art. Imagine twenty thousand of them breaking into the midst of an European army, confounding the ranks, overturning the carriages, battering the warriors' faces into mummy, by terrible yerks from their hinder hoofs; for they would well deserve the character given to Augustus: *Recalcitrat undique tutus.* But, instead of proposals for conquering that magnanimous nation, I rather wish they were in a capacity, or disposition, to send a sufficient number of their inhabitants for civilising Europe, by teaching us the first principles of honour, justice, truth, temperance, public spirit, fortitude, chastity, friendship, benevolence, and fidelity. The names of all which virtues are still retained among us in most languages, and are to be met with in modern, as well as ancient authors; which I am able to assert from my own small reading.

But I had another reason which made me less forward to enlarge his Majesty's dominions by my discoveries. To say the truth, I had conceived a few scruples with relation to the distributive justice of princes upon those occasions. For instance, a crew of pirates are driven by a storm they know not whether; at length a boy discovers land from the top-mast; they go on shore to rob and plunder; they see an harmless people, are entertained with kindness; they give the country a new name; they take formal possession of it for their king; they set up a rotten plank or a stone for a memorial; they murder two or three dozen of the natives, bring away a couple more by force for a sample, return home, and get their pardon. Here commences a new dominion acquired with a title by divine right. Ships are sent with the first opportunity; the natives driven out or destroyed; their princes tortured to discover their gold; a free licence given to all acts of inhumanity and lust, the earth reeking with the blood of its inhabitants: and this execrable crew of butchers employed in so pious an expedition, is a modern colony, sent to convert and civilise an idolatrous and barbarous people.

But this description, I confess, doth by no means affect the British nation, who may be an example to the whole world for their wisdom, care, and justice in planting colonies; their liberal endowments for the advancement of religion and learning; their choice of devout and able pastors to propagate Christianity; their caution in stocking their provinces with people of sober lives and conversations from this the mother kingdom; their strict regard to the distribution of justice, in supplying the civil administration, through all their colonies, with officers of the greatest abilities, utter strangers to corruption; and to crown all, by sending the most vigilant and virtuous governors, who have no other views than the happiness of the people over whom they preside, and the honour of the king their master.

But, as those countries which I have described do not appear to have any desire of being conquered and enslaved, murdered or driven out by colonies; nor abound either in gold, silver, sugar, or tobacco; I did humbly conceive they were by no means proper objects of our zeal, our valour, or our interest. However, if those whom it more concerns think fit to be of another opinion, I am ready to depose, when I shall be lawfully called, that no European did ever visit these countries before me. I mean, if the inhabitants ought to be believed.

But, as to the formality of taking possession in my sovereign's name, it never came into my thoughts; and, if it had, yet, as my affairs then stood, I should, perhaps, in point of prudence and self-preservation, have put it off to a better opportunity.

Having thus answered the only objection that can ever be raised against me as a traveller, I here take a final leave of all my courteous readers, and return to enjoy my own speculations in my little garden at Redriff; to apply those excellent lessons of virtue which I learned among the Houyhnhnms; to instruct the Yahoos of my own family, as far as I shall find them docible animals; to behold my figure often in a glass, and thus, if possible, habituate myself, by time, to tolerate the sight of a human creature: to lament the brutality of Houyhnhnms in my own country, but always treat their persons with respect, for the sake of my noble master, his family, his friends, and the whole Houyhnhnm race, whom these, of ours, have the honour to resemble in all their lineaments, however their intellectuals came to degenerate.

I began last week to permit my wife to sit at dinner with me, at the farthest end of a long table; and to answer (but with the utmost brevity) the few questions I asked her. Yet, the smell of a Yahoo continuing very offensive, I always keep my nose well stopped with rue, lavender, or tobacco leaves. And, although it be hard for a man late in life to remove old habits, I am not altogether out of hopes, in some time, to suffer a neighbour Yahoo in my company without the apprehensions I am yet under of his teeth or his claws.

My reconcilement to the Yahoo kind in general might not be so difficult, if they would be content with those vices and follies only, which Nature had entitled them to. I am not in the least provoked at the sight of a lawyer, a pickpocket, a colonel, a fool, a lord, a gamester, a politician, a physician, an evidence, a suborner, an attorney, a traitor, or the like; this is all according to the due course of things: but when I behold a lump of deformity, and diseases both in body and mind, smitten with pride, it immediately breaks all the measures of my patience; neither shall I be ever able to comprehend how such an animal, and such a vice, could tally together. The wise and virtuous Houyhnhnms, who abound in all excellencies that can adorn a rational creature, have no name for this vice in their language, which hath no terms to express anything that is evil, except those whereby they describe the detestable qualities of their Yahoos, among which they were not able to distinguish this of pride, for want of thoroughly understanding human nature, as it sheweth itself in other countries, where that animal presides. But I, who had more experience, could plainly observe some rudiments of it among the wild Yahoos.

But the Houyhnhnms, who live under the government of reason, are no more proud of the good qualities they possess, than I should be for not wanting a leg or an arm, which no man in his wits would boast of, although he must be miserable without them. I dwell the longer upon this subject, from the desire I have to make the society of an English Yahoo, by any means, not insupportable; and, therefore, I here entreat those who have any tincture of this absurd vice, that they will not presume to come in my sight.

FINIS